# THE COUNSELING PRIMER

# THE COUNSELING PRIMER

## Leonard Austin, Ed.D.

Routledge
Taylor & Francis Group
New York   London

Routledge is an imprint of the
Taylor & Francis Group, an informa business

Published in 1999 by
Routledge
Taylor & Francis Group
270 Madison Avenue
New York, NY 10016

Published in Great Britain by
Routledge
Taylor & Francis Group
2 Park Square
Milton Park, Abingdon
Oxon OX14 4RN

© 1999 by Taylor & Francis Group, LLC
Routledge is an imprint of Taylor & Francis Group

Printed in the United States of America on acid-free paper
15 14 13 12 11 10 9 8 7 6 5 4

International Standard Book Number-10: 1-56032-697-2 (Softcover)
International Standard Book Number-13: 978-1-56032-697-7 (Softcover)
Library of Congress catalog number: 98-31563
Cover design by Curtis Tow.

---

**Library of Congress Cataloging-in-Publication Data**

---

Catalog record is available from the Library of Congress

---

Visit the Taylor & Francis Web site at
http://www.taylorandfrancis.com

and the Routledge Web site at
http://www.routledgementalhealth.com

# TO MY MENTORS

*California: Margaret Kubler*

*New Mexico: Truman Hebdon, Talmidge Christensen*

*Australia: John M.R. Covey*

*Wyoming: Gene A. Pratt, Michael Day*

*South Dakota: George Kroetch, Richard Barnes*

*International: Gerome Garcia (1942–1995)*

*I have walked among giants.*

# TABLE OF CONTENTS

# PREFACE

Students have called this book the "Cliff's Notes" of a master's program in counseling. I am pleased with that nickname, as it accurately represents my intention in compiling this material.

For several semesters, I taught a popular course titled "Capstone," which was designed to prepare master's-level counseling students for their written and oral examinations. It was taken in their final semester and also helped them for the National Counselor Examination (NCE). The main focus of the course was to get students to synthesize their entire program of study. However, there was no comprehensive study guide or text that encompassed all the coursework they were expected to know for their exams. Students found it difficult to effectively organize two years of class notes. They needed an organized and succinct study guide.

Students were grateful when I compiled the vital or salient class notes from most of their Council for Accreditation of Counseling and Related Educational Programs (CACREP) courses in counseling. The resulting success of these students on national exams and in job interviews was encouraging. They reported that of all the material available to them for study, this text was the most valuable. After some honing and suggestions from successful students, The Counseling Primer was born.

Students who now are practicing professionals report that The Counseling Primer is a handy tool that "cuts to the chase." It continues to serve them as an easy-to-read resource. Lay counselors, too, have said that this material helps them better understand certain theories and practical applications of counseling principles. I hope you, too, find it of use, and I welcome your comments and suggestions.

Contact address:

Dr. Leonard Austin
5645 Cleghorn Canyon Road
Rapid City, SD 57702
E-mail: laustin@mystic.bhsu.edu

# Chapter 1

# THE COUNSELING RELATIONSHIP

And so the two strangers meet. They look at each other, sniff the air between them. Their invisible antennae gently stretch out, tentatively probing, and gingerly assessing. Their intuitions working consciously and far below consciousness, take stock. One silently thinks, "Is this someone I can believe in? Someone I can trust with my secrets, my guilts, and shames, my tender and deep hopes for my life, my vulnerability?" The other wonders, "Is this someone I can invest in? Someone I can stand by in pain and crisis? Someone I can make myself vulnerable to? What surprise may this person bring forth, and what may that surprise trigger within me?" (Bugental, 1978, pp. 27–28)

## DEFINITION

The counseling relationship begins with those enabling acts that the counselor uses to help clients recognize, decide, know, feel, and choose whether to change or not. Shertzer and Stone (1980) defined the relationship as a counselor's "endeavor, by interaction with others, to contribute in a facilitating, positive way to their client's improvement" (p. 5). A more recent definition by Chapman (1997) reads:

> Counseling is the intentional injection of oneself into the personal life/lives of an individual or group with the expressed purpose of affecting change. This insertion, while deliberate, is predicated upon adequate training, the receipt of professional qualifications, and the adherence to an established code of professional ethics. (p. 1)

Still other definitions of the counseling relationship center around the application of various researched, psychotherapeutic principles to individuals, groups, couples, and families, with a goal of minimizing ineffective and psychopathological behaviors while maximizing optimal mental health.

The basic concepts of the counseling relationship as initially developed by Carl Rogers (1951, 1957, 1961, 1980) have evolved over the years, and today Rogerian concepts "are generally acknowledged by most theoretical approaches as core conditions in the therapeutic process" (Hackney & Cormier, 1994, p. 14). Rogers' relationship-building skills, cited below, form a foundation for all the therapeutic work to follow.

# ESTABLISHING RAPPORT

Most counselor educators agree that establishing rapport is an essential first step to successful counseling. However, it is not some magical gift or a condition that just happens or doesn't. Rapport skills can be learned. Rogerian skills, or conditions, enable the counselor to facilitate an environment of trust and productivity in the counseling session. They are generally considered fundamental to a positive working counseling relationship.

### Core Conditions

Rogers (1959) said the following three core conditions must be experienced by the counselor and perceived by the client. Hackney and Cormier (1994) further affirmed the three as core conditions, saying they are absolutely central to the therapeutic process.

**Genuineness.**   The counselor is congruent, fully present to the client, in harmony with himself/herself, and genuinely interested. The counselor is transparent, is open, and encompasses the attitudes that are being experienced by the client at that very moment in the counseling session. Rogers said, "genuineness or congruence is the most basic of the three conditions" (Rogers, 1959, p. 184).

**Unconditional Positive Regard.**   The counselor embodies a nonpossessive caring or total acceptance of the client's individuality, respecting and accepting of the client regardless of differing values, views, or how the client sees a given situation.

**Empathic Understanding.** The counselor feels what the client is feeling and truly understands the client's intimate experience. The counselor has the ability to emotionally relate and resonate with the client's experience as if it were the counselor's very own experience. In addition, having empathy for a client from another culture includes the ability to relate to the impact of that client's cultural background, race, gender, religion, etc.

## ATTENDING SKILLS

The attending skills of the counselor serve several important functions in the counseling relationship. They encourage the client to continue to talk, they model appropriate in-session behaviors, they communicate respect to the client, they give insight to the counselor, and they help the counselor stay focused on the client. Corsini and Gross (1991) believed that counselors need to possess the following personal attributes before application of attending skills will be successful: self-awareness, centering and relaxing, humor, genuineness, concreteness, nonjudgmental attitude toward self, and nonjudgmental attitude toward others (i.e., respect).

### Listening Skills

Attending skills are called listening skills by some authors. Corsini and Gross (1991) found that listening skills extend far beyond simply hearing what a client has to say. Effective listening skills are exhibited when counselors carefully

observe the client's verbal behaviors,

notice the client's nonverbal behaviors,

observe the client's bodily reactions,

use both open- and closed-ended questions,

encourage the client,

paraphrase what the client has said,

summarize what the client has said, and

reflect back to the client the client's feelings.

**Nonverbal Communications**

Both counselors and clients exhibit nonverbal communication behaviors. When a discrepancy exists between verbal and nonverbal messages, the nonverbal one is probably the most believable. Mehrabian (1971) found that most people retain only 7% of a message from the content; 38% from voice, speed of talk, and volume; and 55% from nonverbal cues (e.g., facial expressions and body language).

Counselors can use nonverbal behaviors to reinforce their words or to offer comfort. Hackney and Cormier (1994) identified several nonverbal behaviors counselors can use to free clients' potential for self-examination and self-understanding. These include direct eye contact, facial expressions (frowns, smiles, raised eyebrows), body positions and movement (intermittent head nods, relaxed posture), and verbal responses (modulated voice, minimal verbal stimuli).

According to Carkhuff (1980, 1983), counselors should attend to the general energy levels of clients in four major areas: grooming, posture, body build, and nonverbal expressions. Specific nonverbal expressions that help counselors understand the condition of clients include appearance of clothes and hair, conditions of hands and fingernails, head and eye movements, speed of movements, facial expressions, gestures, and items clients bring to the session.

Observing clients' nonverbal actions is not a new practice for counselors. In 1905, Sigmund Freud wrote, "He that has eyes to see and ears to hear may convince himself that no mortal can keep a secret. If his lips are silent, he chatters with his finger-tips; betrayal oozes out of him at every pore" (p. 64).

**Verbal Communications**

Besides the specific content of their verbal communications, clients offer several forms of verbal cues that provide important information to counselors. These include pauses, loudness, silences, hesitations, speech rate, inflections, and the specific words clients choose to describe their situations. Paralanguage, which refers to all extra-speech sounds and noises emitted from the client's mouth, including giggles, hissing, "uh," "hm," whistling, humming, etc., can also provide information to an attentive counselor.

**Advanced Attending Skills**

Seasoned counselors, having mastered the basic attending skills and developed their own unique counseling style, will also be able to identify and confront the client's inconsistencies,

identify and confront the client's conflicted emotions,

take the client to deeper emotional levels,

demonstrate case management skills,

question succinctly,

self-disclose sparingly,

willingly address such sensitive issues as sexuality, abuse, religion, or gender,

draw on a client's strengths and past successes,

freely use immediacy,

identify themes and recurring patterns in a client's life,

hypothesize about a client's condition, motives, prognosis, etc.,

increase a client's locus of control,

apply personal theory consistently,

set achievable goals,

align client's values with behavior, and

be timely and appropriate in terminating a client.

## Obstacles to the Attending Skills

Egan (1990) identified obstacles that counselors may encounter as they attempt to apply the basic attending skills listed above:

being preoccupied,

being judgmental,

having bias,

pigeonholing clients,

attending to facts,

rehearsing,

sympathizing, and

interrupting.

# GOALS OF THE RELATIONSHIP

Goals of the therapeutic relationship will depend largely on the concerns of the client and the theory of the counselor. Broad-based goals, however, can be clustered into several categories for ease in conceptualizing the change process:

*Changes in behavior.* Counselors help clients live more productively through focusing on current problems and the factors that influence and maintain them (Corey, 1991).

*Changes in decision-making ability.* Counselors help clients develop critical decision-making skills. For each decision, clients learn to estimate the probable consequences in personal sacrifice of time, money, energy, and risk-taking. Counselors also help clients explore their values as related to situations and to bring these values to full consciousness in clients' decision-making processes (George & Cristiani, 1986).

*Changes in the ability to cope.* Counselors help clients deal more effectively with the inconsistencies of others, current stress, anxiety, and new demands (Meichenbaum, 1986).

*Changes in interpersonal relationships.* Counselors help clients be more effective in their social interactions with others. This may involve addressing such issues as poor social skills, low self-concept, or family/child problems (Shertzer & Stone, 1980).

*Changes in potential.* Counselors help clients develop their special abilities, fulfill their potential, and achieve their possibilities. As Covey (1990) wrote, potential is a fundamental principle in the human dimension. Further, he wrote, "we are embryonic and can grow and develop and release more and more potential, develop more and more talents" (p. 34).

Regarding outcomes of the therapeutic relationship, Rogers (1961) believed change should occur in one or both parties involved, and that the fruits of change include more appreciation of each other, more open expression, and more functional use of the latent inner resources of the individual. George and Cristiani's (1986) synthesis of several theoretical models suggested that most theorists attempt to effect change in clients by helping them to feel better, to function at higher levels, to achieve more, and to live up to their potential.

# THE COUNSELOR'S VALUES

There can be no mistaking that counselors have values, and those values are a factor in the counseling relationship. While counselors may seek to be valueless, nonmoralizing, or ethically neutral in their relationships with clients, "values are basic components of the content of counseling . . . [that] affect decisions as well as actions" (Pietrofesa, Hoffman, & Splete, 1984, p. 33). Counselors should not only be aware of their own values but be honoring of the client's differing values.

Licensed counselors have a public trust placed in them by society. Society expects counselors to have values similar to those of the larger community, and to assist clients in becoming more functional people with improved morality and socially acceptable values. This trust is not unwarranted, as licensed counselors are well-trained, adhere to a code governing their ethical behavior, and have experience in distinguishing normal behavior from abnormal behavior. Poignantly, Boy and Pine (1982) stated:

> It is the client's searching and processing of values that characterizes the client's involvement in counseling. . . . [C]ounseling, then, is a relationship in which the counselor provides the client with a communicating atmosphere that gives the client the opportunity to become involved in the discovering, processing, and synthesizing of values. (pp. 80–81)

Corey (1991) said, "It seems sensible that we make our values known to our clients and openly discuss the issue of values in counseling," but warned, "We also have an ethical obligation to refrain from imposing our values on clients" (p. 19).

# HOW CLIENTS VIEW
# THE COUNSELING RELATIONSHIP

Both clients and the public generally view the counseling relationship as possessing certain characteristics and therefore hold certain expectations of counselors. These expectations include

*Caring:* The relationship will be based on trust, fairness will prevail, confidences will be kept, and outcomes will be helpful.

*Knowledge:* The counselor will be skilled—evidenced by formal training, certification, and experience with previous clients.

*Values:* The counselor's personal conduct and recommendations to clients will be in harmony with the laws, the public good, and principles of wholesome living.

# WHO COMES TO COUNSELING?

Epidemiologic studies by Vessey and Howard (1993) offer insightful information regarding the demographic breakdown of 1,429 people who made at least one mental health visit. Their findings are listed below:

**Gender**

| | |
|---|---|
| Male | 34.4% |
| Female | 65.6% |

**Education**

| | |
|---|---|
| Grammar school or less | 9.0% |
| Some high school | 10.7% |
| High school graduate | 33.5% |
| Some college | 23.2% |
| College graduate | 23.6% |

**Marital Status**

| | |
|---|---|
| Married | 49.5% |
| Widowed | 5.4% |
| Separated or Divorced | 22.1% |
| Never Married | 23.0% |

**Race**

| | |
|---|---|
| White | 89.2% |
| Nonwhite | 10.8% |

**Age**

| | |
|---|---|
| 18 to 20 years | 4.4% |
| 21 to 30 years | 22.0% |
| 31 to 40 years | 33.2% |
| 41 to 50 years | 19.8% |
| 51 to 60 years | 10.9% |
| 61+ years | 9.6% |

# WHAT BRINGS PEOPLE TO COUNSELING?

According to Peterson and Nisenholz (1995), people become clients in three ways:

1. *Self-initiation.* These clients have the greatest chance for success in counseling, as they are motivated by pain and generally trust the counseling process. Kadushin (1969) also found that the probability increases that people choose to go for counseling if they associate with people who value and understand counseling.

2. *Recommendations of others.* These clients do not have sufficient initiative or comfort level with the counseling process to seek out a counseling session on their own. The encouragement or the insistence of others motivates these clients to come to counseling. They may have reached a critical point with family or friends, who insist that the client come to counseling. The motivation is, thus, "other centered."

3. *Coercion.* These clients are referred to counseling by some authority figure—the court system, a social service agency, a teacher referring a student to a school counselor, or a business referring a worker for testing or psychological help. These clients have low motivation to change, as they are not in counseling by choice. They are called "involuntary clients."

# STAGES OF CHANGE

Counselors know that it is only when clients take responsibility for their actions that change takes place. Schlessinger (1997) wrote, "Victimization status is the modern promised land of absolution from personal responsibility" (p. 8).

Prochaska, DiClemente, and Norcross (1992) have articulated the stages through which clients must pass in order to change a behavior. They believed that self-change depends on doing the right things (processes) at the right time (stages). Their model is as follows:

1. *Precontemplative Stage:* Clients in this stage have no intention of changing. They are unaware of having a problem. While others may see their problem, they don't, and usually they come to counseling

only as a result of pressure from others. These clients may wish to change, but that is not their intention. While some theorists view these clients as "being in denial," this model sees them as being in a stage of development in the process of change, rather than as permanently stuck in a resistant state. If clients are unwilling to change within six months, they remain classified in the precontemplative stage.

2. *Contemplative Stage:* Clients in this stage begin giving serious thought to changing their behaviors. They have an idea about what needs to change and how to make that change, but they have not made a specific commitment to take action. They are only contemplating change. They are considering the pros and cons and the amount of time, commitment, energy, and risk that it will take to overcome the problem. They are "giving serious consideration to problem resolution." The contemplative stage can last for years. Counselors can help clients in this stage through consciousness-raising, confronting, encouraging, and education.

3. *Preparation Stage:* Clients in this stage make small behavioral changes. They are preparing to make changes and intend to take action within the next 30 days. Counselors can help clients in this stage by offering behavioral options, using techniques that raise emotions, and alignment of the proposed changes with the clients' values.

4. *Action Stage:* Clients in this stage make successful short-term behavioral changes by applying a lot of time and effort. Changes are visible and often noticed by others. Clients are able to sustain progress for up to a month. While their actions have not yet resulted in permanent change, an acceptable level of behavior modification has occurred. Sustaining an action may require repeated attempts at this stage. Counselors can help clients in this stage by being supportive and understanding, assessing the conditions under which clients are likely to relapse, developing alternative responses for coping, minimizing the probability of self-defeating behaviors, and not giving up on clients' unsuccessful attempts.

In this stage, counselors can give clients a strong sense of future direction by helping them develop a personal mission statement. This will align clients' new behavior with their personal value system. This written statement should reflect clients' major principles, values, and desires for the future. It will give them purpose and a code of conduct that will guide them in making decisions about behavior when confronted with life's challenges in the future.

5. *Maintenance Stage:* Clients in this stage are able to remain free of unwanted behaviors and engage in desired behaviors for more than six months. The ability to maintain new behaviors is not static but continuously fluid. While changes may eventually become permanent, it generally takes three or four attempts at the action stage before clients can maintain long-term change. With addiction behaviors, a relapse to lower stages is too often the rule. Counselors can help clients in this stage by working with them to stabilize behavior, review successes, set future goals, and prevent relapse. Stephen Covey (1990) said, "People can't live with change if there's not a changeless core inside them. The key to the ability to change is a changeless sense of who you are, what you are about, and what you value" (p. 108). The mission statement that was drawn up during the action stage can be used to strengthen a client's changeless core.

After a strong working relationship has been established with the client, this transtheoretical model can give counselors the ability to assess which stage a particular client is in and to then target issues with the intervention techniques that will motivate the client to the next stage. With this information, counselors can do the right things (processes) at the right times (stages).

# WORKSHEET TO FACILITATE CLIENT CHANGE

1.  The counselor must set an environment for the client that is conducive to change. List below three ways in which you will set such an environment.

    _____

    _____

2.  List any anticipated counselor obstacles (issues within yourself) that you anticipate might hinder your work with a client. What within you might block successful attempts to foster a client's growth?_____

    _____

3.  Identify, with the client, areas that need to be changed._____

    _____

4.  Assess which stage a particular client occupies with regard to his/her identified problem._____

    _____

5.  Develop a mission statement to serve as the client's long-term guide for principle-centered living._____

    _____

6.  Target the client's identified problem with specific intervention techniques that will motivate the client to the next stage of change. List below the specific intervention techniques to be used._____

    _____

7.  If a client is in the precontemplative stage, identify ways in which you will motivate him or her toward the contemplative stage (toward giving serious thought to changing a behavior). Would a mission statement motivate the client to change?_____

    _____

# Chapter 2

# THEORIES OF COUNSELING

There is nothing quite so practical as a good theory. (Kurt Lewin, 1946)

---

## PART A. INTRODUCTION

---

### WHAT IS A THEORY?

While a theory has been called "an educated guess," it nevertheless can serve as a bridge in linking beliefs to actions (Belkin, 1988). A theory of counseling assists counselors in four ways:

1. It is a way to predict the probability of something occurring. It lets counselors guess at what will occur when certain conditions exist.

2. It provides a basis on which counselors can make practical judgments.

3. It provides a logical connection between presumed causes and observed effects.

4.  It serves as an explanation for associating several varied or independent observations.

A counselor is guided by the theory that he or she follows. For instance, the counselor who subscribes to a person-centered theory may respond to a client's comment by reflecting feeling or empathizing, whereas a psychodynamic counselor might respond by attempting to interpret the client's unconscious motives. A counselor following a behavioral theory might reinforce, while an Adlerian counselor might look toward the client's early childhood for additional insights.

Whenever a counselor responds to a client or attempts to intervene, the counselor is putting theory into practice. As interventions are successful, counselors tend to repeat them, thus developing and refining a personal theory of counseling. The value of a theory emerges as the counselor experiences the effectiveness of the application of a theory. Theory is aligned closely with the counselor's values.

Theory is useful in organizing observations and as a basis for inexperienced counselors to commence counseling. However, there is a tendency for experienced counselors to cling to a theory even after they have evidence that their theory may not be working. Another pitfall occurs when a counselor is so tied to a theoretical approach that his or her perceptions of reality are altered to fit into the theory.

## FORMULATING A COUNSELING
## THEORY AND PROCESS

### Formulating a Theory

In attempting to develop a theoretical model, it is important to understand the basic components encompassed by most theories.

*Basic nature of people:* Who are we naturally? What is our pure state? What is our basic nature at birth (e.g., original sin, innate goodness, tabula rasa)?

*Personality:* How do personality and character traits develop? How do we get to be the way we are (e.g., nature, nurture, genetics, environment, chance, social learning, luck, etc.)?

*Effective living:* What is normal living? What do healthy, well-balanced people believe and feel? How should effective people live? Toward what goals should we be striving?

*Maladaption:* How do people develop psychological problems? What causes them to be mentally ill, ineffective, or to "go bad"? What is abnormal behavior?

*Change:* How do people get better? What must they do? How do people change? What motivates them to change (e.g., basic needs, insight, pain, love, power, fear, etc.)? What is the process for change? How do counselors assist clients in changing?

*Limitations:* What are the limitations of a particular theory or approach? Does the theory account for differences in culture, spirituality, gender, ethnicity, religion?

### Formulating a Process

By answering the following questions, counselors can hone their theory into a practical and useful tool.

*Goals:* What do you want people to accomplish? Toward what are you moving them? How will you measure your success and failure?

*Counselor's role:* What is your purpose and place in the process (e.g., build a good rapport, teach, coach, help them discover something, confront, be a resource person)? To what extent, and in what ways, do you need to be involved in your client's life?

*Techniques:* What are the techniques, activities, or therapeutic interventions you will use to reach your counseling goals?

## MAJOR THEORY GROUPS

### Cognitive Counseling Theories

Cognitive counseling includes the following theories and proponents: Rational-Emotive Behavioral Therapy, Reality Therapy, Neurolinguistic Programming, Transactional Analysis, Trait-Factor Analysis, Hypnotherapy, Cognitive

Therapy, Cognitive-Behavioral Therapy, Family Systems Therapy, Donald Meichenbaum, Aaron Beck.

### Psychodynamic Counseling Theories

Psychodynamic counseling includes the following theories and proponents: Sigmund Freud, Psychoanalysis, Alfred Adler, Tom Sweeney, Karen Horney, Neo-Freudians, Harry Stack Sullivan.

### Humanistic Theories

Humanistic counseling includes the following theories and proponents: Existential, Affective, Gestalt, Carl Rogers, Rollo May, Victor Frankl, Holistic, Fritz Perls, Eric Fromm, Abraham Maslow, Gordon Allport.

### Behavioral Theories

Behavioral counseling includes the following theories and proponents: Multi-Modal, Behaviorism, Behavior Modification, Systematic Desensitization, Relaxation Training, Self-Control, Objective Psychology, Edward Thorndyke, John B. Watson, John Locke, B. F. Skinner, Arnold Lazarus.

## MOST POPULAR THEORIES, THEORISTS, AND TECHNIQUES

### Most Popular Theories

Young and Feller (1993) surveyed members of two divisions of the American Counseling Association as to their current theoretical orientations. Below is a chart comparing Young and Feller's results to an earlier study by Smith (1982), who also surveyed counseling psychologists as to what theoretical orientation guided their practice.

|  | Smith (1982) | Young & Feller (1993) |
|---|---|---|
| Eclectic | 41% | 32% |
| Psychoanalytic | 11% | 5% |
| Cognitive Behavioral | 10% | 6% |
| Person-Centered | 9% | 22% |

| | | |
|---|---|---|
| Others (not listed here) | 9% | 3% |
| Behavioral | 7% | 3% |
| Adlerian | 3% | 2% |
| Family Systems | 3% | 10% |
| Existential | 2% | 1% |
| Gestalt | 2% | 2% |
| Rational-Emotive Therapy | 2% | 2% |
| Reality Therapy | 1% | 4% |
| Transactional Analysis | 1% | — |
| Multi-Modal Therapy | — | 3% |
| Psychoeducational | — | 3% |
| Ericksonian Hypnosis | — | 2% |

Zook and Walton's (1989) survey of counseling and clinical psychologists revealed the following: Younger clinical psychologists preferred behavioral approaches, while older clinical psychologists preferred psychodynamic approaches. Younger counseling psychologists favored behavioral approaches, while older counseling psychologists favored humanistic approaches.

**Most Influential Theorists**

Below are Young and Feller's (1993) repondents' ten most influential theorists, in order of preference.

First:     Carl Rogers (three times as many votes as second place)

Second:    Three-way tie among Albert Ellis, William Glasser, and Salvador Minuchin

Third:     Sigmund Freud

Fourth:    Two-way tie between Milton Erickson and Virginia Satir

Fifth:     Frederick Perls

Sixth:     Two-way tie between Jay Haley and Carl Jung

**Most Influential Works.**  Below are the books that Young and Feller's (1993) respondents named as having the most influence on their own counseling practice.

First:    *Client-Centered Therapy* (Carl Rogers, 1951)

Second:   *Reality Therapy* (William Glasser, 1965)

Third:    *On Becoming a Person* (Carl Rogers, 1961)

Fourth:   Two-way tie between *Families and Family Therapy* (Salvador Minuchin, 1974) and *Peoplemaking* (Virginia Satir, 1972)

Fifth:    *A New Guide to Rational Living* (Albert Ellis & R. A. Harper, 1975)

Sixth:    Two-way tie between *Problem Solving Therapy* (Jay Haley, 1976) and *Reason and Emotion in Psychotherapy* (Albert Ellis, 1962)

## Most Popular Techniques

Below are the 20 most popular techniques Young and Feller's (1993) respondents use in their counseling practice.

1.   Empathic understanding

2.   Encouragement

3.   Confrontation

4.   Helping clients find better ways of meeting needs

5.   Positive reinforcement

6.   Unconditional positive regard

7.   Identifying and challenging irrational beliefs

8.   Developing meaning in life

9.   Early recollections

10.  Here-and-now awareness

11.  Role-playing

12.  Cognitive restructuring

13. Reframing

14. Providing congruence

15. Identifying mistaken goals of behavior

16. Imagery

17. Coping self-statements

18. Logical analysis of thoughts

19. Interpreting family history/genograms

20. Focusing on "shoulds and oughts"

# PART B. MAJOR THEORIES

## PERSON-CENTERED THERAPY

(Nondirective, Client-Centered, Humanistic, Rogerian, Relationship Therapy)

**Major Proponents**

Carl Ransom Rogers, C. H. Patterson, Betty D. Meador

**Brief Overview**

Person-centered counseling is a nondirective humanistic approach that emphasizes the relationship between counselor and client, with the focus on the client's feelings. Through a constructive relationship with the counselor, the client is able to gain support, encouragement, and understanding.

The counselor is responsible for setting the three core conditions (Rogers, 1957) in the relationship that will free clients to cure themselves and move toward greater self-direction. The core conditions are

- unconditional positive regard,

- genuineness (being congruent), and

- empathic understanding.

Rogers felt that these three conditions must be experienced by the counselor and perceived by the client. When these key conditions are present, the counselor helps the client overcome his or her frightening and negative feelings about the counseling situation and engenders a feeling of trust and rapport. The counselor then helps the client begin to reorganize and restructure his or her subjective world wherever it is incongruent (Belkin, 1988).

A fundamental Rogerian belief is that people are basically good and will move toward self-actualization if provided a situation in which they can be free to be themselves and where love and understanding are present. The counselor becomes the major intervention tool. The therapeutic process is relationship-centered, not technique-centered.

Robert Carkhuff (1969) developed a 5-point scale to measure empathy, genuineness, concreteness, and respect, with counselor responses being viewed as additive, interchangeable, or subtractive. For example, the counselor's "empathy" response may be scored on one of the following levels:

Level 1:    Does not attend to or detracts significantly from the client's affect.

Level 2:    Subtracts noticeably from the client's affect.

Level 3:    Interchangeable with the client's content and affect.

Level 4:    Adds noticeably to the client's affect.

Level 5:    Adds significantly to the client's affect and meanings.

## Goals

The goal of person-centered counseling is the self-direction and full functioning of a client who is congruent and open to experience. The client should be able to set his or her own goals after insight is gained through experiencing the three core conditions.

## Counselor's Role

Person-centered counselors set the three personal conditions required for change to occur: counselor unconditional positive regard, genuineness (being congruent), and empathic understanding. The counselor must maintain a positive and optimistic view while modeling verbal participation and self-responsibility. The personal traits necessary for the counselor to be effective in this approach to counseling are often underestimated. The counselor possessing these core qualities is the primary intervention tool.

## Techniques

Rogerians set the counseling climate through personal embodiment of the three conditions. Other than listening skills, little or no emphasis is placed on techniques. Instead, reassurance, encouragement, acceptance, understanding, and respect are displayed by the counselor. For client- or person-centered counselors, the therapeutic process is relationship-centered, not technique-centered.

**Quote**

The counselor's role is to assume:

> the internal frame of reference of the client, to perceive the world as the client sees it, to perceive the client himself as he is seen by himself, to lay aside all perceptions from the external frame of reference while doing so, and to communicate something of the empathic understanding to the client. (Carl Rogers, 1951, p. 29)

**Key Terms**

Definitions of the following terms associated with Rogerian counseling can be found in Chapter 18: clarification, empathic understanding, genuineness, ideal-self, incongruent, parroting, rapport, reflection of feelings, self-actualization, and unconditional positive regard.

**Effectiveness**

With the emphasis on rapport-building skills, this theory is a popular training tool for students enrolled in master's level counseling programs. It is especially effective with clients who need to feel understood and need to develop trust. Emotional people respond well to this model. Person-centered counseling has been found to be effective across cultures.

**Limitations**

Person-centered counseling requires a full commitment to and a personal embodiment of the core conditions. It is not as easy to do as the basic concepts may imply. It may not be effective with client disorders that require medication or with clients who are not verbal. It also tends to discount the importance of the client's past.

# PSYCHOANALYTIC THERAPY

(Freudian, Psychodynamic)

## Major Proponents

Sigmund Freud, Joseph Breuer, Erik Erikson, Margaret Mahler, Otto Kernberg, Heintz Kohut, Otto Rank, Jacob A. Arlow, Wilheim Reich, Eric Fromm, Karen Horney, Nancy Chodorow, Harry Stack Sullivan

## Brief Overview

Psychoanalysis is a psychodynamic approach that focuses on the psychological conflict. It views the functioning of the mind as an expression of conflicting forces. Some of these forces are conscious, but the major ones are unconscious. Therefore, psychoanalysis emphasizes the unconscious and deals with hidden meanings.

Freudian analysis is a long-term therapy focused on restructuring the personality. Personality is divided into the

*id* (unconscious energy/motivations),

*ego* (mediator between external reality and inner demands), and

*superego* (which strives for perfection not pleasure).

Psychoanalytic counselors believe that people spend their lives trying to overcome their childhood.

The original Freudian view of human nature was deterministic, with an emphasis on addressing irrational forces, unconscious motivations, basic instincts, and biological drives. Later, neo-Freudians expanded the theory and stressed social, cultural, and environmental factors. Karen Horney (1967) developed the first feminist criticism of Freud's theory, emphasizing women's positive qualities and self-evaluation. Later, Nancy Chodorow (1978, 1989) emphasized the importance of emotions for women. Others (e.g., Spotnitz, 1963, 1968, 1976) developed innovative psychodynamic treatment techniques that boosted psychoanalytic popularity in the United States.

Freud held that the specific cause of neurotic behavior was inhibited sexual development. He believed unresolved and repressed emotions related to a client's sexual development manifest themselves in neurotic behavior and are to be addressed in analysis. Sexual drives are seen as powerful motivators.

**Goals**

Psychoanalysis addresses both psychosexual and psychosocial issues that remain unresolved due to some critical developmental task not being met and resolved at an earlier life stage. Other goals include: making the unconscious conscious, strengthening the ego through analysis of resistance and transference, and restructuring the client's personality.

Anna Freud (1946) identified four unproductive defense mechanisms that clients use to lessen anxiety, and which psychoanalytic counselors address in counseling.

> *Repression:* The client holds things in.

> *Reaction formation:* The client is a fake.

> *Projection:* The client blames others.

> *Fixation and regression:* The client is stuck and eventually moves backward or reverts to a less mature level of adjustment in order to feel safe and to get his or her needs met.

**Counselor's Role**

Psychoanalytic counselors seek to make the unconscious conscious by focusing on and interpreting the resistance or defense mechanisms that arise in the therapeutic process. They help clients work through issues of transference, and assist clients in gaining insight by bringing repressed material to a conscious level via such techniques as free association, dream analysis, interpretation, and analysis of resistance and transference.

**Techniques**

Free association, dream work, interpretation, projective testing, and analyzing resistance and transference are basic techniques of psychoanalytic counselors. The counselor also addresses a client's forgetfulness and misstatements (unconscious slips of the tongue, commonly called Freudian slips) to better unveil the unconscious.

**Quote**

> The patient talked and got well—how remarkable this must have seemed to those who heard of it! Despite all the subsequent rebellions and reactions to psychoanalysis over the years, this simple

principle of a "talking cure" as Freud called it, was to remain the guiding principle for most subsequent psychotherapies. (Gary Belkin, 1988, p. 172)

## Key Terms

Definitions of the following terms associated with psychoanalytic counseling can be found in Chapter 18: abreaction, anal stage, Anna O, borderline personality, compensation, countertransference, denial, displacement, ego, ego-defense mechanisms, Electra complex, fixation, free association, genital stage, id, identification, identity crisis, introjection, latency stage, libido, narcissism, object relations theory, Oedipus complex, oral stage, phallic stage, projection, psychodynamics, psychosexual stages, psychosocial stages, rationalization, reaction formation, regression, repression, resistance, ritual undoing, sublimation, superego, third ear, transference neurosis, and unconscious.

## Effectiveness

Psychoanalysis was the seminal psychotherapy from which other theories evolved. It was the first detailed, comprehensive theory of human personality and motivation. It verified the importance of the unconscious on behavior and focused researchers on the crucial impact of early childhood on adult personality. Freud showed that a person does not have to remain stuck (fixated) on a traumatic life event or unresolved childhood issue. Freud's terminology gave us many of the commonplace words of today's counseling field.

## Limitations

Psychoanalytic counselors are encouraged to be in counseling themselves or to have completed a lengthy analysis or other therapeutic process. Clients, too, are encouraged to prepare for lengthy therapy involving much time, energy, and cost. The psychoanalytic view of human nature is sometimes seen as too negative or pessimistic. The emphasis on childhood trauma rather than self-responsibility in adulthood. The focus on instinctual drives ignores social, cultural, and interpersonal factors. There are not many orthodox Freudians still available to clients. Psychoanalytic thought is often at odds with existential thought.

# OBJECT RELATIONS THERAPY

(Self-Psychology)

**Major Proponents**

Melanie Klein, Michael St. Clair, Edith Jacobson, D. W. Winnicott, Margaret S. Mahler, Ronald Fairbairn

**Brief Overview**

There are several object relations theories. Originally based on psychoanalytic concepts, object relations investigated the very early formation and differentiation of psychological structures—primarily an infant's relationship with objects, one of which would later develop into its mother. While Freud saw aggression as an instinct, modern object relations theorists see aggression as a response or reaction to a pathological situation. Freud focused on repressors and neurotic personality disorders, not on an examination of the structures of personality, which modern theorists believe manifest themselves in serious difficulties in adult relationships.

Object relations theorists focus on the relationships of early life, which they feel leave a lasting impression within the psyche of the individual (St. Clair, 1986).

Modern object relations counselors give more emphasis to the influence of the environment in shaping the personality than did traditional psychoanalytic theorists such as Melanie Klein, who retained Freud's belief that gratification of the instincts was the fundamental human need. Modernists believe that the "inability of an individual to make a satisfying connection with his or her family of origin carries over into later life and affects that person's new family system" (Peterson & Nisenholz, 1995, p. 280). Object relations counselors give primary importance to the influence of interactions with the external environment and interpersonal relationships, and secondary focus to innate biological factors in the shaping of human personality.

**Mahler's Stages of Development.**   Margaret S. Mahler's (1979) four stages of development offer an object relations perspective on development from birth to age three.

> *Normal autism* (birth to one month): Child fuses with mother, in an object-less state.

*Symbiosis with mother* (three to eight months): Mother and child reach a dual unity.

*Separation/individuation* (beginning at the fourth month): Child begins awareness of separateness of mother figure.

*Constancy of self and object* (beginning at the thirty-sixth month): Child sees consistency of self versus object.

## Goals

The goal of object relations counseling is to foster the reemergence and ultimate integration of primitive objects that manifest themselves in intense feelings that hinder individuals' relationships and shape how they feel about themselves (St. Clair, 1986). An additional goal is to analyze and interpret the client's early relationships with objects as they manifest themselves in the client's transference relationship with the counselor.

## Counselor's Role

The counselor refocuses the client's development pattern to one that leads to satisfying human relationships rather than gratifying instincts. The counselor centers on early relationships of the client, particularly the relationship between mother and child and how this relationship shaped the client's inner world then and his or her current adult relationships. In addition, the counselor emphasizes the environment, studies the disorders in the client's relationships, and focuses on developmental processes and relationships (Freud's oedipal stage).

## Techniques

Counselors attempt to direct overly attached or overly dependent clients away from the "repeating patterns of relating" that were formulated with their mothers when they were infants. Basic psychoanalytic techniques such as dream analysis, analysis of resistance, free association, analysis of transference, or other techniques that move clients toward independence and appropriate attachment are used.

## Quote

> Whereas Freud identified instinctual gratification as each individual's fundamental need, the object relation theorists (Melanie Klein, Ronald Fairbairn, and others) maintain that a person's need for a satisfying object relationship constitutes the fundamental motive of life. (Peterson & Nisenholz, 1995, p. 280)

## Key Terms

Definitions of the following terms associated with object relations counseling can be found in Chapter 18: ego, environment, instinct, object, object relations, self-psychology, and splitting.

## Effectiveness

Object relations illuminates early childhood development and experiences. It has proven effective with borderline personality disorders, narcissistic personality disorders, schizoid personalities, and attachment disorders.

## Limitations

The obscure jargon of object relations is a major factor in keeping it largely inaccessible to many counselors (St. Clair, 1986). Its concepts do not form a unified, discrete, or universally accepted body of truths, but are rather a collection of suppositions.

# GESTALT THERAPY

## Major Proponents

Frederick "Fritz" Perls, Ralph Hefferline, William Passons, Erving and Mariam Polster, Irma Shepherd, Gary M. Yontef, James S. Simkin

## Brief Overview

*Here and now*

Gestalt counseling is concerned with insight and self-awareness, and focuses on the present not the past. Gestalt counselors believe that becoming aware of what is going on in the present will lead to change. The past being seen as a memory and the future as a fantasy. Fritz Perls (1969), the best known gestalt theorist, believed in a holistic approach to personality development that fosters alignment between a client's public-self and private-self. The public-self is what the client does, and the private-self is what the client thinks. Lessening the polarization of personality dimensions is a goal of gestalt therapy.

Perls taught that an individual's anxiety is the result of "unfinished business." The zeigarnik effect is the tendency of a client to want to have this closure. Tying up of loose ends is thus a major goal of gestalt therapy.

Gestalt counseling is based on phenomenological-existential principles and focuses on awareness. Perceiving, feeling, and acting are distinguished from interpreting. Gestalt counseling uses focused awareness and experimentation to achieve insight.

Like Carl Rogers, gestalt theorists believe in progression toward self-actualization, but while Rogers' vision of self-actualization in terms of potentiality, gestalt therapists say, "Becoming is the process of being what one is and not a process of striving to become" (Kempler, 1973, p. 262).

Focusing on the here-and-now in the counseling session is important to gestalt work. Counselors need to be comfortable in immediately verbalizing their observations to clients. Making clients aware of their nonverbal behavior, word choices, revealing mannerisms, etc., helps keep the focus on the present.

**Keys for Living in the Present.**  Naranjo (1970) laid out nine principles to help clients live more productively in the present.

1.  Live right now (be more concerned with the present than the past or future).

2.  Live here (deal with what is present rather than with what is absent).

3.  Stop imagining (experience the real).

4.  Stop unnecessary thinking (instead taste, see, smell).

5.  Express, don't manipulate (don't be afraid to explain, justify, or judge).

6.  Don't restrict your awareness (give in to unpleasantness and pain, just as you would to pleasure).

7.  Accept no one else's "shoulds" or "oughts."

8.  Take full responsibility for your actions, feelings, and thoughts.

9.  Surrender to being as you are.

**Major Channels of Resistance.**   Effective gestalt counselors focus on resistances that inhibit a client's successful contacts with other people and the environment. Polster and Polster (1973) identified four major channels that clients use to resist being authentic.

*Introjection:* Clients accept the beliefs and standards of others without assimilating them in a manner to be congruent with who the clients are.

*Projection:* The reverse of introjection. Clients disavow certain aspects of themselves by seeing in other people the qualities they refuse to acknowledge in themselves. They avoid taking responsibility for their feelings and who they really are, which in turn keeps them powerless to begin to change.

*Retroflection:* Clients turn back to themselves what they would like to do to others, or do to themselves what they would like someone else to do to them.

*Deflection:* Clients distract, making it hard to sustain a sense of contact with others or the environment (nature). They use humor, abstract generalizations, and questioning to diffuse or blur the distinction between themselves and others. In interpersonal relationships, they display an absence of conflict, going along with what others desire and refusing to verbalize their true feelings.

## Goals

Gestalt counselors help clients becoming whole, mature, integrated, responsible, and authentic. But the main objective is always and only awareness, for that is what brings about the integration of the individual into one whole (gestalt).

Unintegrated clients are considered to be "phony," so counselors focus on completion of unfinished business through awareness and insight, which leads toward authentic reintegration of all their parts The counselor also strives to integrate polarities, a crucial attribute needed for self-regulation. Polarities are considered part of one whole, not as separated pieces, as in the concept of yin and yang. Lack of integration creates a dichotomy in the client, such as conscious/unconscious, body/mind, generous/greedy, introvert/extrovert, and dependent/independent. Through dialogue, the client can integrate parts of him- or herself into a new whole in which there is a differentiated unity.

Simkin and Yontef (1984) wrote: "The goal is for clients to become aware of what they are doing, how they are doing, how they are doing it and, at the same time, to learn to accept and esteem themselves" (p. 279). Gerald Corey (1991) wrote that effective gestalt counseling requires clients to have contact with other people and with nature without losing their own sense of individuality.

## Counselor's Role

The gestalt counselor takes an "I-thou" approach, where both counselor and client speak the same language, the language of "present centeredness," which emphasizes the sharing of direct and immediate experiences that are being felt by either in the session. Emphasis is on being authentic. Early gestalt practice stressed the use of confrontation, even intentionally frustrating clients at times. However, there has been a

> movement more recently toward more gentleness in Gestalt practice, where counselors prefer experiencing the client in dialogue to using therapeutic manipulation and decreased use of stereotypic techniques. Now more time is spent on process than on content. Dialogue is something done rather than talked about. (Pfeifle, 1997, p. 2)

The gestalt counselor observes and points out to clients their unspoken behaviors (nonverbal and body language). In addition, the counselor clarifies various awareness levels and encourages clients to address unfinished business, constantly focusing on the here-and-now. Gestalt counselors help clients relive experiences and finish the unfinished business in their lives, even if that business is with someone who is dead. Gestalt counselors also help clients become aware of the effects of their language patterns.

Successful counseling achieves integration in all the client's vital functions: ideas, emotions, and actions.

### Techniques

**Empty Chair.**   Chief among the gestalt techniques is the empty chair, also called the "two chair" technique. An empty chair is placed in front of a client, who pretends another person is sitting there. The client talks to that person, saying whatever he or she wants to say to that person. Later the client switches chairs and plays the role of the person imagined to be in the empty chair, and responding to what the client said earlier to the empty chair. This part of the exercise is a form of role reversal. The empty chair exercise helps to resolve unfinished business with someone. The technique is particularly effective in allowing clients to speak vicariously to a deceased family member with whom they still have unfinished business, or to someone who is too intimidating to approach in real life.

**Paradoxical Intention.**   The client is instructed to engage in and magnify the very behaviors of concern.

**Dream Interpretation.**   Dream interpretation is also used. The client is asked to become an object or another person in his or her dream and then to verbalize that experience from that new perspective. The interpretation of the dream is done by the client, not the counselor.

**Guided Imagery and Fantasy.**   Clients symbolically (imagine) recreate a problematic life situation and verbalize any thoughts that come to mind.

**Other Techniques.**   All gestalt techniques are aimed toward increasing awareness. They include the use of immediacy, role-playing, projection, personalization, and encouragement to focus on active feelings.

### Quote

> Integration is never completed; maturation is never completed. It's an ongoing process forever and ever. . . . There's always something to be integrated; always something to be learned. (Fritz Perls, 1969, p. 64)

## Key Terms

Definitions of the following terms associated with gestalt counseling can be found in Chapter 18: confrontation, empty chair, Esalen, explosive layer, gestalt, guided imagery (guided fantasy), here and now, immediacy, implosive layer, maturation, paradoxical interventions, personalization, phobic layer, projection, splits, topdog/underdog, and unfinished business.

## Effectiveness

Gestalt counseling works well with clients who can deal in the present or who are in need of redirection from past traumas that may be hindering current progress. Clients who have managed throughout their lives not to confront themselves on incongruent behaviors can be helped through the emphasis on immediacy and confrontation. Counselors who are creative and active can be effective with gestalt techniques.

## Limitations

Gestalt counseling may emphasize emotion too much and cognition too little, although more current practitioners focus cognitive patterns of the past that affect the client in the here-and-now. Effectiveness has been hard to measure and replicate. There is a danger of misuse of gestalt techniques, as they are powerful and may be hazardous with volatile clients. Gestalt counseling may be "too gimmickry-ridden" (Pietrofesa, Bernstein, Minor, & Stanford, 1980, p. 120), and emphasizes technique rather than the client when the counselor has not fully grasped the "I-thou" relationship and given it primary importance.

# ADLERIAN THERAPY

(Individual Psychology)

## Major Proponents

Alfred Adler, Rudolph Dreikurs, Harold H. Mosak, Bernard H. Shulman, Tom Sweeney

## Brief Overview

While Sigmund Freud merely mentioned social ties and social drive, Alfred Adler (1977) considered them crucial. Adler broke with Freud over the belief that people were social beings, and that the social environment was a significant influence on personality development.

Adler emphasized the conscious rather than the unconscious, and considered individuals responsible for their decisions. Each individual's personality is his or her own creation, not determined at childbirth as Freud postulated. While Freud said people were motivated by unconscious sexual drives, Adler said they were motivated by innate social strivings, which he called "social interests."

Adler believed that each person has a sense of inferiority and a need to strive for superiority. Adlerian counselors believe that people choose a lifestyle, a unified life plan, that gives meanings to their experiences and that includes habits, family, career, attitudes, etc. Behavior is seen as purposeful and goal-directed.

Two unique and important Adlerian concepts are *birth order* and *family constellation*. The child's position in the birth order of the family influences the child's perception of the world outside the family. The family constellation influences the child's interactions with and perceptions of the family group. The child's perception of the family environment greatly influences how the child comes to view him- or herself. Early memories are considered to be biased: Only significant childhood events are remembered, and these recollections are strong indicators of present attitudes.

**Birth Order.**   The place of birth offers insight into the personality traits that child will possess and the problems the child will encounter. However, the "ordinal position" is more than the chronological order of birth. The concept encompasses the psychological birth position of the child in the family. As time progresses, the family changes—parents may change, socioeconomic status may change, geography may change, etc.—therefore each sibling is born into a different environment.

Shulman and Mosak's (1977) offered the following key constructs of birth order:

> Children of the same family are not born into the same environment since the family environment changes with time.

> Although birth order is a key influence, it is not a determinant.

> Psychological birth order is more important than chronological birth order.

> Marked differences in the ages of siblings tend to diminish their competitiveness.

> The oldest sibling tends to be dependable, achievement-oriented, hard working, and adult-like, and gets the most attention.

> The second sibling tends to be successful in the oldest sibling's areas of weakness, competes with the oldest sibling, and is forced to share the attention of the parents.

> The middle sibling(s) tend to feel left out, and often cause problems for the parents.

> The youngest sibling tends to be babied, to choose different directions in life from the other siblings, and to seek a unique or special role in the family.

> An only child tends to be selfish, has difficulty sharing and cooperating, is often good at relating to adults and older children, and seeks attention both as child and as an adult.

For more information on Adlerian psychology, contact http://ourworld.compuserve.com:80/homepages/hstein/adler.

## Goals

Adlerian goals include overcoming feelings of inferiority, reducing discouragement, fostering social interests (identifying appropriate social and community interests), explaining clients to themselves, identifying mistaken goals, changing faulty assumptions, and encouraging clients to become contributing members of society.

## Counselor's Role

The counselor's role is aligned with the goals of Adlerian counseling, which are to encourage and increase the client's social interactions, point out mistaken client goals, minimize feelings of inferiority, and bring clients to insight. In addition, the counselor helps clients to reduce feelings of discouragement and change faulty motivations.

## Techniques

While client responsibility is emphasized, the counselor's attitude is one of collaboration. The counselor examines family constellations, dreams, early childhood memories, and spirituality. The counselor also challenges mistaken notions, fosters social change, and corrects mistaken assumptions.

Adlerian techniques include those that lead clients toward insight, such as discussing life histories, homework assignments, and paradoxical interventions. The counselor is an equal with the client; they are in a collaborative effort. An important question to focus the therapeutic process is: "What would be different if you were well?"

## Quote

> The individual with "psychopathology" is discouraged rather than sick, and the therapeutic task is to encourage the person, to activate one's social interest, and to develop a new lifestyle through relationship, analysis, and action methods. (Harold H. Mosak, 1984, p. 56)

## Key Terms

Definitions of the following terms associated with Adlerian counseling can be found in Chapter 18: communality, compensation, faith in others, family constellation, inferiority complex, life tasks, lifestyle, private logic, social interest, spitting in the client's soup, striving for superiority, and will to power.

**Effectiveness**

Adlerian counseling is a positive approach. A high value is placed on the client and counselor's relationship. Talking about spirituality in a session can be encouraging to clients. The family constellation and birth order concepts have spurred much fruitful research. Adlerian concepts are often used in parent education groups.

**Limitations**

Adlerian counseling is dependent on insight to produce change. It is an educational rather than therapeutic process. Adlerian confrontation can be seen as highly judgmental (George & Cristiani, 1986). Some basic Adlerian concepts are considered vague and not precisely defined. Adlerian precepts are difficult to validate empirically. Some clients may resist the in-depth look at their childhood.

# RATIONAL EMOTIVE BEHAVIOR THERAPY (REBT)

(formerly RET)

## Major Proponents

Albert Ellis, J. A. Bard, Russell Grieger, W. Dryden

## Brief Overview

Rational Emotive Therapy (RET), recently renamed Rational Emotive Behavior Therapy (REBT), is a cognitive approach founded by Albert Ellis, who is one of the pioneers in modern psychotherapy.

REBT holds that clients have the potential to be rational thinkers. When they think irrationally, however, which Ellis believes they do often, problems occur in their ability to live effectively. In childhood, clients learn irrational beliefs, or faulty cognitions, and are continually reinforcing those irrational beliefs through adulthood.

One example of irrational or faulty thinking is the tendency for people to "catastrophize" (imagine something terrible will happen if a certain self-expectation is not met). Irrational "self-talk" also is seen as a source of emotional disturbance.

**Fifteen Irrational Beliefs.** The following beliefs are considered to be anxiety producing and irrational. REBT counselors strive to diminish and rid clients of these thoughts.

1. It is a "dire necessity" for an adult to be loved or approved of by every important person in the community.

2. A person needs to have someone stronger than him- or herself on whom to be dependent.

3. A person's past history is the key determinant of present behavior and past experiences should continue to effect the present.

4. It is simply awful, or catastrophic, if events in this life are not the way a person would like them to be.

5. Unhappiness is externally based and a person has little control over his or her sorrows or pain.

6. Something that is hazardous or induces fear should be the cause for terrible concern and anxiety.

7. Rather than address life's difficulties and hard decisions, it is easier to simply avoid them.

8. People should be competent, adequate, and achieving in all ways in order to have positive self-esteem.

9. Certain people are "evil" or "bad," and they should be severely punished or blamed for their wicked ways.

10. There is one correct answer, one solution to a problem, and that if it is not found, trauma will result.

11. A person can go crazy.

12. The world should be fair, just, and impartial.

13. A person's life ought to be easy, comfortable, and painless.

14. A person should become very upset over another person's problems.

15. A person can achieve happiness or success by being reactive, uncommitted, docile, or selfish.

**The A-B-C-D-E System.** Ellis has simplified his theory into a system that shows the cognitive process through which clients pass.

**A** An Activating event occurs in a client's life.

**B** Beliefs about that event are formulated by the client.

**C** Cognitive Consequences (rational or irrational) occur within the client.

**D** Dispute irrational beliefs. The client and/or counselor confront the irrational beliefs about the activating event.

**E** The Effect is a rational cognition, which changes the initial belief (the Belief).

## Goals

The main goal of REBT is to eliminate the client's self-defeating outlook on life. Objectives include getting clients to acquire a more rational and tolerant philosophy, and to understand that it is not the events in their lives that disturb them but rather their reactions to those events. Clients are encouraged to change their emotions by changing the content of their thinking.

## Counselor's Role

In REBT counseling, little stress is placed on mental illness, emotion, or background. Instead counselors focus on items D and B above, confronting the 15 irrational beliefs listed above, and diminishing them. REBT counselors follow the A-B-C-D-E system.

## Techniques

REBT counselors' efforts are directed toward discovering and addressing patterns of irrationality. They listen for evidence of the 15 irrational beliefs and dispute them. Clients are taught how to identify and uproot their irrational "shoulds," "musts," and "oughts," and also how to substitute preferences for demands.

## Quote

> RET holds that virtually all serious emotional problems directly stem from magical, empirically invalidated thinking, and that if disturbance-creating ideas are vigorously disputed by logio-empirical thinking, they can be eliminated or minimized and will ultimately cease to reoccur. (Albert Ellis, 1984, p. 197–198)

## Key Terms

Definitions of the following terms associated with Rational Emotive Behavior Therapy can be found in Chapter 18: catastrophizing, cognitive restructuring, musturbation, and stress inoculation.

## Effectiveness

REBT works well with multicultural clients in getting them to examine their beliefs and premises. It is short-term, discourages dependence on the counselor, and stresses the client's capacity to control his or her own destiny.

## Limitations

Counselors may exercise too much power or control over the client in determining what is rational or irrational thinking. Beginning counselors may tend to shy away from REBT due to the reputation of Albert Ellis, whose style is abrasive, confrontive, and prone to salty language. REBT may not apply to clients with limited intelligence. Psychological harm also can be done to clients who have been beaten by extensive confrontation.

# BEHAVIORAL THERAPY

## Major Proponents

John Krumboltz, Carl Thoresen, Ray Hosford, B. F. Skinner, Edward Thorndyke, John Watson, Joseph Wolpe, Albert Bandura, Arnold Lazarus, G. Terrance Wilson

## Brief Overview

Behavioral counseling has become a less distinctive type of treatment, as behaviorists have incorporated cognitive theory and techniques into their approaches. Today it can be considered "a derivative of learning or behavioral theory that focuses on the individual" (Peterson & Nisenholz, 1995, p. 164). It employs duplicable scientific data, systematic desensitization, classical conditioning, and behavior modification techniques. A shared belief with cognitive behaviorists is that behavior is learned and so can be unlearned or relearned. "Behavioral counseling does not utilize as the fundamental principle the axiom that the client improves by talking, nor does it emphasize the importance of the counseling relationship" (Belkin, 1988, p. 273).

Behaviorists believe people are born capable of ill or good and are products of their experience. Maladaptive behaviors are, therefore, learned behaviors. People are considered the same as animals except human responses to stimuli are more complex and on a higher level of conceptualization.

Joseph Wolpe (1958), in South Africa, developed several original therapeutic techniques and constructs based on Pavlov's earlier works, including systematic desensitization, construction of an anxiety hierarchy, relaxation training, and reciprocal inhibition.

## Goals

The goal of behavioral counseling is to get clients to overcome maladaptive behaviors and learn a behavioral decision-making process. Clients strengthen effective and desired behaviors to prevent ineffective and undesired behaviors. Clients also reverse maladaptive learning, substitute new effective learning behaviors, and reinforce their own progress. Attempts also are made to identify the reinforcements that maintain behaviors.

## Counselor's Role

The behavioral counselor develops a strong personal relationship with the client, and then focuses on modifying observable behaviors and environmental factors that shape the behaviors. The primary task is to get the client, or patient, to learn new responses to old situations.

## Techniques

Techniques such as operant and classical conditioning are used by behaviorists, as well as direct education, reinforcement, behavior modification, social modeling, problem-solving, direct training, positive reinforcement, and decision making. Wolpe's systematic desensitization technique (based on the theory of reciprocal inhibition) is used to reduce a client's anxiety through increasing positive events (e.g., the fear of airplane flying might be met with a carefully planned, pleasant walk through the airport). By taking "baby steps" toward a negative stimulus, clients can draw on the relaxation part of their anxiety/relaxation status.

Behaviorists focus on overt and specific behaviors, and set precise and measurable goals. They establish a treatment program (a process) that is tailor-made to the client's needs, and objectively measure the success or failure of reaching the goals they set. Most behavioral techniques are experimental, but the main focus is on reaching stated goals.

## Quote

Gary S. Belkin (1988) wrote that behaviorists believe that as people

> interact with their environment, which includes significant others, their experiences and resultant behavior are recorded on the slate-initially in chalk, if you will, which can easily be erased. If the behavior is consistently reinforced, the chalk is traced over in paint, still not indelible, but much harder to remove from the slate. (p. 142)

## Key Terms

Definitions of the following terms associated with behavioral counseling can be found in Chapter 18: classical conditioning, cognitive behavior modification, extinction, implosive therapy, law of effect, operant conditioning, reciprocal inhibition, shaping, systematic desensitization, thought stopping, and token economy.

**Effectiveness**

Behavioral counseling can be especially effective in treating alcoholism, drug additions, anxiety, and juvenile delinquency, and in settings such as prisons, rehabilitation clinics, and youth reform camps. It can be adapted to a short-term approach, it is well researched, and it can be integrated into many cultural settings.

**Limitations**

Behavioral counseling deals directly with symptoms, so clients who seek insight may be disappointed. Success is somewhat dependent on the ability to control the environment. Focusing on behavior problems, it does not address broader human problems,.

# COGNITIVE BEHAVIORAL THERAPY

## Major Proponents

Aaron Beck, Donald Meichenbaum, Jacqueline B. Persons, Aldo Pucci

## Brief Overview

Cognitive-behavioral counseling holds that psychological problems occur due to commonplace errors of cognition such as faulty learning, making incorrect inferences (based on inadequate information), and basing behavior on unreasonable attitudes. The internal cognitive communication system (similar to a "preconscious" state) was termed by Aaron Beck (1976) automatic thoughts. Cognitive-behavioral theorists talk in depth about cognitive structures and internal dialogue. They are interested in overt behavior, but also explore the underlying processes (or inner speech) that guide behavior. Disorders are seen as the result of negative cognition, low self-esteem, self-blame, and/or negative interpretations of experiences.

Self-defeating behaviors (SDBs) result from unproductive cognitive thought patterns. They are not the result of a desire to lose (as Freud thought), but the result of an inability to conceive or act upon constructive alternatives. The client must confront and overcome behaviors that sabotage effective living.

## Goals

While clients choose alternatives based on their own self-interests, objective counseling goals are established. Research and assessment of outcome are emphasized more than in most therapies. The goal is to change behaviors and solve problems through teaching client's skills and a philosophy of living that will enhance their ability to achieve goals.

> This in no way implies forcing one's values or morals upon them. This process does not involve imposing the therapist's values of right-and-wrong onto the client. From the first therapeutic session, cognitive-behavioral therapists emphasize that only the client himself or herself can produce emotional/behavioral change. However, cognitive-behavioral therapists also emphasize that we will teach the client how to produce that change within him or herself. (Pucci, 1977, p. 4)

## Counselor's Role

The role of the cognitive-behavioral counselor is to help clients sharpen their discriminations, correct their misconceptions, attack self-defeating behaviors, and develop adaptive attitudes. The counselor attempts to establish an objective relationship with the client, and acts as a guide, an empathic, objective helper. Speech and teaching are vehicles for change. According to Pucci (1997), the counselor believes in

> teaching clients how to help themselves feel better and how to achieve the client's goals. If clients already had the appropriate knowledge to feel and act better, they would not need to seek professional counseling. The idea of sitting back and watching the client learn for themselves [sic] is akin to watching the rat in the cage get shocked until he finally figures out that hitting the bar opens the door to the cage. Clients want to learn how to feel and act better as quickly as possible, and the best way to help them is to teach them how to do so. (p. 4)

## Techniques

Techniques common to cognitive-behavioral counseling include distancing (getting clients to view thoughts more objectively), de-centering (getting clients to stop vicariously experiencing the adversities of others), changing the rules, reality testing, authenticating thoughts, cognitive restructuring, homework, and many REBT techniques.

Cognitive-behaviorists help clients to

gain insight into their views,

give priority to the most upsetting concerns,

practice cognitive/behavioral responses to upsetting actions,

create new thought processes and begin to apply them,

learn to assess and amend views to better align them with objective reality, and

identify their conscious thoughts that occur between a stimulus (action) and their response (how they behave in reaction to that stimulus).

Jonathan Chamberlain (1975) has described in detail many techniques to eliminate self-defeating behaviors. Donald Meichenbaum (1977) has used cognitive behavior modification techniques to shift the client from self-defeating thoughts to coping skills through stress inoculation, in which clients practice positive or reinforcing self-statements.

## Quote

> In essence, the cognitive-behavioral approach views thoughts as behaviors and suggests that what individuals think and, in particular, say to themselves influences what they do. The emphases, therefore, in this approach are to restructure how the clients think about various aspects of life and to improve the nature of self-talk. (Peterson & Nisenholz, 1995, p. 234)

## Key Terms

Definitions of the following terms associated with cognitive-behavioral therapy can be found in Chapter 18: cognitive behavior modification, self-defeating behaviors, and stress inoculation.

## Effectiveness

With its emphasis on changing behaviors and problem solving, cognitive-behavioral counseling meets the needs of people from many cultures. It also lends itself well to short-term therapy.

## Limitations

Counselors may view problem solving narrowly, rather than as part of the larger social and cultural environment of clients (Helwig, 1994). Cognitive-behavioral counseling deemphasizes feelings and insight in its treatment plan.

# MULTIMODAL THERAPY

**Major Proponents**

Arnold Lazarus, L. F. Brunell, D. B. Keat

**Brief Overview**

While basically a behavioral approach, Arnold Lazarus' multimodal therapy goes beyond behavioral ideals to emphasize the total person. It is sometimes classified as eclectic because of the potpourri of techniques that can be used.

Lazarus' holistic approach focuses on seven modalities in which clients can have problems. The acronym for the seven areas is BASIC ID:

**B**    Behaviors (acts, habits, reactions)

**A**    Affects (feelings, emotions, moods)

**S**    Sensations (touch, sight, smell, taste, hearing)

**I**    Images (how the client perceives self, including memories and dreams)

**C**    Cognitions (thought processes, philosophy, insights)

**I**    Interpersonal Relationships (ways the client interacts with others)

**D**    Drugs (biology, nutrition, alcohol, drugs, caffeine, wellness)

Multimodal therapy is distinguished from others in its emphasis on improving the client's quality of life (both emotional and interpersonal), rather than addressing a single symptom or presenting problem.

**Goals**

The main goal of multimodal counseling is to improve the client's richness of life. The goal of wellness is based on improving the personal effectiveness of the whole person, rather than on fixing only a single symptom. Multimodal counseling seeks to work with clients holistically and to get clients to see the interconnectedness and importance of a healthy balanced life.

**Counselor's Role**

In order to assess a client properly and determine total client functioning, the counselor addresses the seven interactive, yet discrete, areas of a client's life (the seven modalities), and devises appropriate interventions.

## Techniques

The counselor begins with an extensive, systematic, written intake evaluation, which comprehensively examines each of the modalities of the client's life. The counselor asks questions, gathers complaints, notes past history, and records symptom-influencing factors in the seven areas. A treatment plan is formulated, and a host of eclectic techniques can be employed; including medication if needed. Other techniques include relaxation exercises, anxiety control, biofeedback, imagery, hypnosis, modeling, assertiveness training, homework, and overt thought-control.

## Quote

> Multimodal therapy is very different from those systems that cluster presenting problems into ill-defined constructs and then direct one or two treatment procedures at these constructs. The basic assumption of the multimodal approach is that durability of the results is a function of the amount of effort expended by client and therapist across the seven dimensions of personality BASIC ID. (Arnold A. Lazarus, 1984, p. 507)

## Key Terms

Definitions for the following terms associated with multimodal therapy can be found in Chapter 18: modalities, quality of life, and eclectic counseling.

## Effectiveness

Studies over the past decade (e.g., Belkin, 1988) have confirmed that multimodal counseling can be effective in communities, schools, and institutions. Beginning counselors find this systematic approach easy to follow and it is an effective mechanism for focusing on several areas of a client's life. Lazarus is credited with effectively combining a holistic approach with behavioral and cognitive underpinnings, and heightening the awareness of "Drugs" as part of the treatment plan.

## Limitations

The multimodal approach has been criticized for omitting two important modalities: spirituality and gender. In addition, much of Lazarus' original work was done with clients from a high socioeconomic level.

# REALITY THERAPY

(Control Therapy, Choice Therapy)

**Major Proponents**

William Glasser, G. L. Harrington

**Brief Overview**

Reality therapy is a short-term therapy focused on present behaviors and getting client to accept responsibility for their behavior, which Glasser equates with mental health. It is a behavioral approach that concentrates on what clients do, not what they feel.

While pure behaviorists view behavior in terms of stimulus and response, reality therapists measure behavior against an objective standard, which Glasser calls their "reality;" whether social, moral, or practical.

**Glasser's Needs.**   Glasser teaches clients more effective ways of meeting their basic needs without causing others to suffer. The basic needs of clients include survival, belonging, power, freedom, and fun. Glasser (1965) said, "Everyone who needs psychiatric treatment suffers from one basic inadequacy: he is unable to fulfill his essential needs" (p. 5). Chief among the needs are two that, if unfulfilled, cause pain. These are the need to be loved and to love and the need to feel worthwhile to self and others. When clients are thwarted in their efforts to satisfy these two needs, they develop a "failure identity" and turn to deviant behavior or withdrawal. This can be changed to a "success identity" if the clients' behavior can change to meet those needs in a socially acceptable way.

Reality therapy holds that clients are in charge of their own fate and must learn to take charge of their own lives (accept self-responsibility). Clients learn to control their perceptions, which leads to control of their behavior, which leads to a success identity.

**Goals**

The main goal of reality therapy is for the client to acquire realistic behaviors (to "get real"), and to develop an internal locus of control. Clients plan for change, find alternative behaviors, and develop a successful identity. Clients acknowledge their basic needs and strive for better ways of meeting those needs.

## Counselor's Role

In reality therapy, the counselor is warm and involved, and uses confrontation, debate, advice giving, education, and self-disclosure. Because the ability to be responsible is a learned skill, a key counselor role is to teach clients responsible behavior. Initially that responsibility rested with the parents but now falls to the counselor. If responsibility was taught ineffectively in the home, clients will have an evolved sense of irresponsibility, ranging from simply irresponsible to mentally ill (neurotic or even psychotic).

Reality therapy counselors need to be resourceful and able to identify resources for the client's use. The reality therapy counselor models responsible behavior and clarifies, stimulates, sets goals, and educates.

## Techniques

Reality therapy counselors encourage their clients to face reality, to stop behaviors that they know are not productive, and to find productive alternatives.

**Eight Step Process.** The counselor moves the client through an eight-step process.

1. Create a relationship. (Make friends and ask what they want.)

2. Focus on present behaviors. (What needs are not being met?)

3. Evaluate current behaviors by asking, "What are you doing about it now?" (Avoid blaming past events or failures.)

4. Create a plan of action. (Make a plan to do better. Disregard behaviors that are not working and focus on new behaviors that might work.)

5. Commit to the plan. (Get a commitment from the client to follow the plan.)

6. Accept no excuses. (Fix responsibility on the client.)

7. Use no punishments. (The consequences of failure should be the ones that occur naturally.)

8. Refuse to give up. (Assure clients: "I will stick with you!")

## Quote

> Contrary to common sense, feelings do not happen to us. Therefore, one of the difficulties people have in understanding reality therapy is that we don't concentrate on feelings alone, but always on the total behavior of the person. In doing so, we always include the three psychological components of behavior which are what the client does, thinks and feels. All of these are chosen. (William Glasser, 1984, p. 331)

## Key Terms

Definitions of the following terms associated with reality therapy can be found in Chapter 18: responsibility, irresponsibility, and therapy.

## Effectiveness

Reality therapy works well in identifying problems and making plans consistent with different cultural values. It has a short term focus. The "contract approach . . . can lead to specificity and accountability" (Corey, 1991b, p. 387). It avoids blaming and punishment and asks clients to make value judgments about their behavior. A plan of action and commitment are essential ingredients, insight alone is not sufficient.

Glasser's original success came in working with adolescent girls in a southern California inpatient juvenile facility. Other reported successes of reality therapy include work in multicultural settings (Corey, 1996) as a form of brief therapy in college counseling centers (Austin, 1992) and in addressing issues faced by freshmen college students (Austin, 1993).

## Limitations

Reality therapy may be more a process model or technique than a theory. It has been criticized as too simplistic and as having too few theoretical constructs. It does not mention the unconscious, gender considerations, or the spiritual side of clients. Cultural environment factors can also be overlooked. The model tends to deal only with conscious, or surface, issues. It is very value-laden, and allows powerful or manipulative counselors to disregard a client's goals.

# EXISTENTIAL COUNSELING

## Major Proponents

Rollo May, Irvin Yalom, Paul Tillich, Victor Frankl, Ludwig Binswanger, and others listed below

## Brief Overview

The basic premise of existential counseling is that each person carves his or her own destiny and that one's essence, one's inner being, is the product of one's actions (Belkin, 1988). Phenomenology (the study of our direct experiences taken at face value) forms the basis of the existential movement. The idea that people have agency (free will and choice) and that people are responsible for their own destiny are essential components of existentialism. Clients are searching for meaning in their lives and struggle with being alone and feeling unconnected to others.

Soren Kierkegaard, a 19th-century Danish theologian and philosopher, was the first to develop a philosophy based on the notion of pursuing becoming an individual, formulating truth as a guidepost, and emphasizing the necessity of commitment. His approach was later named "existentialism" by German and French theorists Martin Heidegger and Jean Paul Sartre. The approach was later formalized into a therapeutic process by Swiss psychiatrist Ludwig Binswanger.

While Freud believed in an organism's "will to pleasure," and Adler believed in "will to power," existentialist Viktor Frankl (1963) believed in a "will to meaning." While each offers an explanation of the basic drive people have toward "authentic existence," existentialists like Frankl hold that analyzing the meaning in people's lives is of paramount importance.

Frankl (1959), a psychiatrist, developed logotherapy, a form of existentialism that he discovered as a result of his imprisonment in Nazi death camps. Logotherapy holds that mental and emotional disorders are really symptoms of an underlying sense of meaninglessness or emptiness. Covey (1990) wrote that logotherapy helps eliminate the emptiness in people by assisting them to detect their own unique meaning and their own unique mission in life.

## Goals

The central goal of existentialism is to help clients find and develop meaning in life as a way of reducing the anxiety associated with the threat of "nonbeing." Clients seek to better understand their own being (awareness of who one is, who one is becoming) and to be cognizant of their ability to freely and responsibly choose and set goals. Nietzsche has said, "He who has a why to live for can bear with almost any how" (Frankl, 1963, pp. 121, 164).

## Counselor's Role

Since each client is seen as a "total person," who is the product of his or her choices rather than of external circumstances, the counselor first seeks to fully understand clients and then to show them

*where* they have failed to realize their potential,

*when* they have failed to realize their potential,

*the degree* to which they have failed to realize their potential, and

*how* they can help themselves to more fully experience their existence.

Hypnotherapy counselors act as guides, emitting calmness in a soothing voice. They enable clients to create an image in their minds of both the problem (an undesired situation) and the solution (interventions that could alleviate the problem). Counselors assist clients in integrating imagined new behaviors into their lives.

## Techniques

Existential techniques follow understanding. Existentialists use a wide variety of techniques including

- free association (Freud),

- interpretation (Freud),

- hypnotherapy (Erickson),

- confrontation (Perls), and

- being open and inquiring.

Paradoxical intention (Frankl, 1967) invites clients to do intentionally that which they anticipate fearing doing, or that which they secretly say they wish to do. Clients may be asked to think about something when those thoughts are the client's worst fear.

The focusing technique (Gendlin, 1981) is a guided exercise that focuses clients on their internal body awareness identifying the focal point in the body of their energy source, so they will be in touch with their "felt sense" and make positive changes to that force center from an internal perspective.

## Quotes

> Approaching human beings merely in terms of techniques necessarily implies manipulating them. Approaching them merely in terms of dynamics implies reifying them, making human beings into mere things. And these human beings immediately feel and notice the manipulative quality. (Viktor Frankl, 1967, p. 139)

> I do not like to work with patients who are in love. Perhaps it is because of envy—I too crave enchantment. Perhaps it is because love and psychotherapy are fundamentally incompatible. The good therapist lights darkness and seeks illumination while romantic love is sustained by mystery and crumbles upon inspection. I hate to be love's executioner. (Irwin Yalom, 1989, p. 1)

## Key Terms

Definitions of the following terms associated with existential counseling can be found in Chapter 18: focusing, hypnotherapy, paradoxical intention, will to meaning, and Sunday neurosis.

## Effectiveness

Because client-centered counseling techniques often are used by existentialists, clients frequently learn to view themselves with greater honesty. Existentialism is open to experimentation and new ideas to reach goals, with many existential techniques still evolving.

## Limitations

Existentialists use many techniques and abstract concepts that are not easily tested. There is a heavy emphasis on understanding people, perhaps at the expense of finding solutions. Existentialism "is not a school of therapy nor is it a unified and systematic theory" (George & Cristiani, 1986, p. 73).

# JUNGIAN COUNSELING

(Analytical Psychology, Individuation Therapy)

## Major Proponents

Carl Gustav Jung, Aryeh Maidenbaum, Yoram Kaufmann

## Brief Overview

Jungian counseling holds that humans are not only unique individuals but also people who are connected to all humankind, past and present, and therefore have a "collective unconscious" that influences current individual behavior. Carl Gustav Jung viewed counseling as a healing process brought about through clients transforming themselves, gaining knowledge of themselves, recognizing themselves, and progressing toward self-integration. The basis for counseling is experiencing; mere intellectual understanding is insufficient.

A spinoff of Freud's ideas, Jungian psychology has as its goal clients becoming who they really are through making their unconscious conscious. Jung thought Freud placed too much emphasis on sexuality and too little on spirituality. Jung taught about a transpersonal or collective unconscious while retaining the Freudian belief in a personal unconscious.

Jung taught that products of the unconscious are symbolic and can be taken as guiding messages. Neuroses, then, not only are indications of psychic malfunctioning, but also show the way out of the conflict underlying them, if symbolically understood (Corsini, 1984). Jung also was a pioneer in studying attitudes, human functions, and intuition. He was one of the first to focus on the psychology of life after childhood, especially mid-life.

## Goals

The primary goal of Jungian counseling is the transformation of the self, which requires increasing self-knowledge, recognition of the true self, and integration of the self into a whole. The counselor and client view counseling as a healing process.

## Counselor's Role

Jungian counseling (a.k.a. analytical psychology) considers itself to be phenomenological in that the counselor must not hold preconceptions about human behavior. Jungian counselors follow the winding ways of the psyche, no matter where that journey may take them.

## Techniques

The counselor follows unbendingly the direction (guidance) of the unconscious. This models to clients a belief in the existence of a guiding force, the self, that points the way. Painful though it might be, the self shows clients a way of being that is more meaningful and encompasses more wholeness.

Carl Jung developed such techniques as dream work, storytelling, and symbolic tales, metaphors. The Myers-Briggs Type Indicator (MBTI), a widely respected personality test, is based on Jung's theory.

## Quotes

> Learn your theories as well as you can, but put them aside when you touch the miracle of the living soul. (Carl Jung, 1954)

> Theories in psychology are the very devil. It is true that we need certain points of view for orienting and heuristic value; but they should always be regarded a mere auxiliary concept that can be laid aside at any time. (Carl Jung, 1954, p. 7)

## Key Terms

Definitions of the following terms associated with Jungian counseling can be found in Chapter 18: anima, animus, archetypes, collective unconscious, persona, personal unconscious, the self, the shadow, and yin and yang.

## Effectiveness

Jung introduced the concepts of introversion and extroversion, and of a collective unconscious consisting of archetypes. Jungian counseling has been effective with clients who value the unconscious and who have a broad sense of spirituality.

## Limitations

The emphasis on dreams, fantasies, and drawings may not be suited to certain cultures or to a brief solution focus. Clients who are highly cognitive may be uncomfortable, even resistant, to this mode of counseling. The looseness and etherealness associated with Jungian counseling has also received criticism.

# TRANSACTIONAL ANALYSIS (TA)

## Major Proponents

Eric Berne, Thomas Harris, John and Katherine Dusay, Roy Grinka, Adelaide Bry, Robert and Mary Goulding

## Brief Overview

Transactional analysis (TA) proponents believe that the way in which people interact with others is both a symptom and a cause of psychological difficulties. TA analyzes the transactions (the most basic units of social interaction) between people and attempts to diagram the communication patterns between people's ego states. Ego states are the unique coherent systems of thought and feeling people manifest through their corresponding patterns of behavior. Each person has three ego states; Parent, Adult, and Child. From one of these three states a person responds to others, and this formulates a pattern of behavior that may be effective or ineffective.

**The Three Ego States.**  TA counselors believe personality has three distinct ego stages, or patterns of behavior, which clients use to communicate with others:

1.  Parent (filled with values, shoulds and oughts, and behaviors that are internalized from childhood; conforms to what people believe their parents would have them do).

2.  Adult (deals with facts not feelings, focused on data, decision making, and regulating the activities of the Child and Parent ego states).

3.  Child (expressed as the little boy or girl within us, fun loving, responds in one of the following two ways: a) the Natural Child who strives for total freedom and moves toward natural impulses such as love, affection, aggression, creativity, and spontaneity, or b) the Adopted Child who strives to prevent the Parent ego state from reprimanding. [The "Little Professor" is the term used to describe the emerging Child that negotiates between these two child ego states]).

**Four Life Patterns.**  The four life patterns of TA explain the strengths and weaknesses of interpersonal relationships (i.e., the way we communicate). They are developmental, with the goal being to reach the last ego state ("I'm OK, You're OK."). They include

1. I'm Not OK, You're OK,

2. I'm Not OK, You're Not OK,

3. I'm OK, You're Not OK, and

4. I'm OK, You're OK.

## Goals

The goal of TA is to get clients to stage four, "I'm OK, You're OK" (the mature Adult ego state level). But first the counselor must help clients get in touch with their feelings, or achieve "emotional literacy." Counselors teach the language and concepts of the ego states, get clients to recognize their current ego state, and help them settle on appropriate future interactions with others. Counselors also heighten clients' awareness so they are able to make better decisions regarding future behaviors.

## Counselor's Role

TA counselors are active in helping resolve conflicts between the three ego states, and therefore must be proficient in interpersonal transactions and life scripts. The counselor creates an environment in the sessions that fosters an Adult to Adult relationship and is free of game playing.

## Techniques

The concepts of games, life scripts, and scripts are explained to clients and are used to assist them in understanding the complexities of the three ego states and the four life patterns. The counselor teaches the concepts, assists with diagnosis, interprets patterns, and confronts where appropriate. The games clients play in order to avoid intimacy are emphasized (Berne, 1964). Contracts, questionnaires, questioning, and a "script checklist" also are used.

## Quote

The basic interest of transactional analysis is the study of ego states.
(Eric Berne, 1972, p. 11)

## Key Terms

Definitions of the following terms associated with transactional analysis can be found in Chapter 18: complementary transaction, crossed transactions, games, life scripts, and strokes.

**Effectiveness**

Clients tend to like the structure of TA groups. The contracts that clients create can be tailored individually to many cultural differences and values. This approach is conducive to short-term treatment and parallels certain aspects of Erikson's psychosocial development theory. In the group setting, the counselor gets to see individuals interacting with others and can analyze certain elements of personality structure and interpersonal relationships.

This is the only counseling theory ever to have two books on the national bestseller list for longer than a year: *Games People Play* (Berne, 1964) and *I'm OK, You're OK* (Harris, 1969).

**Limitations**

Clients who are seeking an affective approach may be disappointed. The strong emphasis on cognition may not be effective with some groups. Minority clients may have difficulty understanding some TA concepts and processes. There is little scientific proof for the Parent, Child, Adult patterns of behavior. After TA reached its peak in the late 1980s, it has continued to decline in popularity.

# TRAIT-FACTOR ANALYSIS

(Directive Counseling)

## Major Proponents

E. G. Williamson, Francis Galton, Carl Spearman, Donald A. Paterson

## Brief Overview

Trait-factor analysis is a cognitive, problem-solving approach. It is the only general counseling approach to originate in vocational counseling. It applies a mathematical approach to counseling through measurement and prediction. It uses data gathering, synthesis, diagnosis, and planning a program for the client. It measures and correlates multiple trait variables, such as memory, spatial relations, verbal, etc., and correlates them with interests, attitudes, and temperament. The groupings are then used to assess underlying patterns of people's personality and to predict behavior. These data are also used to help clients make personally effective decisions. Individuals are seen as a composite of abilities, aptitudes, interests, and potential.

## Goals

Williamson (1939) said trait-factor analysis was created to assist clients to achieve excellence and reach their full potential. Other goals include increasing rational behavior (Ewing, 1977), achieving self-understanding, choosing appropriate goals for living, striving for the good life, and making decisions based on rational evaluation of choices.

## Counselor's Role

Rapport is important, but the emphasis is on diagnosis, clarification, assessment, analysis, prognosis, psychometrics, synthesis, follow-up, and eclectic choices of techniques. The counselor acts as diagnostician and teacher, and is active in facilitating the formation of an action plan. The counselor establishes rapport, cultivates self-understanding, advises, and checks on the client to see if the advice is being followed.

## Techniques

The six-step trait-factor process is:

1.  *Analysis:* compile data and integrate it into a comprehensive record.

2. *Synthesis:* order/arrange data to assess strengths and weaknesses.

3. *Diagnosis:* identify the problem and causes; the counselor uses intuition and expertise at this stage.

4. *Prognosis:* predict client's chances of success or failure in moving to resolve an identified problem.

5. *Resolution:* provide direct help for an identified problem.

6. *Follow-up:* find the outcome of counseling and help the client deal with future problems (Pietrofesa, Bernstein, Minor, & Stanford, 1980).

## Quote

> [W]ithout in any way neglecting the affective richness of the full life of the human being still I feel that man's capacity to strive to become rational is among his greatest—if not the greatest—assets and capabilities. This is the reason why counseling to me, in the one-to-one relationship at least, takes the form of helping the individual to make a rational evaluation of optional choices with full awareness of alternatives. (E. G. Williamson, 1970, p. 311)

## Key Terms

Definitions of the following terms associated with trait-factor analysis can be found in Chapter 18: directive counseling, development of excellence, and personal cosmology.

## Effectiveness

Trait-factor analysis is effective in dealing with clients who are rational and who are concerned with solving problems. Self-responsibility is a key component, and final decisions are left to the client.

## Limitations

Although Trait-factor analysis is used little today, the many tests that counselors use in working with clients are to some degree based on its assumptions. The role of counselor as advice giver may not be best suited to emotion-oriented people.

# NEUROLINGUISTIC PROGRAMMING (NLP)

**Major Proponents**

John Grinder, Richard Bandler

**Brief Overview**

Neurolinguistic programming (NLP) is a unique methodology that blends psychology, linguistics, and communications. It is based on a communications theory that uses the five sensory channels, or modalities (i.e., visual, auditory, kinesthetic, gustatory and olfactory), to establish and maintain rapport with the client and to help the client do so with others. It also paces the client's verbal cues. NLP examines the structure of language and how clients use language to represent their reality.

In 1975, California linguistics professor John Grinder and math/computer scientist Richard Bandler drew on the work of Milton Erickson, Virginia Satir, and Fritz Perls to investigate what people did compared to what people said they did. The authors discovered that clients, in their verbal interactions with counselors, present sentences that do not necessarily or accurately represent their real experiences. These inaccurate interactions are called "false representations."

**False Representations.**   The following are deceptions clients frequently use in their language:

*deletions*—leaving out important parts,

*distortions*—blaming others for things that are in the client's control, and

*generalizations*—statements that fail to identify anything specific in the experience.

**Presuppositions.**   NLP counselors model and teach behaviors to clients. Failure does not exist, as all responses can be utilized. NLP counselors make the following assumptions about clients:

Clients can succeed if they break tasks into small units,

Clients always communicate using all their sensory modalities,

Clients' behavior is useful in some context, clients' behavior is toward
    positive intentions,

Clients' choosing is better than their not choosing,

Clients embody all the resources they need if they can access them when needed,

Clients make their best choices (but better choices, once learned, can increase their effectiveness),

Clients respond to their own reality, not to actual reality (NLP is the science of changing client's ineffective reality or "maps"), and

Clients are not wrong or broken—they work perfectly.

## Goals

Clients are helped to see their behaviors from a new perspective by placing a new valuation on ineffective behaviors. Counselors help clients differentiate between desirable behaviors and undesirable behaviors by separating intention from behavior. Clients are to adopt new ways of behaving in situations where previously they thought they had no alternatives. Another goal of NLP is to decrease false representations (deletions, distortions, and generalizations).

## Counselor's Role

The counselor's role is to identify the client's predominate sensory intake mode and respond to the client in that same mode. This increases trust and rapport. NLP counselors notice clients' eye movements, which indicate their representational system (e.g., when clients focus their eyes up and to the left they are using a visual system, drawing on their memory; while looking up and to the right indicates they are creating a story).

Through an examination of a client's "structure of language" and how he or she uses words to represent reality, NLP counselors attempt to gain access to a client's "deeper structure." When initially evaluating the client's "surface structure" (the verbal statements he or she makes), the NLP counselor views the client's optimistically—as functioning well, not as wrong or broken. The counselor focuses on how clients function now, and assists them to function more effectively.

## Techniques

Two major techniques are employed by NLP counselors—anchoring and reframing.

**Anchoring.** This is when a counselor reinforces a client through the use of touch, sound, facial expression, posture change, etc., hoping that when the counselor uses that expression again the client will be reminded of the favorable emotions he or she was sensing at the time the original "anchor" was used. For instance, a counselor may touch an angry client on the knee each time the client successfully mentions resolving his or her anger in a successful manner. Then, whenever the client faces a new dilemma, the counselor will use the anger to recall the favorable affect within the client and ask, "What would be a way in which you could resolve this current situation?" The goal of using anchors is to create/evoke new feelings and subsequent behaviors in situations where the client previously experienced undesirable reactions. NLP uses the term "anchoring" in a somewhat different context than other theories.

**Reframing.** The counselor helps the client get a new view of the problem. In NLP this can take the form of getting clients to revisualize a significant memory. The client then is led to changing the way he or she views and interprets the scene. In cases of a traumatic event (car accident, abuse scene, etc.), scenes may be replayed and changed in order to give the a client a new memory that is less debilitating. Clients thus see behavior from a different point of view, and thus place a new value on the behavior. This technique may demonstrate whether a behavior is desirable, or it may point to new behaviors in situations where previously only one option was apparent.

## Quote

> Clients are seen as presenting sentences that do not accurately represent their experiences by using deletions (leaving out important parts), distortions (assigning responsibilities to others that are within the client's control), and generalizations (statements that fail to identify anything specific in their experience). (George & Cristiani, 1986, p. 100)

## Key Terms

Definitions of the following terms associated with NLP can be found in Chapter 18: association, chunking, disassociation, modality, representational systems, resourceful, and visualization.

## Effectiveness

Bandler and Grinder (1975) claim NLP can cure phobias in less than an hour, help children overcome learning disabilities in less than an hour, eliminate habits, change interpersonal communication patterns, and cure psychosomatic problems in a few sessions. Most other theorists believe that language and word choice are not accidental and that there are revelations in body and eye movements.

## Limitations

Counselors must be able to identify the client's representational system and be comfortable and effective in responding in his or her modality.

# FEMINIST THEORY

## Major Proponents

Phyliss Chesler, Carol Travis, Paula Caplan, Mary Gergen, Laura S. Brown

## Brief Overview

Feminist counseling is both a process and theory. Based on recognition of the inferior status of women, it analyzes the forms and causes of female inequality and offers strategies for change. The goal is recognition and validation of a woman's reality, women's interpretations, and the contribution of women.

Contemporary feminism arose from the 1960s civil rights movement and its focus on individual rights and equality. Male-centered mental health systems and theories of development were challenged by women who felt that psychotherapy was a form of social control and a way of keeping women in prescribed roles. Early efforts at raising women's consciousness took place in the social context in which they exist. Feminist counselors believe that women should be empowered to change the social context that suppresses them.

Feminist counseling theory stresses the need for equality of "personal power" in intimate relationships. It substitutes "clear generational boundaries" for "hierarchies" in order to minimize power differentials between people. It advocates increasing the father's involvement in the family in nurturing rather than authoritarian roles. It considers unequal social power and sex role socialization to be the source and cause of many of women's problems.

Feminist counseling is not simply a set of counseling techniques or conclusions. Rather, it is a lens through which different realities of women are viewed and understood. It differs from most traditional (male-generated) counseling in that it:

refuses to diagnose clients as sick;

seeks to counteract the injurious effects of traditional socialization;

rejects traditional personality theory, the medical model, and diagnostic labels;

abandons the hierarchical relationship between counselor and client; and

defines the "personal" as the "political"—views women's experiences as being shared by every woman, not as private "hang-ups."

As many feminist counselors will readily agree, this model is political in nature, because the politics of life bear so strongly on women's issues.

## Goals

The goals of feminist counseling are to change the individual through increasing competence and control and to change society through increasing a woman's ability to affect political change. While insight is valued in counseling, it is not the ultimate goal.

## Counselor's Role

The image of the counselor as expert is used to effect change. Feminist counselors, while stressing the commonality of women's experiences, also teach the concept of "expert power" with knowledge and skills being "owned" by the counselor. Communications between counselor and client are open, honest, and direct.

Since feminist theory sees the social context as the prime determinant of behavior, counselors examine the systems that affect women's lives (family, school, job, etc.) and emphasize the biological and physiological aspects of a woman's life that might affect behavior and feelings.

The counselor's role is to help clients see that the past is continually recreated in the present.

## Techniques

The feminist counselor does the following:

gently questions unexamined assumptions,

shares appropriate statistics pointing to injustice and sexism (to help clients, couples, or families, explore new definitions of their problems),

reframes and relabels,

models instrumentality and competence (to promote the client's self-mastery and control of resources),

highlights the historic and social nature of past events that shape present behavior,

emphasizes the here-and-now,

seeks for clients to have insight and increased understanding, and

uses "referent power" (the counselor's self is used as a point of identification to help clients in their own self-examination).

## Quote

> Women are generally the most frequent consumers of mental health services, yet they are often subjected to mistreatment in the therapeutic relationship. Evidence has shown that women and men are expected to adhere to traditional gender-role norms in the psychotherapeutic situation. When out-of-role behavior is exhibited, clients are frequently labeled sicker than if their behavior had conformed to expected stereotypes. (Florence Denmark, 1994, p. 333)

## Key Terms

Definitions of the following terms associated with feminist counseling are found in Chapter 18: feminist modeling, women's ontology, and front range.

## Effectiveness

Feminist counseling is especially effective with women who are motivated for change and need empowerment. Women in male-controlled environments gain strength and find camaraderie with the counselor, who is of assistance when the client asserts more personal power. Men too benefit from the feminist perspective when counselors are able to sensitize men to the plight of women.

## Limitations

Susan Chamberlain-Hayman (1998) has said that feminist counselors need to consider the reality in which women live and the fact that women often structure their lives around the need for support and connection. Through the empowerment of feminist counseling, a woman may reject her current support and connection systems (her cultural environment). When experimenting with new behaviors, she may disrupt her safe, current environment to such an extent that she damages her significant relationships, financial status, and long-standing cultural support systems (e.g., church, extended family, friends).

Some critics believe this approach is more a process than a theory and that it downplays the importance of clients seeing themselves as part of a family system. It also can overestimate the power one individual has within the family unit. Overbearing counselors may tend to push their own agenda rather than honor the client's goals.

# CHRISTIAN COUNSELING

## Major Proponents

Paul Meier, Frank Minirth, Eugene Kelly

## Brief Overview

Like secular counseling, Christian counseling draws on a variety of therapeutic approaches. While Christian counseling takes many forms, there is some commonality of constructs.

There is general acceptance of Jesus Christ as the Son of God, the Redeemer, through whom salvation will come to those who believe and act according to His teachings. Many counselors believe the word of God is found in the Bible (Old and New Testaments) and is the resource to which client's must look for direction in resolving their personal concerns. It is through the Holy Ghost that biblical truths and the Will of the Father and Son are revealed. Clients are empowered to change through repentance.

The client's personal conscience alone is not the guiding force, for a conscious that is not in harmony with God's teachings (as revealed in the Bible or through a "witness of the Holy Spirit") is invalid. Aligning behavior and intent with God's Will is what is sought, not relying on the power of self. Because of this belief, fundamental Christians are often at odds with secular humanists and ideas that promote strong self-reliance.

While Christianity holds that all people are sons and daughters of God, there is nevertheless the belief that in their natural state people are selfish, weak, in need of God's grace, and have a tendency to ignore God's laws. "The natural man is an enemy to God," says the Bible (Romans 1:28–32). Secular solutions are viewed as rehabilitative rather than preventative (Maxwell, 1988).

Through a gift from God called "free will," or free agency, clients may choose to act responsibly or to be disobedient to God's laws. While problems do not disappear through obedience and full acceptance of God's Will alone, they are lessened, and clients are empowered and better able to cope (enduring to the end).

Christian counselors do not assume that all mental illness is due to sinful behavior or that disorders are a result of parental indiscretions. Powerful influences from early childhood and organic causes can also influence behavior. Sin can cause psychopathology, however, and sin can be the precursor to guilt, stress, shame, marital difficulties, anxiety, and more debilitating disorders.

## Goals

The goal of Christian counseling is to have clients understand God's Will and implement it through emulating Jesus Christ. He is the ideal, and to live with Him after this life, a person must live by his laws, do as he would do, and endure to the end. The Holy Spirit enters those who seek this path and serves as a guide to move people toward a Christ-like life.

## Counselor's Role

Christian counselors are directive and focus on getting clients to understand that the Bible and a strong belief in God both lead to healthy living in this life and secure a better reward in the life to come (Heaven). Overcoming a "weak will" and accepting God (or Christ) are essential to progress. Counselors point out the benefits of having God's love in one's life. They focus on removing sin with its attendant guilt feelings related to a separation from God. They also get clients to assume responsibility for who they are (a child of God), which is done through faith in his name, repentance, baptism, receiving the gift of the Holy Ghost, and enduring through obedience. Some denominations believe in being "saved by grace," which is accomplished through "confessing His name" and then remaining loyal to the end.

## Techniques

A Christian counselor typically begins by listening to the client while building Rogerian type rapport. The counselor helps the client gain insight by balancing the focus on the past and the present. The counselor assists clients in formulating a specific plan of action based on the client's feelings and ideas and on God's Will for them. God's Will is based on the Word of God (scriptures) coupled with the client's personal inspiration (revelation through prayer). Counselors often pray with a client, and for a client. Counselors model, encourage, and monitor living of a spiritual or Christ-like life—one that is full of charity, service, "spreading the word," etc., not coveting or pursuing the riches of the world. Counselors encourage clients to attend church or adopt other activities that will bring them into regular contact (fellowship) with other Christians.

## Quotes

> The true religionist is actually the ultimate realist, for he has a fully realistic view of man and the universe; he does not focus on facts that fade with changing circumstances or data that dissolve under pressures of time and circumstance. (Neal A. Maxwell, 1978, p. 1)

> It is the misapprehension of most people that if you are good, really good, at what you do, you will eventually be both widely known and well compensated. It is the understanding of almost everyone that success, to be complete, must include a generous portion of both fame and fortune as essential ingredients. The world seems to work on that premise. The premise is false! It is not true! The Lord taught otherwise. (Boyd K. Packer, 1989, p. 28)

## Effectiveness

Christian counseling deals effectively with a client's past through forgiveness. This allows absolution of past indiscretions upon full repentance. Once free of guilt (1 John 1:9), clients can look forward to a brighter future (Phil. 3:13–14). The emphasis on Christian service to fellow man can focus clients outward, which also has therapeutic value (increases self-esteem and gratitude). The Christian principle of restitution also has proven to be an effective tool in rehabilitating some criminals.

## Limitations

It is difficult to get clients to live a balanced life when the fervor associated with the goals is so demanding. Exercising faith to obtain a reward after this life requires that clients are able to delay gratification.

Christian counselors who, as is too often the case, lack academic training in counseling, can exhibit rigidity or too much zeal over the gospel, leaving clients feeling hopeless or frustrated. A narrow interpretation of God's Will may disavow the holistic nature of true Christianity. Some clients with hostile feelings toward religion will not be responsive to Christian principles, and some counselors may be intolerant of non-Christian lifestyles and alternative solutions.

# ECLECTIC COUNSELING

(Integrative Counseling)

## Major Proponents

Frederic Thorne, John C. Norcross

## Brief Overview

Eclectic counseling holds that no single theory is sufficiently comprehensive to account for the complexities of human behavior. Eclectic counseling selects concepts and methods from a variety of systems and borrows from other theories to help clients look honestly at their behavior and lifestyle and make decisions about the ways in which they want to modify the quality of their life.

Surveys during the 1980s (Smith, 1982; Young, Feller, & Witmer, 1989; Zook & Walton, 1989) consistently revealed that 30% to 50% of counselors consider themselves to be eclectic in their therapeutic practice. Of those practicing this method of counseling, Norcross and Prochaska (1988) found that 40% of their respondents favored the term integrative, while only 25% favored eclectic.

While other theories may effectively explain aspects of the human experience, eclectic practitioners feel that an effective counseling approach requires the best methods and techniques from all the theories to explain the rich, dynamic complexity of psychological development. Each theory makes a significant contribution toward greater understanding, but eclectic counselors tend toward theories with concepts that illuminate needs and transitions along the life span.

The mission of the eclectic counselor is to determine "what treatment, by whom, is most effective for this individual with that specific problem (or set of problems) and under which set of circumstances" (Paul, 1967, p. 111).

## Goals

The goals of eclectic counseling are as diverse as the theoretical approaches, but many counselors follow a modified cognitive-behavioral approach that stresses specific, concrete, short-term outcomes. Affective eclectic counselors focus on general, global, long-term outcomes.

Eclectic counselors find some consensus in the following list of objectives: examining old faulty decisions and making more appropriate decisions, creating improved social interests, reducing anxiety, omitting maladaptive behaviors and developing new behaviors, finding meaning in life, addressing emotional disturbances, uncovering the unconscious, restructuring ineffective personality, developing trust in oneself, striving for self-actualization, and gaining greater control over one's life.

Clients are asked to look earnestly at their behaviors and lifestyles. In areas of concern to the client, the eclectic counselor asks the client to make adjustments or refinements that lead to a better quality of life.

## Counselor's Role

The eclectic counselor has a broad knowledge of many counseling theories and techniques. The counselor selects principles and methods from several leading theories and integrates them into a treatment plan. Eclectic counseling offers more than "a bag of tricks." For example, the counselor may be dealing with both cognitive and affective issues while administering assessment instruments.

Eclectic counselors play many roles: expert, information giver, comforter, educator, resource person, guide, etc. The key role, however, is to assist clients in recognizing their strengths and discovering what is hindering them from relying on their strengths. The counselor helps the client clarify what type of a person the client wants to be.

## Techniques

The counselor's own personality and style are integral to the healing process, and practitioners who use an eclectic model are encouraged to use the techniques with which they are more familiar. Corey (1991) said counselors should be able to justify the techniques they use, and those may include "reflection of feeling and simply listening to a client's verbal and nonverbal messages . . . but to restrict yourself to these procedures exclusively is to hamper your effectiveness" (p. 436).

## Quote

> An eclectic counselor critically selects concepts and techniques from a number of counseling approaches, taking research findings into account, and blends them together with personal ideas and adaptations into a consistent whole. (F. Robinson, 1965, p. 338)

## Key Terms

Definitions of the following terms associated with eclectic counseling can be found in Chapter 18: systematic eclectism, integrative counseling, and zeitgeist counseling.

## Effectiveness

Eclectism's emergence as a major movement in counseling has freed counselors to use a variety of techniques to good result. In addition, counselors have found solace in being able to pursue their own style of counseling without feeling guilty or disloyal to a specific theory.

## Limitations

Critics have questioned the degree to which it is possible to be eclectic without losing all sense of structure. Inexperienced counselors may attempt to mix theories that hold incompatible underlying assumptions. If eclectic counselors choose techniques on the basis of their subjective appeal, clients can become confused.

# Chapter 3

# GROUP WORK

---

## PART A. INTRODUCTION

---

In individual counseling, you want the client to say whatever comes
to mind. But everything can't be said in a group. An important function of the group is learning what can and cannot be said in group.
(Kirman, 1988, p. 390)

## BENEFITS OF GROUP COUNSELING

Below are several benefits that counselors and client's enjoy through participation in a group experience. The group setting can

provide fellowship,

teach listening skills,

provide a sense of belonging,

parallel real-life situations,

develop rapid intimate relationships,

provide opportunities for peer confrontation,

conform participants to positive peer-group norms,

provide encouragement and praise from other group members,

provide a safe place to experiment with new behaviors,

provide an opportunity to confront the bias of a counselor in safety,

facilitate group interaction and other social skills,

provide positive and negative feedback from other group members,

meet the needs of a specific age group or those with a specific disorder,

decrease prejudice by learning of similarities with others, and

relieve feelings of personal isolation (especially helpful for sexual abuse victims and teen mothers).

## Yalom's Curative Factors

The benefits to be derived from membership in a group can be enormous. However, therapeutic change in groups is a complex process that occurs through an intricate interplay of counselor-guided experiences and members' personal experiences in the group. Irvin Yalom (1985) lists 11 curative factors that enable group members to participate, heal, change, and grow.

*Altruism.* Members increase their sense of self-worth through sharing and "giving of themselves" in the group. Through contributing they gain a sense of being of value to the group.

*Universality.* Members come to counseling with a sense of uniqueness, maybe even isolation, and find relief when they discover that others share similar issues and thoughts.

*Interpersonal learning.* Members learn both how they are perceived by others and the new qualities they will need in order to get along better with others.

*Imparting information.* Members benefit from direct instruction, receiving advice from others, psychodynamics, and didactic tutoring.

*Development of socializing techniques.* Members learn new skills depending on their willingness to receive feedback, instruction, etc.

*Imitative behavior.* In the spirit of Bandura's (1989) social learning theory, members copy behaviors of the leader and other group members.

*Group cohesiveness.* This is analogous to "relationship" in individual counseling. Members who feel they are a part of the group, who feel a sense of "we-ness" in the group, value and depend upon it and therefore learn from it.

*Catharsis.* Members learn how to express negative and positive feelings appropriately. They learn not to keep feelings and thoughts stuffed inside.

*Family reenactment.* The group conjures up memories and interaction styles similar to members' family-of-origin issues. Opportunities therefore exist to understand those relationships and work on them.

*Instillation of hope.* Members develop expectations for positive outcomes through their faith in the group process and through witnessing other members' successes.

*Existential factors.* Members learn that life can be unfair, that life is faced alone, that pain and death are a part of life, and to develop internal locus of control.

When these existential factors have been used in the group setting, Corey (1995) believes people are likely "to become increasingly self-aware and that expansion of awareness results in greater freedom to choose their own directions in life" (p. 254). These group factors are easily integrated into other theoretical frameworks, such as person-centered, psychoanalytic, and gestalt therapies (Van Deurzen-Smith, 1990). They also lend themselves to techniques found in psychodrama, cognitive-behavioral, Adlerian therapy, and reality therapy (Corey, 1995).

## GROUP LEADERSHIP

Groups can be conducted by one or more leaders. The advantages and disadvantages of having a co-leader are listed below.

**Advantages of a Co-Leader**

Some of the advantages of co-leading a group are that when two counselors are present in the same group there can be

an increase in energy in the group,

another viewpoint for feedback,

the perspectives of two genders,

a doubling of the peripheral consciousness of leaders (their ability to see all members reactions),

additional life experiences in the group,

two role models for members to emulate,

two leaders in whom members can confide outside of group sessions, and

the opportunity for leaders to recreate or imitate members' interactions.

In addition, dual leadership is an effective way to train new group leaders.

**Disadvantages of a Co-Leader**

The disadvantages of co-leadership include the possibility of

conflicting theoretical orientations,

power struggles between co-leaders,

differences between the co-leaders about blocking a group behavior, and

increased costs from paying two leaders.

# DIFFERENCES BETWEEN GROUP
# AND INDIVIDUAL COUNSELING

Group counseling tends to be more instructive and informative, while individual psychotherapy attempts to create a more confidential and personal relationship. Group counseling differs from individual counseling in several other ways:

Groups create a type of cooperation not found in individual counseling.

Groups enable the counselor to work with more people in agencies and schools.

Groups produce more effective results with certain minority populations.

Groups are economical in terms of time and money for both client and agency.

# GOALS OF GROUPS

Group goals will differ according to the theoretical model used by the counselor and according to the stated purpose of the group. Individual members may also have private goals they are addressing in the group. Below is a list of general objectives that are common to many types of groups.

- to solve problems;

- to learn more effective social skills;

- to increase self-direction and autonomy;

- to exercise proper decision-making choices;

- to set and reach both group and private goals;

- to discover new ways of resolving old problems;

- to learn to trust oneself in social situations;

- to acknowledge and confirm a unique sense of self;

- to develop trust of others through self-disclosure;

- to learn to genuinely compliment and praise others;

- to learn to confront others in an appropriate manner;

- to sense the commonality of others' needs and problems;

- to view oneself through the eyes of others in the group;

- to increase self-acceptance, self-confidence, and self-respect;

- to become more sensitive to the needs and feelings of others;

- to reveal to oneself, through speech, what one thinks and feels; and

- to clarify one's values and thinking through interactions with others.

# TYPES OF GROUPS

Groups differ with respect to goals, purposes, techniques used, role of the group leader, and the population to be served. Below are brief descriptions of the various types of groups.

### Therapy Groups

In therapy groups the focus is on unconscious factors, the past, remediation, and personality reconstruction in an effort to correct a specific disorder or meet emotional needs. Group members may have severe disorders or may be medicated. Sessions are often held at inpatient facilities. They may also be called "psychotherapy groups" or "therapeutic groups."

### Counseling Groups

Conscious factors, not personality change, are addressed in these groups. The emphasis is on personal, vocational, social, or educational issues. Sessions often are held in schools, agencies, or community facilities. When viewed as guidance groups, information is often centered on how and why the group topic is important. Examples: "Getting Your Child into College," "Passing the GRE Test."

### T-Groups (Training Groups)

Training groups are task oriented, educational, or informational. Sessions are often held in business settings in order to solve problems, arrive at answers, or motivate members toward institutional goals. T-group emphasis is on group process, not personal growth.

### Structured Groups

Structured groups focus on themes (usually on a specific life problem) and generating ideas about how to cope and overcome. "Pre and post" questionnaires, homework assignments, and group exercises are frequently used. Examples: assertiveness training, "Overcoming Perfection," "Women in Transition."

### Personal Growth Groups

These groups are geared for well-functioning clients who seek a brief, yet intense, group experience on interpersonal topics. These groups take a personal growth approach (developmental approach) to topics that focus on facilitating personal growth, increasing sensitivity to the feelings of others, and facilitating greater awareness of self and others.

### Self-Help Groups

Those groups are suited for people not usually served by mental health professionals. Participants share a specific life experience that is discussed and supported in the group. These groups are usually leaderless, functioning without a counselor's guidance. Examples: death of a child, fear of flying, Mended Hearts, Alcoholics Anonymous, Weight Watchers.

### Other Groups

Additional common types of groups include awareness, consciousness-raising, psychoeducational, leaderless, encounter, and marathon groups.

## GROUP LEADER'S SKILLS

> Group counseling techniques cannot be divorced from the leader's personal characteristics and behaviors.... The most effective group direction is found in the kind of life the group members see the leader demonstrating and not in the words they hear the leader saying (Corey, 1995, p. 53).

Group leaders should be trained in group dynamics, group ethical issues, technical procedures, the theories of group counseling (especially their own model), and the stages through which groups pass. Leaders should personally "live growth-oriented lives . . . have the courage to engage in self-appraisal . . . and be willing to seek new experiences themselves" (Corey, 1995, p. 53).

### Functions of the Group Leader

Yalom (1985) believed the following three leadership functions need to be addressed by an effective group counselor.

**Emotional Stimulation.** The leader encourages members to express feelings, beliefs, and values by using techniques such as confronting, challenging, self-disclosing, and modeling. The leader is honest and open, promotes trust in the group, and exhibits caring. The leader is concerned, warm, accepting, and genuine. Ineffective leaders may offer or allow too little or too much emotional stimulation, or may not exhibit enough caring.

**Meaning Attribution.** The leader provides cognitive understanding of the events that transpire within the group by using techniques such as interpreting, clarifying, and restating. The leader puts feelings into words (attributes them to something). Ineffective leaders do not offer sufficient meaning attributions.

**Executive Direction.** The leader provides structure, manages the group progress, suggests limitations, and otherwise provides direction by using techniques such as blocking, pacing, and summarizing. Ineffective leaders may provide too much or too little direction.

## Techniques of the Group Leader

The following are some of the many techniques used by group leaders.

**Active Listening.** Counselors pay attention to verbal and nonverbal messages and to underlying meanings. They focus on the way group members express themselves.

**Clarification and Restatement.** Counselors respond to unclear or confusing messages of members by rewording statements more clearly. They help members sort out their feelings and put them in words. Effective clarification and restatement improve members' self-understanding.

**Confronting.** Counselors point out to group members the difference between their words and their actions (the discrepancies between verbal and nonverbal messages). For example, a counselor might say, "On the one hand, Lorene, you said . . . , but on the other hand, I notice you are . . . ."

**Linking.** Counselors logically connect the comments of one group member to another. This helps build direct communication between members. Group interactions flow more smoothly when members talk to each other, not the leader.

**Protecting.** Counselors protect members from psychological and physical harm. They strive for fairness and emotional safely. Counselors protect members from scapegoating.

**Questioning.** Counselors ask questions that begin with What and How, avoiding both closed-ended and Why questions.

**Summarizing.** Counselors pull together, through verbal summaries, the vital parts of the session's interactions. Summarizing is used most effectively when changing from one topic to another and at the end of a session, when group members are attempting to make sense of what has transpired.

**Supporting.** Counselors personally encourage and reinforce members when members disclose personal information, face a crisis, attempt risk-taking behaviors, or try to integrate what has been learned in the group.

In addition to the skills and techniques listed above, others the group leader may employ include empathizing, reflecting feelings, giving feedback, interpreting, challenging, self-disclosing, modeling, and goal setting.

### Blocking Skills of the Group Leader

Leaders are often required to intervene when a member's conduct becomes counterproductive. In attempting to stop or prevent (block) an unproductive behavior, the group leader gently and sensitively focuses on the behavior, not on the individual. Examples of behaviors that should be blocked include:

*Gossiping:* When members talk about another member in the group without addressing that member directly.

*Group pressure:* When members pressure an individual to make changes or try to make demands of a member.

*Questioning:* When members interrogate others or ask repeated or numerous questions.

*Scapegoating:* When members "gang up" on an individual and vent their feelings in a hostile manner.

*Storytelling:* When members "bird walk," telling unrelated stories or stories within stories that stray from the topic.

# ORGANIZING A GROUP

The counselor has many decisions to make in planning a group. Below are some important issues to address.

*Purpose:* Define the reason(s) for this group. What are its direction, aim, and goals?

*Population:* What issues or disorders do these members have in common? Is the topic age or disorder specific?

*Meeting place:* The setting should be quiet, comfortable, large enough for bodily movements, yet intimate, and to allow for face-to-face interaction.

*Group size:* For adults the best group size is 6 to 10 members (8 is ideal). For children, 3 to 4 is best. Size varies according to the type and purpose of the group, environmental limitations, etc.

*Frequency and length:* How often and how long will the group meet? Corey (1995) suggested that for adults a weekly two-hour group is usually appropriate.

*Duration:* An ending date should be established at the outset. Private practice groups may run 30 to 50 weeks, while groups in colleges may last only a semester (about 15 weeks).

*Open or closed group:* A closed group allows no new members to join after the initial session. In an open group, new members may replace departing members, or additional members may enter throughout.

*Voluntary or involuntary membership:* Voluntary members participate through their own free will and choice. Involuntary members are sent to the group or forced to attend (e.g., court-ordered attendance).

*Structure and format:* What process will be followed when the group meets? What are the rules members should honor? What can they expect? How are members to participate during sessions?

*Advertising and recruiting:* How will the group be announced publicly? Where will the group be advertised in order to reach the targeted population?

*Pre-screening members:* The group leader explains the group's purpose, times, etc., at a private meeting with each member and ensures that the member's needs and the focus of the group are compatible. An assessment tool may be used to determine compatibility.

*Selection of members:* Members are selected on the basis of the pre-screening interview and compatibility with the group's purpose.

*Follow-up and evaluation procedures:* At the outset, a follow-up session is scheduled to assess the outcome of the group and to give members a clear picture of the impact that the group has had on them.

## RIGHTS OF GROUP MEMBERS

### Information

Group members have the right to the following information prior to the first meeting of the group:

purpose of the group,

venue/time/length/duration,

leader's qualifications,

goals of the group,

size (number of participants),

confidentiality and its limits,

general format or topics to be addressed,

cost of the group, and

the policy on participation during the group.

### Expectations

Group members have the right to expect that the following will be safeguarded by the group leader:

the right to leave when they desire,

freedom from pressure from members or leader,

the right to say, "I pass," at any time, and

confidentiality of what transpires in the group.

## STAGES OF A GROUP

The stages through which groups pass are not the same as those in individual psychotherapy. Below is a general model based on the early works of Yalom (1985), Trotzer (1977), and Tuckman (1965).

### General Model for Stages of a Group

**Initial Stage: Orientation and Exploration.** Primary tasks are identifying, including, and establishing trust. The leader's role includes modeling, identifying goals, and giving structure.

**Transition Stage: Dealing with Resistance.** Primary tasks are dealing with group anxiety, resistance, struggle for control, and challenging the leader(s). The leader's role includes intervening timely and sensitively, providing a challenge, and encouraging.

**Working Stage: Cohesion and Productivity.** Primary tasks are establishing cohesion, working together, developing group productiveness. The leader's role includes reinforcing, linking group themes, encouraging risk-taking, and supporting new behaviors.

**Final Stage: Consolidation and Termination.** Primary tasks are members transferring what has been learned inside the group to the outside world and dealing with termination. The leader's role includes helping members adapt to newly learned behaviors and dealing with termination and feelings of loss.

### School Setting Model for Stages of a Group

Another model for the stages of a group includes five stages with rhyming names. This model is popular in school settings.

**Forming.** The awkwardness of joining a group and being in a new situation are addressed.

**Storming.** Members react to the new demands of the mission of the group. They address what has to be done and question authority. They feel increasingly comfortable to be themselves in the group.

**Norming.** Order begins to form in the group process. Members conform their behavior to the group process and to the tasks that need to be accomplished.

**Performing.** Members focus their energies on the group's task, having already worked through issues of membership, orientation, leadership, and roles.

**Mourning (Adjourning).** As the group task nears completion, members address issues related to the group's ending (terminating). The group searches for positive closure and anticipates changes in relationships after the group ends.

### Irvin Yalom's (1985) Group Stages

**Orientation.** In this initial stage, the group searches for structure and goals. There is great dependency on the leader and concern about group boundaries.

**Conflict.** In the second stage, the group deals with issues of interpersonal dominance.

**Cohesion.** The third stage is characterized by harmony and affection. Later, full commitment to the primary tasks of the group emerges.

**Termination.** This final stage is a vital part of the process of bringing about change in members.

## GROUP ETHICS

**Informed Consent.** Prior to the first meeting, group leaders should provide members with information about the group, including their rights and expectations.

**Social Relationships.** Group members should be informed that forming relationships with other members or the leader(s) outside the group sessions is not permitted for the duration of the group.

**Confidentiality.** Counselors must clearly communicate to group members that while confidentiality is important and required in group work, it cannot be guaranteed. However, group members are charged with the same obligation that leaders are to keep confidences.

**Values.** Because of their position of leadership and trust in the group, group leaders should explain (prior to the group's commencement) any personal values or constructs (religious views, cultural assumptions, political outlook, etc.) that may impair their ability to be impartial or that may affect group members adversely.

**Organizational Ethics.** The Association for Specialists in Group Work (ASGW) (1989), a professional subdivision of the American Counseling Association (ACA), has its own Ethical Standards for group workers, which should be reviewed by all counselors who conduct groups.

## GROUP TERMS

Definitions of the following terms associated with groups can be found in Chapter 18: active listening, altruism, band-aiding, bird walking, blocking, catharsis, cohesiveness, existential factors, family reenactment, giving feedback, gossiping, groupthink, imitative behavior, intellectualization, linking, mind reading, modeling, group norms, peripheral consciousness, protecting, scapegoating, storytelling, summarizing, supporting, and universality.

# PART B. GROUP COUNSELING THEORIES

## PERSON-CENTERED GROUPS

### Goals

Person-centered group members build trust and then put aside their "safe selves" and progress toward a fuller and more genuine expression of their feelings. They gain insight into themselves, becoming aware of their problems and resolving to move toward wholeness and self-actualization.

### Context

Emphasis in a person-centered group is on feelings, meanings, insight, affect, and personal attitude. Change occurs as both the leader and members create Rogers' three core conditions: unconditional positive regard, empathy and understanding, and genuineness in their dealings with each other.

### Leader's Role

Since the group is to move toward its own goals, the leader's task is to respect that direction while modeling the three core conditions. The group is member centered and process oriented, with a focus on exploring feelings and thoughts. The leader creates a safe climate so members can truly be themselves. The leader is process oriented.

### Member's Role

Members develop their own goals, express feelings, support and encourage others, self-explore, move from safe disclosures to greater genuineness, and increase their efforts to become more internally focused.

### Techniques

Few formal activities are planned, but the leader and members do the following: actively listen, show respect, embody the three core conditions, reflect, clarify, self-disclose, and encourage.

# PSYCHODYNAMIC GROUPS

## Goals

Psychodynamic group members restructure their character and personality by working through repressed conflicts.

## Context

The focus is on the unconscious, past and present, but especially during the early stage (first six years) of the member's life, which determines personality and behavior.

## Leader's Role

The leader assists members with working through transference, addressing their defense mechanisms, and focusing them on recollections of early childhood.

## Member's Role

Group members observe other members' defense mechanisms and give feedback. Members are expected to free associate to their dreams, interpret them for others, and examine their own resistances that prevent the unconscious from becoming conscious.

## Techniques

Often a group "go round" starts a session to assist with a free association activity. Other techniques include interpretation, focusing on resistance, and dream analysis.

# RATIONAL EMOTIVE BEHAVIOR THERAPY GROUPS (REBT)

## Goals

REBT (formerly RET) group members develop a rational philosophy of life, replacing irrational beliefs with a more rational cognitive processing. They learn and apply Albert Ellis' (1984) A-B-C-D-E model in order to better understand how they create and recreate their own cognitive-based problems. Members eliminate self-defeating behaviors.

## Context

Members come to know that external events are not the source of their problems; rather, it is the way in which they respond to, process, and interpret those events that causes problems.

## Leader's Role

The leader shows how emotions and behaviors follow cognition. Members are taught about irrational beliefs and how to identify and overcome them. The leader is active as a teacher and confronts members about their irrational beliefs concerning reality. The leader, like the group, is both process oriented and outcome oriented.

## Member's Role

REBT group members need to be willing to concentrate and work on their thinking processes. They are required to practice outside of sessions and must learn to discuss in a rational and logical manner their own and others' irrationalities.

## Techniques

Several educational techniques are employed, including homework assignments, didactic teaching, group discussion, feedback, confrontation, role-playing, behavior rehearsal, cognitive restructuring, and desensitization.

# GESTALT GROUPS

## Goals

Group members gain awareness of their "here and now" through experiences in the group that focus on their "unfinished business" and through giving expression to repressed parts of their fragmented personalities. By becoming aware of their unconscious, members become more integrated and less "phony."

## Context

In gestalt groups, little emphasis is given to cognitive structuring or behavioral modification. Instead the focus is on the here-and-now (experiential catharsis). The gestalt approach is characterized by action and insight.

## Leader's Role

The leader insures that the group is member and process centered, focusing on the how and what of members' personal experiences. Verbal and nonverbal messages are observed as well as any resistances from members. The leader confronts and points out behaviors that are observed to be unauthentic.

## Member's Role

Members decide what "feeling issues" will be explored in the group, and those issues get acted out in the group. Members talk using "I" statements and act out unfinished business from their early life. Members offer and receive feedback from the group and have the responsibility for becoming aware of and dealing with their own unfinished business.

## Techniques

Techniques used include how and what questioning, fantasy experiences, focusing on what is being felt and experienced right now, dream exploration through becoming part of your dream, role-playing, and practicing new choices.

# BEHAVIORAL GROUPS

## Goals

Behavioral groups follow a contract (a treatment plan with specific goals) that details the group behavior and process that will be followed. Members identify environmental circumstances that maintain maladaptive behaviors, and then explore environmental changes and intervention strategies that will lead to behavior change. Members seeks to eliminate problem behaviors.

## Context

This action-oriented and rational approach to group counseling addresses behavioral learning processes and focuses members on finding ways of changing and learning new behaviors, cognitions, and emotions.

## Leader's Role

The group is leader centered and action oriented. The leader prescreens and interviews members, is active in assisting with goal setting, teaches self-management skills, and reinforces members' efforts. In addition, the leader monitors members' progress with their treatment plan, encourages therapeutic alliances among other members, and follows up after termination of the group to insure members are keeping their contracts and maintaining targeted behaviors.

## Member's Role

Members must agree to the behavioral changes specified in their contracts. They report weekly to the group on their progress (sometimes keeping logs of their progression), practice new behavioral roles, act as a support to others, and agree to meet after termination for a follow-up session.

## Techniques

Use of contracts is expected. Other techniques used include role-playing, assessing, reinforcing, cognitive techniques, desensitization, self-reinforcement, homework, and feedback to monitor progress.

# REALITY THERAPY GROUPS (RT)

## Goals

The first goal of reality therapy groups is for members to ascertain whether their current behaviors are meeting their needs. They learn how their irresponsible behaviors have led to problems. New behaviors are substituted for ineffective or irresponsible choices. Members seek to improve the quality of their lives by increasing control over their conduct.

## Context

The focus of RT groups is on behavior, not affect. Present behavior is examined and new, responsible choices replace poor choices. Group cohesiveness is initially important, but eventually members' personal needs and the new behaviors that will fulfill those needs are brought before the group. The group is leader centered and outcome oriented.

## Leader's Role

The RT group leader encourages members to face reality and evaluate the effectiveness of their efforts in light of basic needs. Appropriate actions are developed to rectify previous irresponsible choices. The group is outcome oriented and leader centered. The leader ensures that the group is rational and action oriented. Past concerns are avoided unless they impinge directly upon present behavior.

## Member's Role

RT group members must be willing to assess what they want and evaluate current behaviors. Honest self-examination is required. Members formulate a plan for change, commit to it, and seek to have greater control of their lives.

## Techniques

The RT group leader encourages open discussion to ascertain needs and then helps members to develop contracts. The leader confronts, avoids punishing, asks if current behaviors are meeting members' needs, uses paradox and role-play, assigns homework, commits members to the process, and gives the contract (plan of action) priority.

# ADLERIAN GROUPS

## Goals

Adlerian group members increase their positive self-esteem (moving away from feelings of inferiority) through an exploration of their early family environment. They gain insight into mistaken goals and self-defeating behaviors by developing greater social interests that lead them to a more meaningful life.

## Context

Also known as Individual Psychology, this approach to group work was developed by Alfred Adler, who created education and child guidance group clinics. Rudolf Dreikurs brought Adlerian group ideas to the US, where the interpersonal and social nature of members' problems was emphasized. Early childhood experiences are discussed, especially birth order and family dynamics, with an eye toward insight and meaning. Today the approach encompasses a holistic view of the person.

## Leader's Role

An Adlerian group leader's role is aligned with the goals of the group members. The leader examines the members' goals in order to understand the members. The leader encourages, supports, and helps members assess and clarify their problems by drawing on their strengths. This gives members the freedom to access and interpret significant early childhood experiences.

## Member's Role

Members agree to be active, state their goals in front of the group, keep commitments, deal openly with their issues of trust, analyze the impact of their family structure on current behavior, and take responsibility for their actions in the group. They examine their mistaken attitudes and admit their faulty motivations.

## Techniques

Adlerian group techniques are educational in nature. Lifestyle and motivations are examined. Other techniques used include confrontation, modeling, paraphrasing, encouragement, catching members in typical behaviors ("catching oneself in the act of being oneself"), acting "as if" (acting the part that you want to become), contracts, and reeducation techniques.

# TRANSACTIONAL ANALYSIS GROUPS (TA)

## Goals

TA group members contract on the work to be done in the group. They relive early life decisions (made in their Child ego state) and then examine how "injunctions" and messages applied when a child may no longer be effective as adults. Members make new decisions that are more appropriate for their current lives. Members apply concepts of TA— which include identifying life scripts, working through impasses, recognizing the ego states, and understanding the games people play—to focus on altering their course of life.

## Context

Eric Berne's (1964, 1972) TA theory as adapted to groups stresses that people are in charge of what they think, do, and feel. Interactions among people are both a symptom and a cause of psychological difficulties, so members experience interacting with others in the group. They make a contract for change, review and challenge their past childhood experiences, and participate in a group process that is both insight/action and rational/affect oriented.

## Leader's Role

The TA group leader teaches the language and process of TA. The leader gets group members interacting with each other and teaches them how they have "given power away." The leader helps members identify goals and commits them to a contract. Members learn from the group leader that they are responsible for what they feel, think, and act. TA groups are leader centered and have both a process and an outcome orientation.

## Member's Role

Members learn about the three dynamic ego states used in TA (Parent, Adult, Child). Members create a contract, examine the games they play, and explore basic TA concepts such as life scripts, basic life positions, and early childhood decision making. Members must decide how they will change and then plan specific ways to change their feeling, thinking, and behavior.

## Techniques

In TA groups contracts are vital. Other TA techniques include imagery, role-playing, fantasy, life script analysis, cognitive and affective techniques, the empty chair technique, desensitization, homework, and psychodrama.

# PSYCHODRAMA GROUPS

## Goals

Members of psychodrama groups release pent-up feelings through catharsis (an explosive moment of insight accompanied by greater self-awareness).

## Context

A basic belief of psychodramatists is that there is value in releasing pent-up feelings through acting out personally relevant situations, and that there are benefits from watching and participating in others members' enactments. Acting, or role-playing, commences when the leader suggests a theme to be explored by group members on a stage or in front of the group. Few or no props or scripts are used. Sometimes an individual will act out a theme or event from his or her own life. The roles should be vibrant, as these recreated situations from a member's past become key vehicles for releasing suppressed energy. Feedback from other group members assists with insight.

## Leader's Role

The psychodrama leader (director) must establish strong group bonding and give permission for spontaneity in order for members to feel comfortable enough to participate. The leader encourages intense emotional participation and catharsis. The leader helps the "protagonist" in the enactment to integrate what has occurred by asking for feedback from the group and providing closure for the session.

## Member's Role

Members must be willing to participate intensively—cognitively, emotionally, and physically. A protagonist (a group member) chooses a specific conflict to portray in the group through acting, fantasy, or other means, and enters emotionally into the live drama, while retaining the ability to determine the level of his or her involvement. Members share and interpret in a personal (not cognitive-analytic) manner. The discussion and processing of the dramas are vital to the education of group members.

## Techniques

The warm-up period may include guided fantasy, musical expression, dancing, light dramatic scenes (e.g., a discussion among family members at the dinner table), drawing, discussion, or creative personal introductions.

Psychodrama has a director/producer (the group leader), a protagonist (a group member), and one or more auxiliary egos (members who represent significant others or objects for the protagonist). It often uses "family sculpture" techniques to replicate a member's family or other meaningful relationships. These can be recreated both physically and emotionally. The scenes chosen are meaningful for the members and should lead them to catharsis.

Other techniques used include action-oriented self-presentations, directed fantasy situations, dream work, symbolic role-playing, and time travel. At closure the leader may employ discussion techniques to cool down or offer praise, do a "magic shop" technique, hold a solution roundtable, provide personal interpretation, offer aftercare, or act as a resource person to members needing post-group assistance.

**Founder**

Jacob Moreno (1946) developed this therapeutic process in which members enact their conflicts or crises before other members in a stage-like setting. Begun in Vienna, and known as the "Theatre of Spontaneity," Moreno's psychodrama focused extensively on the here-and-now. He attempted to bring members to a catharsis through insight and reality testing. Moreno's desired outcome for participants was to reorganize their perceptions, the same as it is in modern psychodrama groups. In 1941, Moreno founded the American Society of Group Psychotherapy and Psychodrama.

# Chapter 4

# FAMILY AND COUPLES COUNSELING

---

## PART A. INTRODUCTION

---

> Let there be spaces in your togetherness. . . . Sing and dance to-
> gether and be joyous, but let each one of you be alone, even as the
> strings of a lute are alone though they quiver with the same music. .
> . . Give your hearts, but not into each other's keeping. . . . Stand
> together yet not too near together: for the pillars of the temple stand
> apart, and the oak tree and the cypress grow not in each other's
> shadow. (Kahlil Gibran, 1968, pp. 15–16)

When working with couples or families, the counselor shifts from thinking in terms of individual experience to a broader, "systems" perspective.
Defining and resolving problems is viewed in the context of the family unit.
Most marriage and family counselors agree that it is best to see family members altogether in a session rather than see members individually. Many also
believe that family behavioral patterns are the dominant force in personality
development.

# FAMILY COUNSELING

## Differences from Individual Counseling

Couple and family counseling differ from individual counseling in the following ways:

A family member's problem or pathology is seen within the broad social context of that individual, particularly within the family context.

While the presenting problem may be focused on one individual, the counselor's attention is directed to the family unit.

A brief counseling model is used to move rapidly toward resolution of current or short-term family problems.

The identified client (identified patient) is the family.

## Stages of Family Counseling

While the stages outlined below are not discrete and may differ in order according to the counselor's approach, they are common to many approaches to working with families.

**Referral Phase.** The interactional process by which the family enters counseling. What are the issues that brought the family to counseling?

**Joining Together.** The personal rapport or empathy that counselors develop with the family. According to Garfield and Bergin (1978) this is the most important variable in determining the effectiveness of counseling.

**Making a Therapeutic Agreement.** Hanna and Brown (1995) found that how clearly goals and expectations are communicated between the counselor and the family affects how cooperatively the family will work together.

**Gathering Information about Family and Individuals.** The counselor decides if information will be gathered from the past, present, or future. The counselor then questions, makes observations, and applies theory-specific interventions.

**Hypothesizing about Gathered Information.** The counselor helps the family define the problem through questions and observations. What do family members think is currently going on? How do the individuals make sense of their experiences? Selvini Palazzoli, Boscolo, Cecchin, and Prata (1980) said gathered information is neither true nor false, but simply more or less useful.

**Applying Interventions.** Based on the gathered information (data collection) and hypothesizing (making assumptions), the counselor takes action to resolve the presented problem.

**Making the Evaluation.** The counselor encourages explicit feedback from the family in order to avoid impasses and misunderstandings. Family members are the ultimate authority on their own lives and evaluation of effectiveness is based on the individual's perception of whether they have been helped or not.

### What Is a Healthy Family?

Becvar and Becvar (1982) offered several characteristics of a healthy, well-functioning family. Within their broad framework, counselors can use their own styles and apply a potpourri of counseling techniques to move families toward healthy goals. A healthy well-functioning family system embodies the following characteristics:

legitimate sources of authority, which are established and supported over time,

stability and an established system of rules that members consistently follow,

consistent nurturing behaviors,

effective and stable child-rearing practices,

effective marriage maintenance practices,

goals toward which the family and each individual member can strive, and

sufficient flexibility to accommodate normal growth and crises.

### Life Cycle of a Typical Family

As individuals age, they pass through cycles in relation to the family unit. The stages outlined below are adapted from the work of Carter and McGoldrick (1980), who believed that problems in families often result from derailments in the family life cycle and that the goal of family counseling is to return the family to the appropriate cycle.

**Leaving Home of Origin.** The single young adult accepts separate emotional and financial responsibility for self and deals with issues of separation from the family of origin.

**Joining of Families Through Marriage.** The individual commits to a new family with its new family systems.

**Families with Young Children.** The individual and spouse deal with children entering into the system.

**Families with Adolescents.** The individual and spouse are confronted with the need to change parenting skills and to increase the flexibility of family boundaries. They also negotiate issues dealing with their aging parents.

**Launching Children.** The individual and spouse deal with being alone again, having no children at home. They experience frequent comings and goings of others in their life. This phase is sometimes called "the empty nest syndrome."

**Families in Later Life.** The individual and spouse confront changing generational roles. They face issues of health and renewal.

### Confidentiality in Family Counseling

Ethical guidelines state that counselors must not disclose information about one family member to another without prior consent. Family members also should have an opportunity to discuss the limits of confidentiality and create a covenant as to what will not be discussed outside the counseling sessions, and how members will deal with breaches in that policy.

## COUNSELING COUPLES

The dynamic in dealing with couples is different from that in individual counseling, group therapy, or family counseling. Counselors are faced with dealing with the relationship between just two people. The effective couples counselor needs to be aware of his or her position in the triad.

### Role of the Counselor in Counseling Couples

In working with couples, counselors do the following:

encourage couples to look at their marriage more realistically and objectively, act initially as a "sounding board" for feelings and complaints,

help couples identify the real, rather than the reported problems,

help couples realize how each partner contributes to the conflict,

empower couples to take personal responsibility for their portion of the outcomes,

teach fidelity and personal integrity,

help both partners deal with their own solutions,

help couples identify problems that arise from lack of character, integrity, or commitment to the relationship,

understand that neither partner is solely to blame for the problems in the relationship, and

act as a "mirror" to couples so that they learn to see the relationship and themselves from a new perspective.

### What Is a Functional Couple?

Sternberg (1988) identified ten rules that counselors can use when counseling couples who are seeking a more satisfying love relationship. Successful partners do the following:

1. Make their relationship an important priority in their lives.

2. Do not take their relationship for granted.

3. Actively seek to meet each other's personal needs.

4. Know when (and when not) to change as a response to their partner.

5. Value themselves.

6. Love each other, but not their idealization of each other.

7. Tolerate what they cannot change.

8. Are open to each other.

9. Create good times together and grow through the bad times.

10. Abide by the Golden Rule.

### Gender Issues in Traditional Marriages

When couples are in conflict, gender differences can be at the heart of their concerns. Counselors should be sensitive to research that suggests that women are more expressive and affectionate than men in marriage and that difference bothers women (Santrock, 1992). Women express more tenderness, fear, and sadness than men (Cancian & Gordon, 1988), and they want more warmth and openness from their husbands (Santrock, 1992). Men, on the other hand, cited *controlled anger* as a common emotional orientation (Cancian & Gordon, 1988), and "frequently respond that they are open or that they do not understand what their wives want from them" (Santrock, 1992, p. 500).

According to Jacobson, Holtzworth-Monroe, and Schmaling (1989), women are more likely to favor counseling as a way to resolve problems, and they push for egalitarian relationships, while men are less inclined to seek counseling and prefer to maintain traditional gender roles.

One widely circulated maxim from the 1980s with regard to gender differences was: "Women want to be listened to, men want to be appreciated."

However, counselors should always be sensitive to individual differences. Many individuals (as well as couples and families) do not conform to the norms of research or of stereotypes.

### Areas of Specialization

As marriage and family counseling has branched off from individual psychotherapy, subdivisions of marriage and family counseling have emerged as counseling specialties.

**Pre-Marital Counseling.**   Counseling before the marriage addresses such issues as finances, having children, the role of in-laws, sex, goals, economics, balance of power in chores, division of responsibility, decision-making process, fidelity, priority of the spousal relationship, migration, establishment of family traditions, support of educational and occupational goals, parenting, religious involvement, and contingency plans for trouble.

While these may be new concerns for couples first planning marriage, couples entering into a second marriage are usually aware of the importance of these issues. They can empower or destroy a relationship. All couples should discuss these issues during courtship.

Potential benefits to premarital counseling are that it offers:

a chance to define the roles in the marriage (e.g., duties, needs, and expectations of the partner),

forethought about children (Do they want children? When? How will they be raised, disciplined, schooled? What will be the role of religion in their lives?),

an opportunity to decide how arguments and differences in the relationship will be resolved before they occur; and

time to openly discuss important issues (e.g., sex, money, traditions, children, religious issues, in-laws, etc.).

**Second Marriage Counseling.** This counseling specialty has also been called "Blended Family Counseling." It address such issues as healing wounds from the previous marriage, personal "baggage" that may be brought to the current marriage, issues of disciplining children from a spouse's previous marriage.

**Intergenerational Counseling.** This specialty focuses on working with problems that confront not only husband and wife but also grandparents, parents, significant relatives, and children.

**Divorce Counseling.** This specialty focuses on helping those whose marriages have ended to deal with their emotional wounds and to face the future with renewed confidence and hope.

## FAMILY COUNSELING TERMS

Definitions of the following terms associated with family counseling can be found in Chapter 18: alignment, architects of the family, boundaries, classical conditioning, coalitions, cognitive behavior modification, extinction, family sculpture, first order reality, genograms, metacommunication, operant conditioning, power, reframing, second order reality, structural maps, theory of reciprocal inhibition, and time series design.

# PART B. CONJOINT AND FAMILY COUNSELING THEORIES

> The truth is that the different systems of family therapy are more alike in practice than their theories suggest. Moreover, each new approach tends to become more eclectic over time. Practitioners start out as relative purists, but eventually discover the validity of theoretical concepts from other approaches and the usefulness of other people's techniques. (Nichols & Schwartz, 1991, pp. 512–513)

In recent years there has been an increased movement toward an integrated model of conjoint and family counseling. Although there are still strong networks of counselors loyal to one pioneer or theory, the majority of marriage and family counselors today are trained in a diversity of styles.

The models and theories of family counseling described below vary in concept, terminology, and process. Successful family therapy may hinge on the counselor's ability to integrate the reality of the family with a theoretical model.

## PSYCHODYNAMIC THEORY

**Major Proponents**

Nathan Ackerman, James Framo, Robin Skinner

**Brief Overview**

Derived from the psychoanalytic movement, this approach emphasizes the infant's ego development (object relations) within the family context. Members of the family are viewed by practitioners as a central part of the infant's movement through the various stages of early childhood development.

**Key Concepts**

Couples usually bring to counseling introjects (imprints or early childhood memories) from parents or others, which need to be addressed. In many cases, the counselor attempts to make that which is unconscious conscious. Psychodynamic counseling reveals to couples defense mechanisms that are affecting the relationship.

## Goals

Disorders, or maladaptive behaviors, of individual family members disrupt the family homeostasis (balance). It is members' efforts in their individual roles that determine whether the family will move toward homeostasis (a key goal for psychodynamic counseling). Individual members may either help resolve or contribute to conflict. Psychodynamic counselors restructure an individual's character and personality, so as to move the family toward homeostasis.

## Counselor's Role

Ackerman (1966), widely acknowledged as the father of family counseling, believed that counselors should take an interactive approach and act as a catalyst for change. The single most important function of a counselor is to bring balance to the family unit.

## Techniques

Issues of transference are confronted by the counselor in the session. Counselors attempt to bring the clients to insight through analysis of resistance and free association.

## EXPERIENTIAL FAMILY COUNSELING

**Major Proponents**

Virginia Satir (Humanistic Family Counseling) and Carl Whitaker (Experiential)

**Brief Overview**

Experiential family counselors focus on the subjective needs of each individual family member and work to facilitate a family process that will address the self-concept of each member. Emotional expression is considered vital to the growth process.

**Satir's Model.**   Virginia Satir (1972) listed four aspects of the family that are subject to change, correction, and improvement:

1.   Each family member's feelings of self-worth.

2.   The communication abilities of each family member.

3.   The family system.

4.   The way things are done within the family (the family rules).

The family rules, according to Satir, are the most difficult to uncover in counseling because they are often unspoken or not consciously known. Satir's goal was to have all family members, including parents (whom she called the "architects of the family"), understand the rules that govern the family's emotional interchanges. These rules include freedom to act, freedom to express what one is seeing or hearing, freedom to agree or disapprove, and freedom to ask questions.

**Whitaker's Model.**   Carl Whitaker (Whitaker & Bumberry, 1988) was another strong proponent of experiential family counseling. Whitaker held that growth is an interpersonal process, and he used aggressive encounter as the vehicle for change. Whitaker said he is comfortable being confrontive, even argumentative, in order to encourage honest expressions of emotions instead of concealing pain or distrust. Whitaker used symbolism to make unexamined experiences more conscious for clients. Whitaker's motto might well have been: Anything worth knowing can't be taught; it must be experienced.

**Key Concepts**

A family is dysfunctional when family rules are not clearly understood.

There are no bad family members, only bad family rules.

Families need to be able to alter discrepancies between the intent and impact of their messages (Hanna & Brown, 1995).

Trust will be established in families when members are willing to take risks.

Families have the resources within themselves to flourish, grow, and increase in self-concept. Discrepancies (poor family communications) block family members from healthy functioning.

Satir held that family members under duress will adopt one of five different styles of communication. These styles are patterns of response clients will use to avoid the threat of being rejected. They include

- the Placater (the family member that tries to please),

- the Blamer (the fault-finder, dictator, boss),

- the Super-Reasonable,

- the Irrelevant, and

- the Congruent Communicator (the most healthy style).

**Goals**

The goals of experiential family counselors are personal growth and self-responsibility. The expression of emotions is the vehicle for exploration of issues. Satir's goals centered on relieving family pain, increasing personal growth, and heightening self-concept. Whitaker's goals were to develop interpersonal competence and self-responsibility through "awareness changes" in the family.

**Counselor's Role**

When the counselor is open and spontaneous, family members learn to behave in like manner. Satir taught that the family counselor should be internally open, model openness and congruent communication, and serve as a resource for members.

The counselor helps family members to clarify values so they can more easily communicate with one another. The counselor also attempts to get family members to adjust to family events in such a way that individual achievement (personal satisfaction) occurs, and to analyze family interactions with an eye toward development of each family member's individual self-worth.

Carl Whitaker taught counselors to model openness and directness, to be highly engaged, to use confrontation, and to employ argumentation to bring awareness to family members. The counselor also challenges ineffective traditions and urges movement toward new goals.

### Techniques

Satir used family sculpting, acceptance, and family communications training, while Whitaker used modeling behavior, confrontation, argumentation, and cotherapy.

# STRATEGIC FAMILY THERAPY

(MRI Interactional Family Therapy)

## Major Proponents

Jay Haley, Cloe Madanes, Paul Watziawick, Don Jackson, Milton Erickson, and the Mental Research Institute (MRI)

## Brief Overview

**Haley's Model.** In Jay Haley's approach, the counselor develops in advance a specific strategy to resolve the presented problem as efficiently as possible. Strategic counseling views the family as a system with several subsystems. It centers on aspects of family communications: communication problems, mutual interpretation of messages, and giving feedback.

**The MRI Model.** The Mental Research Institute's approach addresses family communication patterns and postulates that power and control characterize relationships in families.

## Key Concepts

Symptoms are seen as messages, and solutions are sometimes the problem. A chief concern is the utopian syndrome, which occurs when problems are attributable to a family member's idealistic view of how things ought to be. Most family conflicts are based on family members' perceptual differences.

## Goals

The goals of strategic family counseling include interrupting (eliminating) sequential patterns of behavior (problematic sequences) that cause a family to be stuck at a particular stage in the family life cycle. Changes in thinking and interactional communication patterns are sought. Families are to be left with skills that will help them stop dysfunctional sequencing and improve their communication skills.

## Counselor's Role

The strategic family therapist "serves as a stage director who provides directives to the family. The therapist hypothesizes about each problem and provides a directive to the family in an attempt to solve it" (Hanna & Brown, 1995, pp. 8–9). The counselor redefines the family's presenting problem from one that is focused on an individual's situation (e.g., one child's anger) to a behavioral or interactional problem that can be alleviated (e.g., discovering the precipitating interactions that lead to anger). In addition, the counselor examines the metaphors that a family uses (e.g., a headache may be a symptom or symbol for "I want more attention"), reframes, and assesses which family interactions are successful.

## Techniques

The counselor uses direct suggestions: addressing shame (inducing restitution), giving assignments, and reframing. The strategic family counselor also uses the following types of *paradoxes*.

*Therapeutic double-bind:* The counselor allows the client to do something that the client knows he or she should quit. This technique catches the client in a "therapeutic dilemma."

*Prescribing the symptom:* The client is told to continue a problematic behavior. This technique leads to the eradication of the behavior or to admitting no control over it.

*Relabeling:* The counselor reframes the meaning of a situation or event so that it is perceived in a different way by the client.

# FAMILY SYSTEMS THEORY

(Intergenerational Family Theory)

## Major Proponents

Murray Bowen and Ivan Boszormenyi-Nagy

## Brief Overview

In this well-developed family counseling theory, family problems are seen in a multigenerational and extended family context. The focus is on family beliefs, conflicts, and losses transferred from one generation to another. Family generations are seen as connected through needs, emotional communication, and learned behavior.

Bowen's theory gives special emphasis to the family's emotional inheritance. The emotional composition of a family is key to its dysfunctional behaviors.

## Key Concepts

Important concepts in family systems theory include family losses, relational ethics, differentiation, and a family ledger. The counselor's ability to gather family information is crucial, so a family story can be developed.

Murray Bowen (1978) described the following concepts of family systems theory:

**Differentiation.**   To what degree can clients distinguish between their intellectual (thinking) and their emotional (feeling) processing? If there is little distinction between these two, it is probable that clients will experience involuntary emotional reactions and become dysfunctional. Responding to a family situation out of *emotion* rather than *rationality* creates an imbalance of emotionality over rationality.

**Triangles.**   Interlocking triangles are common building blocks of a family's relationship system. Whenever the emotional relationship between two members (usually the parents) becomes too intense or distant, a third person (usually a child) can be brought in to restore equilibrium (stability) in the system.

**The Emotional System of the Nuclear Family.**   Adults tend to choose marriage partners with equal levels of differentiation, which results in undifferentiated partners. Their triangle is likely to be too intense, which creates a family tradition of similar characteristics (children who are unstable, too fused or intense, overly emotional, etc.).

**Family Projection Process.**   The unstable or "fused" couple may focus attention on one of the children.

**Emotional Cutoff.**   Children selected for the "projection process" may try to "detriangulate"—separate or isolate themselves, emotionally or physically withdraw.

**Multigenerational Transmission Process.**   The poorly differentiated child (often from poorly differentiated parents) may select a mate who is also poorly differentiated. This can lead to a multigenerational problem (occurring through several generations) with the "weak links" always marrying weak links.

**Sibling Position.**   Roles tend to be associated with birth order. For example, if two individuals of different birth order marry, there is a higher likelihood they will complement each other.

**Societal Regression.**   To Bowen, society is regressing because it has not yet learned to differentiate effectively between emotional (feelings) and intellectual (thinking) decision-making.

## Goals

Intergenerational family counseling seeks to decrease emotional reactivity, address issues of loss, and restore trust and fairness in a family. A strategy is developed in counseling that can be executed over time by the family to help them meet their goals. Goals are often reached outside of the counseling sessions.

## Counselor's Role

The counselor's role is active and involved. The counselor gathers family data, facilitates change, and tracks emotional sequences within the family of origin, spouse, and children. The counselor seeks to unmask family myths, rules, and extended family patterns. In addition the counselor may investigate death and loss issues in the family. The counselor acts as coach or guide, focusing foremost on the parents, even when the child is the "identified patient."

## Techniques

Family systems counseling uses questioning, tracking of family sequences, directives, genograms, letter writing (to the living or the dead), and "multidirected partiality" (evidenced by counselor not taking sides, but seeking understanding of each point of view, and allowing each member to confirm or correct the counselor's understanding). Counselors gathering information about the nuclear family and coach the family in strategy development.

# STRUCTURAL FAMILY COUNSELING

## Major Proponents

Salvador Minuchin and J. Colapinto

## Brief Overview

Structural family counselors believe that if change occurs in the family, change will occur in its members. The family has subsystems derived from rules that have evolved in the family. These subsystems may be spousal, parental, sibling, etc. They carry out the family's functioning patterns, and have their own rules and boundaries. The rules may be for all family members (generic) or individualized (idiosyncratic). The rules tell family members when, where, and how to interact. They form "transactional patterns." Rigid rules (or boundaries) may lead to family members drawing away (disengaging), while too loose rules (or boundaries) may result in enmeshment or codependency.

Structural family counseling holds that psychosomatic illnesses are brought on by and maintained in the family unit.

## Key Concepts

A key concept of Minuchin's work is family boundaries, which are established and maintained through multiple contexts of communication and behavior within the family. Boundaries assure a sense of privacy and autonomy for family members but also can become too closely tied to intimacy and nurturing needs. Healthy families honor members' boundaries, and most family problems are related to boundary violations.

Areas stressed in structural family counseling include boundaries, hierarchy, subsystems, alignments and coalitions.

Important processes for families to negotiate are

• coming to agreement on the problem,

• being able to identify the participants involved in the problem, and

• pledging to cooperate in solving the problem.

## Goals

The main goals of structural family counseling are to strengthen the parental subsystem and realign the family structure through assessing family boundaries, coalitions, and hierarchies.

## Counselor's Role

The counselor acts as stage manager in family transactions. The counselor is also a director who creates dramas designed to help clients develop more functional family structures. The counselor tracks sequences, reframes (relabels perceptions), and directs. The counselor also examines and "rebalances" the boundaries between the family subsystems.

## Techniques

The counselor uses unbalancing, joining, relabeling, reframing, and enactments of both actual dysfunctional and proposed or desired family interactions. The counselor challenges the transactional patterns of family members, clarifies boundaries, and reorganizes the family unit. The counselor alters ineffective or inappropriate rules of family interaction by examining

how family members relate to one another,

who is aligned with whom against whom, and

the nature of the parental dyad.

# MILAN SYSTEMATIC FAMILY THERAPY

## Major Proponents

The Milan Team: Mara Selvini Palazzoli, Luigi Boscolo, Giuliana Prata, and Gianfranco Cecchin

## Brief Overview

This approach is based on hypothesizing, circularity, and neutrality. It requires the counselor to be proficient in asking questions that draw comparisons between people, points in time, or definitions of the problem.

Originally developed in Italy by the Milan Team for working with anorectic patients and their parents, this model later evolved to encompass communications theory, system theory, and linguistics. A distinguishing feature is the use of paradox to achieve better family communications

## Key Concepts

The communication patterns between family members are either consonant (both the message and its emotional intent are communicated) or dissonant (the objective message differs from its emotional intent).

## Goals

The main goals are to relieve symptoms, maintain or establish balance in the family system, and examine and expose the methods by which family members keep the family system in balance.

## Counselor's Role

The counselor looks for family rituals and family games, then attempts to change both, plus the relationships that sustain them. The counselor also examines how symptoms have formed in the family over time, and the outside forces that currently impinge on the family unit. Counselors examine the roles of symptoms in the family, and the extended family relationships. Counselors must be able to effectively hypothesize.

## Techniques

The Milan system uses circular questioning, externalization, positive connotation, and paradoxical interventions. Reframing and directives are also employed. Often a team of counselors is used to observe and provide input to the lead counselor.

The Milan Team is noted for a rather unique technique that has yielded interesting results. During the course of family counseling, the parents are asked to continue to come to counseling sessions secretly, without their children (the identified problem) knowing about it. Children's symptoms decreased when the parents were able to keep their visits a secret, but when the parents failed to come or keep the secret, the symptoms recurred.

# BEHAVIORAL APPROACHES

Family and systems therapists assert that problems of an individual can best be understood and successfully treated by changing the entire interpersonal system within a family. . . . However, behavior therapists reject the assumption that every problem requires a broad-scale intervention in the family system. The findings of well-controlled outcome studies clearly show that this is not always necessary. (G. Terence Wilson, 1984, pp. 242–243)

## Major Proponents

Robert Liberman, Richard Stuart, Masters and Johnson, Gerald R. Patterson, Donald Meichenbaum, and John Gottman

## Brief Overview

This approach utilizes typical behavioral concepts. It attempts to move family members toward becoming "reinforcing agents." The focus is on changing behavior. Behaviorists rely on empirical research and continual measurement of outcome. They offer several paradigms for training family members to function better.

Cognitive behavioral family counseling centers on thoughts and actions, and includes operant conditioning and Bandura-like social learning principles. Also called "operant interpersonal therapy" by Richard Stuart (1976), this approach emphasizes ongoing behavioral exchange and contracting.

## Key Concepts

Behavior is viewed as adaptive and always serving a function. This approach is committed to the scientific method.

## Goals

The goals of behavioral family counseling is behavioral change, with a focus on individual change that will in turn change the family.

## Counselor's Role

Behavioral counselors are less concerned with inner states and more concerned with how people behave.

**Techniques**

Behavior changes in the family are brought about without insight or cognition, but through focusing on the interactional sequences of the family, and interrupting the ones that are identified with the family's problem. This is done during the counseling session, by "focusing on the emotional nature of out-of-session interactions and the clients' own reactions to them. The tools that the therapist uses are modeling and questions aimed toward fostering interactional and intraphysic insight" (Hanna & Brown, 1995, p. 37).

In working with children, behaviorists may use time-out or other traditional behavior modification methods. For parenting skills, time-out methods and contracts for behavior improvement are used. In conjoint sex therapy, Masters and Johnson (1970) have used behavioral techniques successfully with sexually dysfunctional couples.

# Chapter 5

# DIAGNOSIS

Diagnosis was originally the purview of psychiatry, but as increasing numbers of counselors open private practices and seek insurance reimbursements, they are now diagnosing and classifying clients in order to demonstrate accountability and justify their role to insurance companies and the public.

The purpose of diagnosis is to assess the current level of a client's functioning, identify and label client problems, and establish an appropriate treatment plan.

## STANDARD DIAGNOSTIC CLASSIFICATIONS

The classification systems most commonly used by mental health workers are the *Diagnostic and Statistical Manual of Mental Disorders, Fourth Edition (DSM-IV)* (American Psychiatric Association, 1994) and the *International Classification of Diseases, 9th Revision, Clinical Modification (ICD-9-CM)* (World Health Organization, 1994). The *DSM-IV* coding is included in the ninth edition of the *ICD*. Used in tandem, the two form a standardized diagnostic system available to mental heath and health care professionals. They provide professionals with a common body of language, making communication easier and quicker, especially in terms of assessing, coding, and identifying treatment procedures. They provide the industry with a shorthand that transfers easily across mental health disciplines.

### Diagnostic and Statistical Manual of Mental Disorders

The *DSM-IV* was developed by the American Psychiatric Association. It enables the classification of each individual with mental disorders according to five different areas, or "axes." Axes I and II define and describe mental disorders. Axes III, IV, and V are used for official diagnostic assessments. Axis IV and Axis V are used in special settings or in research.

> *Axis I* identifies psychiatric (clinical) disorders (syndromes). These usually can be diagnosed in infancy or early childhood.

> *Axis II* identifies personality disorders (in the adult) and specific developmental disorders (in the child or adolescent). These disorders may become known only after adolescence. Axis II includes dementia and mental retardation.

> *Axis III* identifies any physical disorder or general medical conditions relevant to understanding or treating the individual. It includes common diseases.

> *Axis IV* identifies the severity of psychosocial stressors. Diagnoses may range from no apparent psychosocial stressors to catastrophic stressors. It also includes stressors in the client's environment (e.g., housing, occupation).

> *Axis V* identifies levels of adaptive functioning, social relations, occupational functioning, and use of leisure time. Functioning may range from superior to grossly impaired. Axis V uses a Global Assessment of Functioning (GAF).

### International Classification of Diseases

The *ICD* coding system is used in the United States and throughout the world. The two types of codes used in the *ICD* are for general medical conditions and for medication-induced disorders. The *ICD* is "a statistical classification not only of mental disorders but of diseases and other morbid conditions; complications of pregnancy, childbirth, and the puerperitum; congenital abnormalities; causes of perinatal morbidity and mortality; accidents, poisonings, and violence; and symptoms, signs, and ill-defined conditions. Its principle use is in the classification of morbidity and mortality information for statistical purposes" (American Psychiatric Association, 1987, p. 433). The unabridged title of the *ICD* helps to clarify the book's contents: *The International Statistical Classification of Diseases, Injuries, and Causes of Death.*

The codes found on Axis I and Axis II of the *DSM-IV* system represent only a small portion of the codes found in the *ICD-9-CM*.

One advantage of using the *ICD* system over the *DSM-IV* system is that the *ICD* offers a higher degree of diagnostic specificity than does the *DSM-IV*, as the *ICD* identifies the specific anatomical site, or the presence of a specific complication.

The *ICD* is not a list or catalog of all the approved terms for describing and recording clinical and pathological observations; instead, it shows the relationship between diagnostic categories and is restricted to a limited number of categories that include the entire range of diseases and conditions of morbidity.

The *ICD* is published by the World Health Organization (WHO). For more information on the *ICD-10* Procedures Coding System, contact Aspen Systems Corporation, Health Information Services, at 800-395-5055.

### Criticisms of Classification Systems

Several theorists have warned against putting labels on clients, claiming that it dehumanizes people and robs them of the self-responsibility needed for healing. Other criticisms of classification systems in general and the *DSM-IV* in particular are listed below.

Agreement among diagnosticians is low.

People's ability to change may be diminished by being given a diagnostic label. A diagnosis may seem to offer proof of their limitations.

Categorization de-individualizes the client.

The demand by insurance companies of diagnoses for reimbursement puts them in control of the therapy and industry, not the practitioners.

The jargon ("psychobabble") used in the *DSM* keeps the public from understanding mental health professionals and from understanding themselves.

Counselors may diagnose a client prematurely in order to obtain insurance reimbursements.

The *DSM* system comes from the medical model of mental health, and counselors see mental health differently—from a human growth and development perspective.

The *DSM* leads to the "pathologizing" of America.

The *DSM* system plays into the myth of mental illness in America. A mental disturbance is only a difference or deviation from the norm. The *DSM* system punishes clients by categorizing, medicating, isolating, and hospitalizing them.

Most problems in people's lives are related to lack of character (having no courage or integrity) not disorders (conditions beyond people's ability to control them).

## MAJOR PERSONALITY DISORDERS

Brief descriptions, loosely derived from the *DSM-IV* and the *ICD-9-CM*, of the major personality disorders follow:

### Characteristics

*Paranoid:* distrustful of others, suspicious, hypersensitive.

*Schizoid:* reclusive, withdrawn, reserved.

*Schizotypal:* oddity of thought/behavior, called *schizophrenia* in the *DSM-IV* (APA, 1994).

*Histrionic:* dramatic, impulsive, overly emotional, seeks approval and praise.

*Narcissistic:* enlarged sense of self-importance, lack of empathy, exploits others.

*Antisocial:* sociopathic, repeated conflicts with others, inability to feel guilt.

*Borderline:* unstable in a variety of areas.

*Avoidant:* hypersensitivity to rejection.

*Dependent:* needy, fails to assume responsibility for one's own life.

*Dementia:* multiple cognitive deficits (especially memory impairment).

*Obsessive compulsive:* inflexible, preoccupied with rules, order, and details.

*Passive aggressive:* passively manipulates or obstructs others.

## Symptoms and Traits

*Ego-dystonic:* the symptoms and traits are perceived by the client as unacceptable and undesirable.

*Ego-syntonic:* the symptoms and traits are perceived as acceptable by the client.

# BASIC HUMAN NEEDS

Clients can also be classified according to their needs. It is important for counselors to understand basic human needs since unmet needs often motivate clients to seek therapy.

Stephen Covey (1990) offers an illuminating story on unmet needs. He said: Imagine all the air were suddenly sucked out of the room you're in right now. How interested would you be in reading this paragraph? You wouldn't care at all! You would only care about getting air. Survival would be your only motivation.

Now suppose you have air. Air is no longer what you need. You are not motivated to find air. That need has been met. He concludes—and this is one of the greatest insights in the field of human motivation—satisfied needs do not motivate. It's only the unsatisfied need that motivates (p. 241).

Theoreticians have devised many classifications of basic human needs. Some of them are described below.

## Maslow's Hierarchy of Needs

Abraham Maslow (1954) developed a noted hierarchy of needs, claiming people are always motivated to higher order needs (Figure 5.1) and that basic needs have to be satisfied before people can reach the highest human need—to become self-actualized (the motivation to develop one's full potential as a human being).

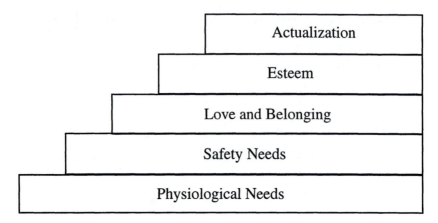

**Figure 5.1.** Maslow's hierarchy of needs.

The first needs are physiological. Safety, love, belonging, and esteem are deficiency needs (what one lacks), and can be met only by external sources. The final need, self-actualization, is a growth need and is never truly satisfied. Its motivation is intrinsic, as people continually strive for self-fulfillment or to fill the measure of their creation.

Maslow said that people progress by filling their needs from the physiological level, to the social level, to the cognitive level. When two or more needs are unmet, people tend to satisfy them in a particular sequence. They begin with the lowest needs and attempt to fulfill higher needs only after the lower ones are met.

Maslow's hierarchy of needs has become a central concept of the humanistic counseling movement; however, like all the need classifications listed below, it is rooted in philosophy not research.

**Glasser's Needs**

William Glasser (1965) wrote that people have two basic needs that, if unfulfilled, cause pain. Behavior is an attempt to fulfill these two psychological needs. They are:

> *The need to love and be loved:* If a person has a complete deficit of love early in life, death can result and if this deficit exists later in life the result can be depression, suicide, or psychosis.

*The need for achievement of self-worth:* If people feel worthwhile to themselves, they are able to love others and in turn be loved.

Later, Glasser reduced these two needs into one basic need: *The need for identity* (Glasser & Zunin, 1973). Glasser felt that our patterns of behavior are formulated in the striving to satisfy our basic needs.

## Jourard's Needs

Sidney Jourard (1963) categorized needs in this fashion:

*Survival needs:* Concerned with self-preservation and safety, including psychological and physical safety needs. When threatened psychologically, a client might become anxious, narrow his or her perceptions, and exhibit inappropriate behavior.

*Physical needs:* The desire for food, shelter, drink, freedom from pain, and sleep. If these basic needs are unsatisfied, they can dominate behavior.

*Need for love and sex:* The necessity to be loved and to love others. These may be intermingled, but they are not always, for sex may be physiological.

*Status, success, and self-esteem needs:* These achievement motivations are designed to create feelings of confidence, competence, and usefulness.

*Physical and mental health needs:* Physical wellness and mental stability create a sense of well-being. If these needs are not met, physical and mental ailments will occur.

*Freedom needs:* Independent beings seek to make their own choices and pursue their own identities.

*Challenge needs:* Goals and life's challenges stimulate growth and keep us from boredom and feeling empty inside.

*Cognitive clarity needs:* Wrestling to resolve dilemmas and life's inconsistencies helps us in clearer decision making.

*Varied experience needs:* The personal stimulation that comes from living life moves us toward a desire to be more full-functioning.

## Horney's Neurotic Needs

Karen Horney (1967) believed that children develop anxiety if they feel isolated and helpless. These insecure children handle their feelings by developing irrational (neurotic) solutions to problems. Horney's 10 neurotic needs are

1. The neurotic need for affection and approval.
2. The neurotic need for a partner to take over your life.
3. The neurotic need for restructuring your life within very narrow bounds.
4. The neurotic need for power.
5. The neurotic need to exploit others.
6. The neurotic need to have prestige.
7. The neurotic need for personal admiration.
8. The neurotic need for personal achievement.
9. The neurotic need for self-sufficiency and independence.
10. The neurotic need for protection.

## Rogers' Needs

Carl Rogers (1980) said there are two universal needs. They are:

*The need for positive regard,* which comes from others and from self. This develops as our awareness of the "self" emerges in early life, eventually leading us to the desire for acceptance and love from important people in our life.

*The need for self-regard,* which develops from our self-experiences associated with the satisfaction or frustration of our need for positive regard.

## Counselor's Role

In speaking to the issue that clients are generally knowledgeable about their need deficiencies, Gary S. Belkin (1988) said, "Often when individuals come for counseling many of their need-satisfying abilities are impaired. It is not unusual for a client to know exactly what he or she wants, but to lack the emotional, intellectual, familial, or social resources to obtain it" (p. 154). It is the role of the counselor to help clients develop the resources necessary to satisfy their needs.

# Chapter 6

# TESTS, MEASUREMENTS, AND RESEARCH

## TESTS AND MEASUREMENTS

### Purposes of Tests

Counselors use tests to gather information about clients so that realistic decisions can be made about treatment. Some counselors believe that testing, like diagnosis, is an external method of understanding clients and has little to do with the fluid dynamic that goes on inside clients.

The testing and measuring of clients by counselors has increased in recent years, necessitating the addition of courses in testing and measurement to master's-level counseling programs. Career counselors have long been familiar with testing instruments and the positive purposes they serve.

Below is a list of some of the purposes for which counselors may engage in testing and measuring clients.

to determine if a client should be in counseling.

to ascertain if the client's needs are within the range of a counselor's competency.

to help determine the counseling process and techniques to be used.

to uncover the client's strengths and weaknesses (improving the client's self-awareness).

to confirm previous test results or the counselor's personal observations.

to assist the client in making specific career or educational decisions.

to predict future performance.

to assist in evaluating the outcome of counseling interventions (to measure counselor effectiveness).

Tests are used for the following broad purposes:

placement (in education or workplace settings),

admissions (to schools, specialized degrees),

counseling (see list above),

educational planning,

diagnosing,

licensure and certification standards, and

self-understanding and self-improvement.

## Ethical Issues

Counselors should remember that some tests have been shown to be biased against people of color, women, and those with strong religious beliefs. Tests by their very nature are biased, as they attempt to discriminate performances, one person from another. Many early tests used by counselors were developed and normed on white middle-class males. A classic example of test bias was found in the Dove Counter-Balance Intelligence Test, which proved that African Americans in Watts, California, scored higher than whites when questions were centered on black American cultural issues.

Caution should be used when testing, for tests can be used or misused to label, stereotype, or invade privacy. In addition, new risks to confidentiality exist with the increased use of electronic mail, WebCounseling, computer testing, computer disk security and interoffice data sharing.

## Assessment

Testing is part of a larger process know as assessment, or appraisal. Testing and assessment are not synonymous. Assessment in counseling is a multifaceted process that involves far more than the administration of a single test or inventory. Assessment is the process of collecting data (information) for the purposes of making decisions.

Assessment may involve many different methods of studying individuals. Standardized instruments, self-report inventories, interview information, observation, counseling sessions, case study techniques, and other nonstandardized tools of assessment may be used. Counselors use assessment skills when recording, analyzing, compiling, and interpreting data.

## Computer Appraisal

Computer programs can administer, score, and interpret many of the clinical instruments named in this section. Advantages of taking and scoring tests on a computer are

test scores/results are available faster,

the process is less expensive,

there is proven effectiveness in the area of career counseling, and

many clients are less intimated than when talking to a counselor.

Disadvantages include

the accuracy of test interpretation has been questioned,

the software may be used by untrained personnel, and

confidentiality of client records is uncertain.

## Types of Tests and Inventories

**Achievement Tests.** These tests measure the effects of learning or a set of experiences. Achievement tests are often used diagnostically. Examples include

California Achievement Test (CAT)

Stanford Achievement Test

Iowa Tests of Basic Skills

College-Level Examination Program (CLEP)

College Board's Advanced Placement Program

**Aptitude Tests.**   These tests predict future performance and measure the effects of general learning. Examples include:

Multiple Aptitude Batteries:

Career Ability Placement Survey (CAPS)

Differential Aptitude Test (DAT)

General Aptitude Test Battery (GABT)

Flanagan Aptitude Classification Tests (FACT)

Armed Services Vocational Aptitude Battery (ASVAB)

Individual Aptitude Tests:

Purdue Pegboard

General Clerical Tests

Musical Aptitude Profile

**Intelligence Tests.**   Intelligence tests, and even the definition of intelligence, are controversial. Some researchers believe that intelligence is the ability to think in abstract terms. Others believe it is the ability to adapt to the environment. Still others believe that it is the ability to learn or adjust. The research of Howard Gardner (1983) into multiple types of intelligence has further eroded the eminence of traditional intelligence testing.

On traditional tests, the average intelligence quotient (IQ), or score is 100, with normal in the range of 85 to 115. Today most IQ test scores are derived from comparing test scores of people within the same age cohort. There are several different types of IQ tests. The following tests measure general IQ:

Individual Intelligence Tests:

Stanford-Binet Intelligence Scale

Toni2

Raven's

Wechsler Preschool and Primary Scale of Intelligence (WPPSI)

Wechsler Intelligence Scale for Children-Revised (WISC-R)

Wechsler Adult Intelligence Scale-Revised (WAIS-R)

Group Intelligence Tests:

Otis Self-Administering Tests of Mental Ability

Cognitive Abilities Test

The following tests measure specialized abilities:

American College Test Program (ACT)

Scholastic Aptitude Test (SAT)

Miller Analogies Test (MAT)

Graduate Record Examination (GRE)

Kaufman Assessment Battery for Children (KABC)

System of Multicultural Pluralistic Assessment (SOMPA)

**Personality Tests.** There are three different types of personality tests: projective, inventories, and specialized.

Projective Tests:

Incomplete Sentences Task

Draw-a-Person Test

Rorschach Diagnostic Test

Thematic Apperception Test (TAT)

Inventories:

Myers-Briggs Type Indicator (MBTI)

Minnesota Multiphasic Personality Inventory (MMPI)

Millon Clinical Multiaxial Inventory

Sixteen Personality Factors (16PF)

California Psychological Inventory (CPI)

Specialized Tests:

Tennessee Self-Concept Scale

Luria-Nebraska Neuropsychological Battery

Bender-Gestalt Test

**Interest and Values Inventories.** These tests include preferences, likes, dislikes, and general values. They include:

Study of Values

Career Assessment Inventory (CAI)

California Occupational Preference Survey (COPS)

Strong Interest Inventory (SII)

Self-Directed Search (SDS)

Campbell Interest and Skills Survey

Kuder Occupational Interest Survey

Work Values Inventory (WVI)

Minnesota Importance Questionnaire

Career Orientation Placement and Evaluation Survey (COPES)

## Testing and Measurement Terms

Definitions of the following testing and measurement terms can be found in Chapter 18: assessment, bell-shaped curve, correlation coefficient, criterion-referenced, ipsative score interpretations, kurtosis, mean, measures of central tendency, measures of variability, median, mode, nonstandardized tests, norm, normative score interpretations, percentile or percentage, regression toward the mean score, scores, skew, social desirability, sociogram, sociometry, standardized score, standard deviation, standard error of measurement, standardized tests, rust statement, and validity

## Suggested Readings on Testing and Measurement

Aiken, L. R. (1994). *Psychological testing and assessment (8th ed.).* Boston: Allyn & Bacon.

Anastasi, A. (1989). *Psychological testing (6th ed.).* New York: Macmillan.

Cronbach, L. (1990). *Essentials of psychological testing (5th ed.)*. New York: Harper & Row.

Drummond, R. J. (1992). *Appraisal procedures for counselors and helping professionals (2nd ed.)*. New York: Macmillan.

Fraenkel, J. R., & Wallen, N. E. (1993). *How to design and evaluate research in education*. New York: McGraw-Hill.

Hopkins, K., & Stanley, J. (1990). *Educational and psychological measurement and evaluation (7th ed.)*. Englewood Cliffs, NJ: Prentice-Hall.

Salvia, J., & Ysseldyke, J. E. (1995). *Assessment (6th ed.)*. Boston: Houghton Mifflin.

# RESEARCH

**Purpose of Research**

Research helps counselors understand their clients and the counseling process. It assists counselors in identifying their own prejudices and in understanding the biases of clients. It also helps counselors discard outdated therapeutic ideas and offers them better methods. Research keeps counselors stimulated, engaged in the learning process, and willing to try new methods to achieve greater results. In the end, research benefits the counselor, the counseling process, and the client.

**Definition**

Research involves answering a question or testing a proposal. An idea, called a hypothesis, is proposed and then tested in some manner. The results of that test are evaluated to decide if the original question was answered and how it was answered. The results of the research confirm or refute the concepts (theories) that guided the research. The hypothesis is either substantiated, modified, or rejected.

Research is "any sort of careful, systematic, patient study and investigation in some field of knowledge, undertaken to discover or establish facts and principles" (Marshall, 1995, p. 7).

Research used in counseling can be either process research or outcome research:

**Process Research.**  Process research looks at change, whether it occurs in or outside of a counseling session. It examines what factors contribute to better mental health and what factors cause malfunctioning. It looks not at the results of counseling, but at how client change occurs. It focuses on the process of counseling.

**Outcome Research.**  Outcome research often compares one treatment to another to determine if one is better or worse for a client with a specific problem or disorder. It evaluates what has occurred as a result of counseling. Outcome-oriented research examines what approaches are best with what clients.

## Types of Research

The following are the major types of research investigation methods:

**Correlational.**   This research method looks at relations among two or more variables, and determines the degree of relationship between variables using a correlation coefficient statistic.

**Qualitative.**   This type includes descriptive and historical research methods. It attempts to create a holistic picture of a process or culture, an existing state of events, or events from the past. Historical research usually involves the analysis of primary and secondary document sources, old newspapers, and genealogies.

*Types of Sources.*   There are three major types of resources from which information is gathered:

> *General references:* sources that a researcher consults to locate other sources (e.g., encyclopedias, almanacs).

> *Primary sources:* sources from which the researcher gets direct information (e.g., conversations or correspondence with participants, publications that report the results of an investigation).

> *Secondary sources:* "second hand sources" (e.g., publications in which authors describe the work of others).

**Ethnographical.**   This is a form of qualitative research in which data are obtained through observation, interviews, and a systematic search of documents. Primary and secondary sources of information are used to report on events or populations.

**Experimental.** This method is used to determine cause-and-effect relationships between variables by manipulating the variables (using a control group and experimental treatment group). Quasi-experimental research is akin to experimental research, except the ability to place random subjects in the two groups is impaired (e.g., no control group is possible).

**Meta-Analysis.** This research method is a culmination of many studies. It usually involves a comparison of findings across many studies, perhaps examined all at once.

**Survey.** This method uses interviews, questionnaires, polling, instruments, etc., to sample and evaluate attitudes, perceptions, etc. Survey research is characterized by low response rates and questionable generalizability.

**Evaluation.** This method attempts to measure the worth of a delivery system, program, process, product, or technique through systematic and careful data collection.

## Methods of Research

There are two primary methods of research (or reasoning or logic):

**Inductive.** This method moves from specific information to general assumptions. It leads to theory building. It begins at a practical real-world level and is usually descriptive, correlational, or historical.

**Deductive.** This method moves from general assumptions to specific application. It begins at a broad level (often a theory) and attempts to determine relationships between elements of that theory.

## The Scientific Method

The generally accepted process of conducting research, known as the Scientific Method, is outlined below.

1. Identify the problem.

2. Review the literature (includes defining the problem to be studied).

3. Formulate a hypothesis.

4. Project possible consequences.

5.  Test the hypothesis by

   a.  collecting and organizing the data (information),

   b.  analyzing the data,

   c.  formulating conclusions from the data, and

   d.  verifying, modifying, rejecting, or accepting, the original hypothesis.

**The Research Process**

In formal papers, such as dissertations, the following format is used to organize and present research to readers. It is similar to the Scientific Method listed above, but is formatted differently so as to present research in a more readable style.

1.  Statement of the problem.

2.  Statement of the hypothesis.

3.  Definitions of terms in the study.

4.  A review of previous literature on the topic.

5.  Details of the research design that will be followed.

6.  Explanation of the sampling.

7.  Instrumentation.

8.  Procedures.

9.  Analysis of the gathered data.

10. Summary and recommendations.

**Sampling**

Choosing the sample is an important part of the research design. Once a population has been chosen for study, subsets of the population are selected to sample and study. The appropriate type of sampling method is crucial to valid generalization of the findings of a small sample to a larger population.

**Kinds of Sampling.** Four kinds of sampling are identified below:

*Random sampling* (random selection): All subjects in the population have an equal chance of being selected for study. This method attempts to ensure fairness. It usually involves using a table of random numbers (often computer-generated) select or assign individuals or groups to categories.

*Stratified sampling:* Subgroups are identified within the total population that can later be sampled and studied.

*Proportional stratified sampling:* Samples are randomly selected from each subgroup, and are proportionate to (have equal representation as) the other subgroups.

*Cluster sampling:* Naturally occurring groups of subjects are sampled. This used to be called Area Sampling.

**Sample Sizes.** Below is a table showing minimal numbers suggested for each type of research.

| Type of Research | Minimal Sample Size |
|---|---|
| Experimental | 15 per group |
| Casual-Comparative | 15 per group |
| Correlational | 30 per variable |
| Survey | 100 per subgroup |

## Research Controversies

Why do people behave the way they do? How do they grow and progress? The following are three broad categories of controversies that research seeks to resolve.

**Nature versus Nurture.** Is human development influenced more by nature (inherited traits, genetics, capacities, limitations) or by nurture (environmental, cultural, social factors)? Many believe that nurture and nature interact, rather than conflict or function separately. Because research finds it hard to prove which of the two is responsible for a particular developmental change or situation, controversy continues to surround such topics as what causes alcoholism, homosexuality, propensity for criminal activity, etc. The implications of whether something is caused by nature or nurture are enormous.

**Continuity versus Stages.** Is there continuity in behavior change (a gradual continual growth process) or are there distinct stages or tasks that must be addressed and mastered before being able to progress to the next or to a higher level?

**Deviant versus Different.** Is behavior that is out of the ordinary (abnormal) simply different (an alternative) or is it deviant (undesirable)?

## Ethical Issues in Research

The Committee on Scientific and Professional Ethics of the American Psychological Association (APA) has published a list of concerns of which mental health researchers need to be mindful when conducting studies. These concerns can be fit into three major categories:

1.  protection of the participants from harm,

2.  ensuring confidentiality of gathered materials (e.g., access to the data will be permitted only to the researchers), and

3.  withholding information from subjects that might jeopardize their objectivity or be deceptive (this might be justifiable if no risk to the subjects is involved).

In an effort to monitor and ensure researcher compliance with accepted ethical standards, of research, most universities now require project approval from an ethics committee prior to proceeding with research on human subjects. Ethics committees usually consider such issues as informed consent, potential dangers to those being studied, debriefing of participants afterwards, and whether the potential findings are worth the effort involved. Not only is research on humans carefully monitored, especially when children are involved, but research involving animals is increasingly being screened to ensure no unnecessary cruelty.

## Research Terms

Definitions of the following research terms can be found in Chapter 18: analogue study, ANCOVA, ANOVA, computer analysis of data, control group, degree of freedom, experimental group, data, demand characteristics, double-blind study, error types, ethnography, ex post facto, external validity, halo effect, Hawthorne effect, hypothesis, instrumentation, levels of measurement, levels of significance, Likert scale, MANOVA, multiple regression, needs assessment, nonparametric tests, null hypothesis, observer bias, parameter, pilot study, placebo, population, power-based tests, Pygmalion effect, reliability, scattergram, speed-based test, statistical analysis, t-test, theory, validity, and variables.

## Suggested Readings in Research

Ary, D., Jacobs, L. C., & Razavich, A. (1990). *Introduction to research in education.* New York: Holt, Rinehart, & Winston.

Campbell, D., & Stanley, J. (1966). *Experimental and quasi-experimental designs for research.* Chicago: Rand McNally.

Cronbach, L. (1990). *Essentials of psychological testing (5th ed.),* New York: Harper & Row.

Fraenkel, J. R., & Wallen, N. E. (1993). *How to design and evaluate research in education.* New York: McGraw-Hill.

Gay, L. R. (1991). *Educational research: Competencies for analysis and application (3rd ed.).* Columbus, OH: Charles E. Merrill.

Keppel, G. (1991). *Design and analysis: A researcher's handbook (3rd ed.).* Englewood Cliffs. NJ: Prentice-Hall.

Kerlinger, F. (1986). *Foundations of behavioral research (3rd ed.).* New York: Holt, Rinehart & Winston.

# Chapter 7

# PROFESSIONAL AFFILIATIONS

## PROFESSIONAL ORGANIZATIONS

### American Counseling Association (ACA)

Formerly called the American Association for Counseling and Development (AACD), the ACA is a professional umbrella organization of counselors. It has over 58,000 members in four geographical regions in the United States and internationally. ACA consists of subdivisions (see below) that offer memberships, journals, and conferences. These subdivisions address the needs of counselors who practice in different settings. All subdivisions combine for an annual national ACA Convention.

American College Counseling Association (ACCA)

American College Personnel Association (ACPA) (disaffiliated July 1, 1992)

American Mental Health Counselors Association (AMHC)

American School Counselor Association (ASCA)

Association for Adult Development and Aging (AADA)

Association for Assessment in Counseling (AAC)

Association for Counselor Education and Supervision (ACES)

Association for Counselors and Educators in Government (ACEG)

Association for Gay, Lesbian, and Bisexual Issues in Counseling (AGLBIC)

Association for Humanistic Education and Development (AHEAD)

Association for Multicultural Counseling and Development (AMCD)

Association for Specialists in Group Work (ASGW)

Association for Spiritual, Ethical, and Religious Values in Counseling (ASERVIC)

International Association of Addictions and Offender Counseling (IAAOC)

National Employment Counseling Association (NECA)

## National Board for Certified Counselors (NBCC)

The NBCC was incorporated in 1982 as a result of the ACA's professional concerns and efforts in the area of credentialing. It is a nonprofit organization that establishes and monitors a national counselor certification exam, and promotes professional credentialing standards for counselors.

After meeting NBCC standards and obtaining certification, member-counselors are required to maintain and renew certification through continuing education programs. The NBCC provides a national standard for counselors in the United States. This allows the public to have confidence in its members, knowing they meet nationwide training standards and abide by a professional code of ethics.

In 1985, NBCC became accredited by the National Commission for Certifying Agencies (NCCA). The NCCA is an independent, nongovernmental, national regulatory organization that monitors the credentialing processes of its accredited agencies. Accreditation in the commission represents the foremost organizational recognition within the field of national certification.

**Requirements for Certification with NBCC.** As of March 1997, NBCC has certified more than 25,000 counselors. To become a National Certified Counselor (NCC), candidates must

Verify via official transcripts graduation from a regionally accredited university with a minimum of 48 semester or 72 quarter hours in the following eight course areas:

1. Human Growth and Development

2. Social and Cultural Foundations

3. Helping Relationships

4. Group Work

5. Career and Lifestyle Development

6. Appraisal

7. Research and Program Evaluation

8. Professional Orientation and Ethics

Document two years of post-master's counseling experience with 3,000 client contact hours and 100 hours of supervision.

Document two terms of supervised field experience in a counseling setting. (Three years of post-master's counseling experience with supervision may be substituted for the first practicum).

Supply two professional references. One must be a recent supervisor.

Fulfill one of NBCC's eligibility options. The most common option is passing the National Counseling Examination (NCE).

**The National Counseling Exam.** The NCE is a multiple choice test consisting of 200 questions. It lasts approximately four hours, and a fee is charged. The exam is administered through the NBCC twice yearly at numerous sites around the country. It focuses on the eight course areas as listed above, and on the following five work behaviors:

1. Fundamental Counseling Practices

2. Counseling for Career Development

3. Counseling Groups

4. Counseling Families

5. Professional Practice

Valuable seminars to help counselors prepare for the NCE examination are available from Andrew Helwig (e-mail: AHelwig@carbon.cuDenver.edu). Additional internet information on the NCE can be obtained at: http://www.nbcc.org/require.htm.

**NBCC's Specialty Areas.** The NBCC also offers certification in five specialty areas. Certification in one of the five areas attests to educational background, knowledge, skills, and competency in that specialty. These areas are:

*Certified Clinical Mental Health Counselor.* CCMHC's purpose is to identify (a) professional clinical mental health counselor competencies, (b) methods of measuring knowledge underlying these competencies, and (c) areas where additional professional clinical mental health counseling training may be needed. CCMHC members have been recognized by the Office of the Civilian Health and Medical Program of the Uniformed Services (CHAMPUS) and others as authorized mental health providers. Requirements for certification include NCC certification, experience, coursework, examination, and demonstrated clinical skills.

*National Certified Career Counselor.* NCCC's purpose is to identify (a) professional career counselor and career development competencies, (b) methods of measuring knowledge underlying these competencies, and (c) areas where additional professional career counseling and development training may be needed. Requirements for certification include NCC certification, experience, coursework, professional assessments, and examination.

*National Certified School Counselor.* NCSC's purpose is to (a) promote the school counselor's professional identity, visibility, and accountability on a national level, (b) identify to the counseling profession and to the public those counselors who have met national professional school counseling standards, (c) advance cooperation among school systems, professional organizations, and other credentialing professional development agencies, and d) encourage the professional growth of school counselors. Requirements for certification include NCC certification, experience, coursework, self-assessment, and professional assessments.

*National Certified Gerontological Counselor.* NCGC's purpose is to (a) promote the gerontological counselor's professional identity, visibility, and accountability on a national level, (b) identify to the counseling profession and to the public those counselors who have met national gerontological counseling standards, (c) encourage the professional growth of gerontological counselors, and (d) advance a positive, wellness-enhancing attitude toward older person among professional organizations and other credentialing and professional development agencies. Requirements for certification include NCC certification, experience, coursework, self-assessment, and professional assessments.

*Master Addictions Counselor.* MAC's purpose is to (a) identify to the counseling profession and to the public those counselors who have met national professional addictions counseling standards, (b) promote the master's-level addictions counselor's professional identity, visibility and accountability, and (c) encourage the professional growth of addictions counselors. Requirements for certification include NCC certification, experience, coursework, professional assessments, and examination.

### Council for the Accreditation of Counseling and Related Educational Programs (CACREP)

CACREP was incorporated in 1981. It is legally separate from, but an affiliate of, the American Counseling Association (ACA). The mission of CACREP is to promote the professional competence of counseling and related practitioners through the development of preparation standards for counseling and related educational programs, encouragement of excellence in counseling and related preparation programs, and accreditation of counseling and related professional preparation programs.

CACREP grew from efforts in the 1970s of the Association for Counselor Education and Supervision (ACES), one of the subdivisions of the ACA. More than 100 of the 500+ counselor education training departments have one or more specific programs accredited by CACREP (Hollis, 1997). These are located in 40 states plus the District of Columbia.

As a specialized accrediting body recognized by the Commission on Recognition of Post-Secondary Accreditation (CORPA), CACREP grants accredited status to graduate-level programs in five professional counseling fields.

**Areas of CACREP Accreditation.** As of January 1996, there were 251 master's-level accredited CACREP programs and 34 doctoral-level programs. All the doctoral programs emphasize counselor education (Hollis, 1997). CACREP areas of master's level accreditation include

Community Counseling

Community Counseling: specialization in Career

Community Counseling: specialization in Gerontology

School Counseling

Mental Health Counseling

Marriage and Family Counseling

Student Affairs Practice in Higher Education

## American Association of Marriage and Family Therapists (AAMFT)

The AAMFT was created in 1942. It is a professional organization for marriage and family counselors. Its purpose is to advance the marriage and family profession through promoting marital and family wellness. AAMFT sets professional standards for graduate education, supervision, professional ethics, and the clinical practice of marriage and family counseling. The Commission on Accreditation for Marriage and Family Therapy Education (COAMFTE) accredits graduate programs in marriage and family counseling. The four categories of membership are Clinical, Associate, Student, and Affiliate. An Approved Supervisor status also is available to Clinical members who are seeking to supervise marriage and family counselor trainees.

## National Academy for Certified Clinical Mental Health Counselors (NACCMHC)

NACCMHC requires a master's degree in a 60-credit-hour mental health curriculum, and two years of post-master's work internship/experience (3,000 hours), and 100 hours of individual supervision.

## The American Psychological Association (APA)

The APA is the largest scientific and professional organization representing psychology in the United States, and it is the world's largest association of psychologists. APA's membership includes more than 142,000 researchers, educators, clinicians, consultants, and students. Through its divisions in 49 areas of psychology and its affiliation with 58 state, territorial and Canadian provincial associations, APA works to advance psychology as a science, as a profession, and as a means of promoting human welfare.

The APA accredits three areas: Clinical, Counseling, and School Psychology. APA information can be found on the internet at: http://www.apa.org.

# LICENSURE AND CERTIFICATION

## Licensure

Licensure controls titles and functions. Licensed professionals have met criteria established by state law for the use of an occupational title. Most states have specific criteria to become a Licensed Professional Counselor (LPC) or a Licensed Professional Counselor in Mental Heath (LPC/MH) counselor. Licensure protects the public from untrained and unethical counselors and insures that counselor preparation and a standard of excellence of service are maintained. Licensure ensures that training consists of a uniform and rigorous core of knowledge and clinical experience. In addition to the training, most states require the successful completion of the NBCC's National Counselor Examination (NCE) or the National Clinical Mental Health Counseling Examination (NCMHCE) for licensure. Application to take these tests is made through the state licensure boards. Additional requirements can include a specific number of supervised clinical experience hours, graduation from a CACREP program, specific coursework, etc. Many states license the following:

Licensed Mental Health Counselor (LMH)

Licensed Professional Counselor (LPC)

Licensed Professional Counselor/Mental Health Counselor (LPC/MH)

Addictions licenses

## Registry

Some states register professional counselors, with requirements similar to those of licensure.

## Certification

Licensure and registry are legal standards determined by each state. While certification also may be legally based, most often it is based on peer recognition. The recognition is by a professional organization of peers. For example, the NCC is an organization's certification issued by the NBCC, which is composed primarily of a group of peer professionals. While terminology may be confusing, generally mental health professionals are "licensed" while school counselors are "certified."

The National Certified Counselor (NCC) credential, often referred to as a "license," is national and voluntary certification. State laws do not govern this credential. The NCE is designed to be general and to assess the types of cognitive knowledge that should be mastered by all professional counselors, regardless of their professional specialization.

Drug and Alcohol Counselors are licensed or certified on a state-by-state basis.

**School Counselors**

School counselors are granted certification by most states upon completion of predetermined training qualifications. In some states, school counselors may receive certification without having to pass a state or national examination.

Approximately 35 out of 50 states do not require teacher certification for school counselor certification. In states that do require teacher experience prior to entering a school counseling program, students often spend four to five years getting an undergraduate teaching degree, then teach a year or two, then go back to graduate school and earn a 48-hour master's degree (which usually takes two years to complete) in order to be hired as a school counselor.

**Reciprocity**

Many states' credentialing agencies and licensure boards honor the licenses and certifications of other states. They acknowledge the credentials as being equivalent.

# TYPES OF MENTAL HEALTH PROFESSIONALS

The following types of mental health professionals are adopted from Meier, Minirth, Wichern, and Ratcliff (1995); and J. Schoen (personal communication, November 20, 1996).

**Certified School Counselors.**  A school counselor offers direct services (individual, group, and classroom psychological education), indirect services (consults with teachers and parents and coordinates events), and performs clerical duties (testing, scholarship administration, etc.) in schools. A master's degree is the minimum requirement.

**Chemical Dependency Counselor.** A chemical dependency (CD) counselor works with alcohol and drug-related dependency issues. There are often several levels of CD certification. Counselor certification varies from state to state, and some states do not require a master's degree.

**Child Psychiatrist.** A child psychiatrist specializes in treating emotional and behavioral disorders of children. An M.D. degree followed by psychiatric residency is required.

**Clinical Psychologist.** A clinical psychologist works primarily with the diagnosis and treatment of severe mental illness. He or she assesses and treats mental, emotional, and behavioral disorders ranging from short-term crises (e.g., adolescent rebellion) to more severe conditions (e.g., schizophrenia, borderlines, bipolar disorders). Some clinical psychologists specialize in areas such as depression or phobias. A doctoral degree is required.

**Counselor (see Licensed Professional Counselor)**

**Counseling Psychologist.** A counseling psychologist works with severe mental illnesses, relationship issues, adjustments to life, and career counseling, and does personal and marriage counseling. He or she helps people with personal changes or with changes in their lifestyle, and consults with medical doctors on physical ailments that may have underlying psychological causes. A doctoral degree is required.

**Developmental Psychologist.** A developmental psychologist examines psychological development, life span issues, and the aging process. A doctoral degree is required.

**Educational Psychologist.** An educational psychologist is involved in research, school testing, attention deficit hyperactivity disorder (ADHD) assessments, and issues related to how effective teaching and learning takes place. He or she consults with teachers, parents, and individual education program (IEP) teams; does psychological and individual intellectual testing related to education; and works directly with public schools and private schools. Some states use the title Psychological Examiner or School Psychologist. A master's degree is the minimum requirement, but usually a doctorate is required.

**Engineering Psychologist.** An engineering psychologist applies psychological concepts and research to the field of man and machines. A master's degree is the minimum requirement, but usually a doctorate is required.

**Forensic Psychologist.** A forensic psychologist applies psychological principles to legal issues, police work, and causes of death. A master's degree is the minimum requirement, but usually a doctorate is required.

**Health Psychologist.** A health psychologist explores the social factors as well as the biological and psychological factors that affect health and wellness. A master's degree is the minimum requirement.

**Industrial Psychologist (or Organizational Psychologist).** An industrial psychologist's interests center on the workplace and psychological precepts and research that affect the world of work and its workers. A master's degree is the minimum requirement.

**Licensed Professional Counselor.** A licensed professional counselor (LPC) works with adjustment, marital, and career concerns, some testing with individuals, families, and with groups. They also work with communication issues, stress, and treat clients for anxiety and depressive disorders. They have high proficiency in conducting groups and delivering seminars and workshops.

LPCs are licensed by the state. Most states require a master's degree and successful passage of the NCE. LPCs are usually affiliated with the ACA rather than the APA.

**Licensed Professional Counselor/Mental Health.** LPC/MH counselors must first satisfy the requirements of an LPC, then various lengths of additional supervised training hours, and perhaps an additional exam. LPC/MH's receive insurance reimbursement privileges. A master's degree is the minimum requirement.

**Marriage and Family Counselor.** A marriage and family therapist (MFT) or counselor focuses on marital and divorce issues, communication skills, child-raising concerns, blended family issues, and parenting skills. A minimum of a master's degree is required, in addition to supervision hours in counseling couples and families.

**Measurement Psychologist.** A measurement psychologist focuses on the methods and techniques of obtaining and analyzing psychological data. A master's degree is the minimum requirement.

**Neuropsychologist.** A neuropsychologist explores the behavioral consequences and relationships of the brain and the central nervous system functioning. He or she is often employed in hospital settings. A doctorate is required.

**Organizational Psychologist** (see Industrial Psychologist).

**Pastoral Counselor.** A pastoral counselor does premarital and marital counseling and is concerned with spiritual issues, difficulties with religious doctrines, and grief counseling. He or she is often employed by a specific religious denomination. Pastoral counselors are often ministers without academic counseling degrees.

**Psychiatrist.** In most states, a psychiatrist is the only mental health professional who can prescribe medications. Concerned with the biological basis of mental illnesses (brain abnormality or biochemical dysfunction), psychiatrists follow the medical model. They see patients who are taking or need medication, who have bipolar disorder, physical ailments related to psychological problems, hyperactivity, severe personality disorders, or who are homicidal, suicidal, or psychotic and need immediate inpatient care. They see patients for medication checks. An M.D. degree is required, followed by a psychiatric residency.

**Psychological Examiner** (see Educational Psychologist).

**Psychologist.** A psychologist does psychological testing and marital counseling. He or she deals with early childhood problems, emotional and behavioral disorders, and severe and/or persistent mental illness in clients. Psychologists follow a medical model. A doctorate and licensure are required. Usually psychologists are affiliated with the APA, not the ACA. Most of the occupations listed in this section that have Psychologist in the title require a doctoral degree.

**Psychometrician.** A psychometrician plans and monitors comprehensive strategies for the development of examinations, constructs tests, conducts research projects related to examination reliability and validity, and develops testing methodologies and scoring strategies. A master's degree is the minimum requirement.

**Rehabilitation Counselor.** A rehab counselor works primarily with stroke and accident victims, people with mental retardation, and clients with developmental disabilities caused by accidents, birth defects, handicaps, cerebral palsy, epilepsy, and autism. A master's degree is the minimum requirement.

**Rural Psychologist.** A rural psychologist focuses attention on rural communities, nonurban populations, interfamily businesses, and life issues embodied in an agricultural setting. A master's degree is the minimum requirement.

**School Psychologist** (see Educational Psychologist).

**Social Psychologist.** A social psychologist studies problems as they relate to people's mental, behavioral, spiritual, and physical life and their social interactions with others. A master's degree is the minimum requirement.

**Social Worker.** Often referred to as an MSW (master's of social work); involved with child welfare, family services (home-based programs), protective services, gerontology assistance, and members of a family who are incarcerated or need legal assistance. MSWs work with individuals, groups, and do marital counseling. They are often associated with community agencies and social service agencies. Generally, an MSW degree is required.

**Sports Psychologist.** A sports psychologist works with athletes to hone their focus and motivation. He or she also assesses coach–player relationships and addresses anxiety, performance enhancement, and fear of failure associated with performance and competition. A master's degree is the minimum requirement.

**Therapist.** A term often used in place of counselor (see Licensed Professional Counselor).

# Chapter 8

# ETHICAL AND
# LEGAL ISSUES

The first ethical responsibility of every counselor is to be as emotionally healthy as possible. The counselor is the example, the model of ethical behavior for the client during the counseling process. There is no ethical technique, only ethical counselors.

An important element in the healing process is the strength and confidence that clients perceive in the counselor. The courage for clients to be ethical and face dilemmas with resolution is modeled by a counselor who embodies these characteristics.

## ETHICAL STANDARDS FOR COUNSELORS

There are many professional standards to guide counselors in ethical behavior. In fact, as Ted Remley, Jr. (1993) said, "Currently the counseling profession has far too many sets of ethical standards. There is no need for this confusing situation. When professional counselors try to determine the standards required of them as professionals, they are overwhelmed" (p. 4).

Indeed, there are many sets of ethical standards, yet they still cannot cover the numerous situations in which counselors confront an ethical dilemma. How-

**157**

ever, there are general concerns that are basic to ethical behavior for counselors. These include

knowing and practicing the written ethical standards;

representing accurately areas of competence, education, training, licensure, and experience, and correcting any misrepresentations provided by others. (Note: "misrepresentation of professional credentials" is the top ethical code violation of Licensed Professional Counselors);

adhering to professional standards when making professional services available to clients (i.e., providing information that accurately informs the public of services offered, professional qualifications, counseling processes and techniques, billing policies, office hours, emergency procedures, and grievance procedures);

using an appropriate diagnostic system to assess client's problems;

developing an appropriate treatment plan tailored to the client's needs;

using a theoretically based approach so as to justify assessment processes, treatment methods, and goal attainment;

terminating clients when services are no longer helpful; and

using appropriate title designations after the counselor's name on correspondence (e.g., LPC, Ed.D., Ph.D., LPC/MH).

## CODES OF ETHICS

A professional code of ethics is a statement of the standards of behavior in a chosen career field. The ethical codes that determine right and wrong behavior for counselors are derived from cultural values, legal edicts, and the knowledge of those experienced in the field. They are standards of worthy conduct based on a consensus of society's values and norms.

The American Counseling Association (ACA) has an extensive code of ethics to which all practicing counselors should adhere. In addition, specific professional settings have additional ethical codes. For instance, the following groups have also developed a code of ethics: school counselors, group workers, social workers, consultants, counseling psychologists, the American Psychological Association, counseling supervisors, and marriage and family counselors.

Ethical codes are helpful in guiding the counseling process toward noble ends. For instance, clients with whom a counselor has had a previous relationship, or with whom a counselor may be unable to be objective or effective should immediately be referred to another counselor.

In 1997, students in the master's degree program in counseling and human resource development at South Dakota State University reflected on what the ethical codes meant to them. They said:

> They keep me at a "professional distance" so I can be objective; without worrying about political considerations.

> They remind me that I am a role model, a professional.

> They allow my theory to work better, unfettered by my personal interests in the client.

> The ethical codes keep my goals, role, and boundaries clear.

> The codes are a standard by which I can measure my own professionalism, growth, and unity with my colleagues.

## Ethical Standards for WebCounseling

The newest area to require guidelines for counselor behavior is the computer field. Only very recently have ethical standards emerged that cover counseling through electronic means. The practice of webcounseling has been defined as "the practice of professional counseling and information delivery that occurs when client(s) and counselor are in separate or remote locations and utilize electronic means to communicate over the Internet" (National Board for Certified Counselors, 1997).

In 1995, the National Board For Certified Counselors (NBCC) appointed a WebCounseling Task Force, which examined the practice of online counseling. As a result, in late 1997, the NBCC Board of Directors formally adopted the following "voluntary standards," which they expect will change as new information and electronic proficiencies evolve. Webcounselors shall

1.   Review pertinent legal and ethical codes for possible violations emanating from the practice of webcounseling and supervision.

     Liability insurance policies should also be reviewed to determine if webcounseling is covered. Local, state, provincial, and national statutes as well as the codes of professional membership organizations, professional certifying bodies, and state or provincial licensing boards should be reviewed. Also, as it is not yet determined whether webcounseling takes place in the webcounselor's location or the webclient's location, webcounselors should consider carefully local customs regarding age of consent and reporting of child abuse.

2. Inform webclients of encryption methods being used to help insure the security of client/counselor/supervisor communications.

   Encryption methods should be used whenever possible. If encryption is not made available to clients, clients must be informed of the potential hazards of unsecured communication on the internet. Hazards may include authorized or unauthorized monitoring of transmissions and records of webcounseling sessions.

3. Inform clients if, how, and how long session data are to be preserved.

   Session data can include webcounselor and webclient email, test results, audio/video session recordings, session notes, and counselor/ supervisor communications. Electronic sessions can be easily and inexpensively preserved, which increases their potential use in supervision, research, and legal proceedings.

4. In situations where it is difficult to verify the identity of webcounselor or webclient, take steps to address impostor concerns, such as by using code words, numbers, or graphics.

5. When parent or guardian consent is required to provide webcounseling to minors, verify the identity of the consenting person.

6. Follow appropriate procedures regarding the release of information for sharing webclient information with other electronic sources.

   Because of the relative ease with which email messages can be forwarded to formal and casual referral sources, webcounselors must work to insure the confidentiality of the webcounseling relationship.

7. Carefully consider the extent of self-disclosure to the webclient and provide the rationale for that level of disclosure.

   Webcounselors may wish to ensure, minimally, that the webclient has the same data available about the counselor as would be available if the counseling took place face to face (e.g., ethnicity, gender, age). Reasons for limiting disclosure should be presented. Webcounselors should protect themselves from unscrupulous users of the internet by limiting potentially harmful disclosures about themselves and their families.

8. Provide links to websites of all appropriate certification bodies and licensure boards to facilitate consumer protection.

9. Contact the National Board for Certified Counselors or the webclient's state or provincial licensing board to obtain the name of at least one counselor-on-call within the webclient's geographical region.

   Webcounselors should contact a counselor-on-call to determine his or her willingness to serve (either in person, over the phone, or via email) and should also provide the webclient with local crisis intervention hotline numbers, 911, and similar numbers in the event that the counselor-on-call is unavailable.

10. Discuss with webclients procedures for contacting the webcounselor when he or she is offline.

    This includes explaining exactly how often email messages are to be checked by the webcounselor.

11. Mention at their websites any presenting problems they believe to be inappropriate for webcounseling.

    While no conclusive research has been conducted to date, those topics might include sexual abuse as a primary issue, violent relationships, eating disorders, and psychiatric disorders that involve distortions of reality.

12. Explain to clients the possibility of technology failure.

    The webcounselor should instruct webclients about calling if problems arise, discuss the appropriateness of the client calling collect when the call is from around the world, point out differences in time zones, discuss dealing with response delays in sending and receiving email messages.

13. Explain to clients how to cope with potential misunderstandings arising from the lack of visual cues from webcounselor or webclient.

For example, the counselor could simply say, "Because I couldn't see your face or hear your tone of voice in your email message, I'm not sure how to interpret that last message."

(Webcounseling standards are reprinted with the permission of the National Board for Certified Counselors, Inc.)

Wayne Lanning (1997), a member of the original Web Counseling task force, said:

> The thought of replacing the face to face component in counseling is very threatening, or at least disturbing. A bit of reasoned reflection, however, soon reveals that counseling services offered over the internet do not involve different ethical principles than face to face counseling. Only the application of those principles may be different. The primary issue that involves something not faced is how to manage the licensing of the practice of counseling when it is not limited geographically to state boundaries. The use of a computer or the internet is not an intervention any more than using one's voice or a book is an intervention. They are all tools we may choose to use to make an intervention. It may be, however, that special training/education ought to be obtained before attempting to deliver intervention by means of the internet.

## Ethical Standards Regarding Sexual Intimacy

The ACA (1995) code of ethics states, "Counselors do not have any type of sexual intimacies with clients and do not counsel persons with whom they have had a sexual relationship." The code also says that counselors do not engage in sexual intimacies with former clients within a minimum of two years after terminating the counseling relationship, and that counselors who engage in sexual relationships with clients after two years following termination still have the responsibility to thoroughly examine and document that such relations do not have an exploitative nature, based on factors such as

duration of counseling,

amount of time since counseling,

termination circumstances,

client's personal history,

client's mental status,

adverse impact on the client, and

actions by the counselor during counseling suggesting a plan to initiate a sexual relationship with the clients after termination.

Remember, it is always the counselor's responsibility to ensure that sexual intimacies with clients do not occur. The power in the relationship must always be assumed to rest with the counselor. Several useful maxims to govern a counselor's sexual behavior are listed below:

Do not counsel clients with whom you have previously shared intimacies.

Do not be a voyeur.

Do not drink with, or party with, current, future, or past clients.

Do not share your personal intimacies, or problems, with clients.

Do not have sex with clients, ever.

Do not have sex with a professor, colleague, boss, trainee, or intern.

### Ethical Standards for Making Referrals

Making timely referrals is an important element of successful case management. Counselors begin with the end in mind and see termination as a goal. Professional counselor behavior includes knowing when, how, and to whom to refer clients. Referrals should be made when the client would be better served by another professional or when a client's needs are beyond the scope of a counselor's skills. The list of types of professional helpers and their areas of specialty in Chapter 7 can assist counselors in making appropriate referrals.

## UNETHICAL CONDUCT

In addition to the many issues already cited, unethical or unprofessional conduct by counselors can involve other types of unprofessional activities and incompetence.

### Unprofessional Activities

Behavior that is unprofessional on the part of a counselor includes

- exploiting relationships with clients for personal gain or financial advantage,

- using any confidence of a client to the client's disadvantage,

- having dual relationships with clients or relationships that may impair or diminish the counselor's professional judgment or objectivity (i.e., counseling an employee or supervisor, a close friend, a family member, or engaging in close personal relationships with clients),

- failing to safeguard the rights of each member of a family when engaged in family therapy,

- failing to notify and assist the client in seeking appropriate alternative services (making a referral) when termination or interruption of service to the client is anticipated,

- failing to terminate a client when it is obvious that the process no longer serves the client's interests or needs,

- delegating professional responsibilities to another person knowing that person is not qualified by training or experience,

- failing to make clear to the client that all decisions are the right and responsibility of the client,

- failing to prescreen group counseling members, and

- failing to be aware of each group member's status during the group process.

## Counselor Incompetence

Behavior that exhibits incompetence and that also may be illegal on the part of the counselor includes

- seeking work positions for which he or she is not professionally qualified;

- failing to have sensitive regard for the beliefs of clients (moral, social, religious) or imposing his or her own beliefs on clients;

- engaging in dishonesty, fraud, deceit, or misrepresentation while performing professional activities;

- failing to recognize potential or actual harm to clients when diagnosing, treating, or advising on problems outside the recognized boundaries of the counselor's competence;

- practicing inhumane or discriminatory behaviors toward clients (e.g., on the basis of religion, sex, age, gender, sexual preference, or national place of origin);

- failing to seek appropriate professional assistance for his or her own personal problems when they are likely to result in inadequate services for clients;

- using an institutional affiliation to solicit clients for private practice;

- practicing in an area in which he or she has no professional training or competence;

- practicing while under the influence of unprescribed medications, illegal drugs, or alcohol;

- failing to recognize the need for continued training, knowledge, and relevant techniques necessary to treat clients from different cultural backgrounds; and

- accepting or giving a fee for making or receiving a referral.

## RESOLVING ETHICAL DILEMMAS

No code of ethics is broad enough to encompass every possible unethical situation. Counselors will draw on their training, personal experiences, and intuition to help resolve ethical dilemmas. However, the oath below can serve as a guideline to assist in that resolution.

**Counselor's Oath**

I will comply with the ACA Code of Ethics and Standards of Practice.

I will comply with the code of ethics of my specialty area.

I will consult/inform my supervisor of serious ethical dilemmas.

I will consult with other peer professionals.

I will answer the question, "What is the greater good?"

I will answer the question, "Who benefits most from my decision?"

I will carry liability insurance.

I will not be motivated by the threat of a lawsuit, or be motivated by the "easy way out."

# CONFIDENTIALITY AND PRIVILEGED COMMUNICATION

## Confidentiality

Keeping confidences is an ethical behavior that protects clients from unauthorized disclosures of information. Clients have a basic right to privacy, which is the assurance that what they say in a counseling session will remain private.

The concepts of confidentiality and privileged communications are based on the fourth amendment of the US Constitution, which guarantees citizens the fundamental right to privacy. Clients have the freedom to choose the time, place, and extent to which their beliefs and behaviors will be made known (or withheld) from others. A breach of client confidentiality is considered an "invasion of privacy."

Many counselors inform clients at the outset of the process that any of the following situations may warrant an exception to confidentiality:

- when a counselor is "court ordered" (required by law) to reveal,

- to disclose information to others specifically designated in written consent from the client,

- when the counselor is a defendant in a disciplinary action (criminal or civil) arising from counseling,

- when there is "clear and imminent danger" to the client or others (i.e., the client is threatening harm to self or others),

- when discussing case notes with another professional for purposes of consultation, or

- when child abuse is suspected (laws vary greatly from state to state on this issue).

**Buckley Amendment.** The Family Educational Rights and Privacy Act of 1974, known as the Buckley amendment, protects the confidentiality and privacy of clients. It also grants to students 18 years and older, and their parents, access to the school records of the student.

**Keeping Records Confidential.** Confidential storage of records includes computer data, videos, case notes, drawings, written data, audio tapes, and examination results. Minimal protection is a locked file cabinet, not just a locked office door. Client information should be kept for ten years, or as dictated by state statutes. Records cannot be sold to another counselor even upon a counselor's retirement. Access to computer disks and to hard drives should also be secured, even from extraneous office personnel. Passwords should be changed regularly.

**Confidentiality in Groups.** The ethical code of the Association for Specialists in Group Work (1989) requires group counselors to protect members by defining clearly what confidentiality means, why it is important, when the leader is required by law to break confidentiality, and how confidentiality is to be enforced and disciplined within the group. Counselors should also encourage group members to raise any questions they might have about confidentiality.

**Confidentiality in Family Counseling.** Counselors should not disclose information about one family member to another family member without prior consent.

**Release of Information.** A release form should be signed by the client whenever counselors attempt to obtain confidential records (case notes, test results, videos, data, etc.) from other mental health professionals or institutions, whenever counselors use the client's materials (tapes, case notes, etc.) in training sessions or for supervision purposes, or whenever they counsel minors (the signature of a parent or guardian is required).

**Breaches of Confidentiality.** Counselors are unethical in their conduct related to confidentiality if they

- fail to obtain written, informed consent from each client before electronically recording sessions,

- fail to obtain written, informed consent from each client before permitting a third party to observe a session,

- fail to store or dispose of client records in a way that maintains security and confidentiality,

- fail to ensure that the content of the information is accurate and unbiased,

- fail to guard fully the identity of the client when using material from a counseling session for training or educational purposes,

- fail to obtain consent from each family member who is competent when disclosing information from family counseling, and

- fail to obtain consent from the parents or guardian of a minor.

## Privileged Communication

Privileged communication is a legal right protecting the client's communications from being disclosed in a court of law without that client's consent. The "privilege" belongs to the client, not the counselor. The client is usually the only person who can waive this privilege. A client's communications are not privileged if the professional with whom he or she is dealing is not legally certified or licensed by the state in which the counseling takes place. Privileged communication is a status granted by state law (usually via a licensure law) to counselors who meet licensure requirements. Privileged communication in counseling is similar to the legal right awarded to the medical and legal professions.

# CLIENTS' RIGHTS

The basis for clients' rights is the Bill of Rights, particularly the first and fourth amendments to the Constitution of the United States. These guarantee freedom of speech, freedom of the press, and the right of petition, and freedom from unreasonable searches and seizures.

## Counselor's Duty to Warn

In 1976, Mr. P. Poddar was a client of a University of California psychologist. While in counseling, Poddar murdered Tatiana Tarasoff. The psychologist knew of Poddar's threats to harm Tarasoff, but failed to warn her in advance. Following her murder, the Tarasoff family successfully sued the U.C. Board of Regents when the court ruled that the psychologist's failure to warn her was professionally irresponsible. Since then, other court cases have upheld and expanded the Tarasoff ruling. Counselors today, therefore, are often required to break confidentiality in order to warn people of impending danger.

**Counselor's Duty to Protect**

Counselors sometimes have the obligation to protect clients, especially if they are in danger of physically harming themselves or if they threaten suicide. Counselors are also obliged to protect others from their clients. Counselors therefore need a plan of action for themselves (e.g., a knowledge of local referral sources) and a plan of action for their clients (e.g., giving them the name of another counselor they can contact in the counselor's absence).

**Statement of Disclosure**

A written statement of disclosure should be given to potential clients before beginning counseling services. In some states, this is required. This statement informs the client and the public about the counselor's professional qualifications, counseling processes and techniques, billing policies, office hours, emergency procedures, and grievance procedures.

**Rights of Group Members**

Clients who meet for group counseling have most of the same rights as those in individual counseling, with the additional rights to

know all group members were prescreened,

know the qualifications of the group leader(s),

know the limits of confidentiality,

know how members will be protected in the group, and

sign an informed consent form.

# ETHICAL RESPONSIBILITIES IN SPECIFIC AREAS

Counselors perform their duties in a variety of work environments, and many of those settings have established ethical guidelines.

## Research Responsibilities

The counselor agrees that when any research is conducted, the rights and dignity of participants will be safeguarded. Counselors doing research will

- be sure participation in research is voluntary, unless involuntary participation will have no harmful effects on the subjects,

- realize that ultimate responsibility for ethical research lies with the principle researcher,

- protect each research participant from unwarranted harm (physical, emotional, and mental), and

- abide by the following basic elements of informed consent:

  a)   provide clients with a fair explanation of the procedures to be followed,

  b)   provide clients with a description of all risks,

  c)   provide clients with a description of the expected benefits,

  d)   tell clients they can withdraw their participation any time,

  e)   treat all data compiled as confidential, and

  f)   acknowledge previous research when reporting research findings.

## Supervision Responsibilities

The counselor agrees that when supervising others, the rights and dignity of supervisees will be safeguarded. Counselors serving as supervisors will

- engage in clinical supervision only after receiving adequate training in supervision,

- maintain ongoing professional development in supervision,

- not engage in dual relationships with supervisees,

- have supervisees inform their clients that they are being supervised,

- make supervisees aware of ethical standards of the profession of counseling,

- establish a plan of action with supervisees for handling crises,

- provide supervisees with ongoing critiques,

- not engage in any activity that impairs the objectivity of the supervisor, and

- never engage in a sexual relationship with a supervisee.

**Measurement and Evaluation Responsibilities**

The counselor agrees that when engaged in gathering, analyzing, and publicizing data, the rights and dignity of clients will be safeguarded. Counselors serving in this capacity will

- inform clients about the purpose of the testing and all proposed uses of the tests prior to their administration,

- evaluate the appropriateness (theoretical base, validity, reliability, etc.) of test instruments used with clients,

- respect clients' rights to know their test results and the conclusions drawn from them,

- use appropriate supervised test-taking techniques with clients when testing through the mail,

- use test instruments that are not beyond the counselor's competence to administer and interpret,

- use electronic data or computer-based systems with which they are familiar, and

- ensure that data are kept secure, and destroyed when no longer needed.

In addition to the ethics that apply to working in different areas, counselors also have ethical responsibilities to themselves and to those with whom they collaborate.

**Professional Development Responsibilities**

Counselors have an ethical responsibility to themselves and to the public to continually upgrade their skills and knowledge in the field. Certified Licensed Professional Counselors (LPCs) and other professionals are required by their licensing or certifying boards to continue to accumulate continuing education units (CEUs) on a regular basis.

## Collegial Responsibilities

The counselor has responsibilities to colleagues—those with whom he or she works, collaborates, counsels, and does research. The ethical colleague will

- not solicit clients currently under the care of another counselor and will communicate with that colleague or agency should such a client or student come to him or her for counseling;

- keep any confidences shared by his or her colleagues;

- as a counselor in an organization, church, agency, school, etc., remain individually accountable for the ethical principles in that setting;

- not take credit for work not personally performed, neither by giving inaccurate information nor by failing to give accurate information;

- take action when it is apparent that another member of the counseling profession violates the code of ethics, first, by discussing the violation with the colleague in question, and, if that action is not satisfactory, by filing a complaint with the licensing board, a supervisor, or some other appropriate authority;

- not harass another counselor;

- understand his or her areas of competence and make full use of other professional resources that may best serve the interest of clients.

# LEGAL STANDARDS OF PRACTICE

There is considerable overlap of ethical and legal practices in counseling. For instance, the law as well as ethical standards requires the reporting of suspected abuse of children 16 years of age or younger. Sexual contact between clients and counselors is also both an unethical and illegal activity in most states. Privileged communication is a legal right offered to counselors in some states, usually through licensure statutes. The laws in many states allow counselors to detain clients for medical observation and assessment. Laws vary from state to state, so counselors must be familiar with, and abide by, state statutes that define illegal activities in the counseling profession.

## Malpractice

Malpractice is the failure to render proper service through either ignorance or negligence resulting in injury or loss to clients. In order to prove malpractice, a client must allege and demonstrate that

- a professional relationship was actually established between the client and counselor,

- the client was truly harmed (evidenced by an actual physical or psychological injury, which must be measured in economic terms),

- the counselor was in the position to have a "legal duty" to the client,

- the conduct of the counselor clearly violated that legal duty through a failure to conform to a legal standard established to prevent "unreasonable risk or harm" (physical or psychological), and

- the counselor's conduct caused the actual injury or there was a "causal connection" between the counselor's negligent conduct and the harm experienced by client.

## Negligence

Negligence is found when a counselor departs from "the usual and customary practice of counseling" rather than pursuing a reasonable and ordinary prudent practice.

## Reporting Child Abuse

Each state has its own statutes regarding a counselor's legal obligation to report suspected child abuse. In many states, the counselor has no option and must report suspected child abuse to a designated agency for further investigation. Some states require reporting when any family member even mentions being abused, whereas other states do not require reporting abuse when the perpetrator reveals the matter in confidence to the counselor.

## Liability

The most frequent types of legal action brought against counselors are sexual harassment, mental distress, abandonment, defamation of character, negligence, and misrepresentation of professional ability. Thus, it behooves counselors to have professional liability insurance (obtainable from ACA at discount rates for students). Most master's degree programs require students to carry liability insurance, especially during their practicum and internship experiences. Legal assistance for ACA members may be available through the ACA's Legal Defense Fund at 800-347-6647.

### Discrimination in Counseling Workplaces

The Americans with Disabilities Act (ADA, 1990) prohibited counselors or clinics employing 25 people or more from discriminating in the workplace. In 1994, the act was expanded to cover employers of 15 people or more. This law protects the disabled, including substance abusers in rehabilitation, AA, etc. The act prohibits discrimination in public and private transportation, too. By definition, a disabled person is substantially limited in one or more major life activities, such as caring for oneself, performing manual tasks, walking, learning, seeing, speaking, hearing, and working.

# Chapter 9

# CAREER COUNSELING

Work is love made visible. (Kahlil Gibran, 1968, p.28)

Career counseling focuses on helping clients obtain greater life satisfaction. A meaningful, rewarding, and economically satisfying career often lies at the heart of a client's satisfaction with life. However, some clients satisfy their personal needs through their leisure time activities. Vernon Zunker (1994) defined career counseling as including "all counseling activities associated with career choices over a life span. In the career counseling process, all aspects of individual needs (including family, work, and leisure) are recognized as integral parts of career decision and planning" (p. 3).

Some counselors have criticized the field of career counseling for being too straightforward, too formulaic, and not allowing room for creativity or personal values. However, these arguments can be rebutted with the realization that career counseling incorporates many aspects of interpersonal counseling and psychotherapy.

In debunking critics of career counseling, Crites (1981) argued that

there is a greater need for career counseling than for individual counseling (a view supported by several surveys),

career counseling is therapeutic since personal adjustment and careers are interrelated, career counseling is the appropriate follow-up activity to individual counseling because new directions in career development often occur following personal change,

career counseling is more successful and carries greater expectancy of success than individual psychotherapy, and

career counseling is more comprehensive (utilizes a broad-based approach with assessment tools).

Career counselors may have more broadly based competencies than individual counselors. They are often perceived by clients as both career counselors and individual counselors.

## CAREER COUNSELOR SKILLS

The National Career Development Association (NCDA) has listed various competencies for career counselors. They include a knowledge of

career counseling theories,

management and administration,

interventions and strategies for change,

career consultation approaches,

employment data, education levels, career resources, and training opportunities, and

how to assess individuals and groups (including assessment tools and instruments).

## CAREER COUNSELING THEORIES

Listed below are the major categories of career theories along with some theorist's names. Career development theories provide the counselor with a beginning point from which to plan helping procedures for clients.

*Personality*          Holland

*Trait-Factor*          Parson, Williamson

| | |
|---|---|
| *Developmental* | Super; Tiedeman and O'Hara; Crites; Gottfredson; Ginzberg, Ginsburg, Axelrad, and Herma |
| *Needs* | Roe, Hoppock |
| *Social Learning* | Mitchell and Krumboltz |
| *Cognitive* | Peterson, Sampson, and Reardon; Gelatt; Knefelkamp and Slepitza |
| *Decision Making* | Gelatt, Tiedeman, and O'Hara |

**Personality Theories**

**Holland's Personality Typology.**  In John Holland's (1985) theory, career choice is an expression of personality. Both people and work environments have personalities (characteristics), and people search for work environments that let them exercise their skills and abilities, express their attitudes and values, and take on agreeable problems and roles. In Holland's personality typology, people are assessed through the Strong Interest Inventory and the Career Assessment Inventory, which culminate in a Holland Code, characterized by six different personality types (R, I, A, S, E, C) as represented in the hexagonal pattern in Figure 9.1. Clients' career choices are also influenced by the stereotypes they hold about different jobs.

The six personality types of Holland's model (shown in Figure 9.1) are defined below.

| Type | Characteristics | Trades | Predominant affect | Motto |
|---|---|---|---|---|
| Realistic | aggressive, prefers abstract vs. concrete work, less sociable, weak interpersonal interactions | photographer, plumber, technician | constrained | "Do it!" |
| Investigative | intellectual, abstract, analytical, sometimes radical, task-oriented, systematic, poor persuasive and social skills | computers, electronics, chemistry, mathematician, lab technician | suppressed | "Explore it!" |

| Type | Characteristics | Trades | Predominant affect | Motto |
|------|-----------------|--------|--------------------|-------|
| Artistic | imaginative, value-laden, self-expression through the arts, independent, extrovert, colorful, verbal, dislikes systematic and ordered activities | writer, critic, musician, artist | labile | "Create it!" |
| Social | likes social interactions and social issues, religious, service/community minded, educational activities, enjoys activities that inform or enlighten others | teacher, college professor, sociologist, counselor, psychologist, funeral director, social worker | warm | "Talk about it!" |
| Enterprising | extrovert, aggressive, likes leadership roles, dominant, persuasive, strong verbal skills, dislikes abstract or cautious activities | personnel manager, sales, insurance/real estates sales, car sales | aggressive | "Implement it!" |
| Conventional | practical, well controlled, sociable, conservative, likes structured tasks, prefers ordered and structured activities | accountant, bookkeeper, receptionist, credit manager, clerical | constrained | "Keep it going!" |

John Holland is also noted for developing assessment tools for career needs, namely the Vocational Preference Inventory, the Self-Directed Search, and the My Vocational Situation.

**Trait-Factor Personality Theory.** Frank Parsons, the "father of guidance," wrote *Choosing a Vocation* in 1909 and developed a cognitive career counseling approach that held that certain occupations require workers to possess certain traits for success. Parsons originally said there was a single "right goal" for every person in the choice of an occupation. This approach is some-

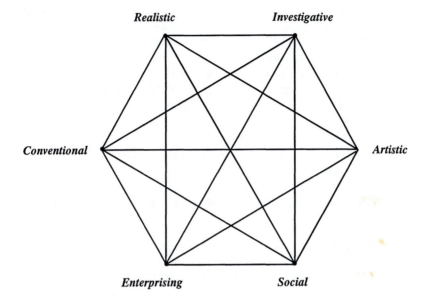

Figure 9.1. Holland Code.

times called an *actuarial* or *matching* approach to career selection since the focus is on matching a client's traits with the requirements of an occupation.

In the trait-factor approach, counselors study the individual, survey occupations, and then match the client with a specific occupation. This led to an increase in occupational information gathering by counselors and in the use of assessment tools and techniques (e.g., tests and inventories) in career exploration. E. G. Williamson (1939) refined the trait-factor approach into six steps: analysis, synthesis, diagnosis, prognosis, counseling, and follow-up.

This model is not often used today in its original form as critics see the idea of only one right occupational choice as naive.

### Developmental Theories

Developmental theorists view the choice of a career as a process, not an event. They also feel the choice of a career is not based on the client's needs.

**Super's Developmental Theory.** In Donald Super's (1980) theory, client's fulfill their *self-concept* when making a vocational choice. Vocational preferences and competencies are based in the situations in which people live and work (and hence in their self-concepts), which will change with time and experience. Thus, *choice* and *adjustment* are continuous, lifelong processes. Super developed an archway model, with the keystone being *the self*, which experiences both social and personal forces. Super originally proposed the concept of *career maturity* but later renamed it *career adaptability*. Super created the Career Pattern Study, which examined the vocational behavior of ninth graders through age 30.

*Vocational Developmental Stages.* The following are Super's vocational developmental stages.

> *Growth* (birth to ages 14–15): development of interests, capacities, and self-concept.
>
> *Exploration* (ages 15–24): tentative choices are made regarding a vocation.
>
> *Establishment* (ages 25–44): work begins on a trial basis, with some stabilization occurring.
>
> *Maintenance* (ages 45–64): a continuous process of adjusting.
>
> *Decline* (ages 65 and older): preretirement, then retirement.

*Vocational Development Tasks.* Super posited these five developmental tasks that people could, to some extent, repeat through:

> *Crystallization* (ages 14–18): vocational goals are formed through awareness, interests, values, and resources. A preferred career plan and how to implement it are developed.
>
> *Specification* (ages 18–21): movement progresses from a tentative or preferred career plan to a specific choice of occupation.
>
> *Implementation* (ages 21–24): training terminates, employment begins.
>
> *Stabilization* (ages 24–35): clients confirm a vocational choice.
>
> *Consolidation* (ages 35 and older): clients establish a career, advance, and achieve status.

Later, Super (1990) modified the five tasks listed above to better incorporate cycling and recycling through the tasks. He reemphasized that ages and transitions are flexible and do not occur in a predictable sequence.

*Major Roles.* Super believed that people play nine major roles in life: 1) child, 2) student, 3) worker, 4) spouse, 5) parent, 6) citizen, 7) "leisurite," 8) homemaker, 9) pensioner.

These nine roles are played out in four locations: 1) home, 2) school, 3) workplace, 4) community.

One criticism of Super's work is that it was based largely on research of only white middle-class college-educated males.

**Tiedeman and O'Hara's Developmental Theory.** David Tiedeman and Robert O'Hara's (1963) model emphasizes *cognitive decision making* and *self-development.* They believed that society and individuals seek the same objective: to see what meaning each may have for the other. Clients go through a period of self-evaluation in regard to a specific occupation. They seek mentally to accept themselves in that field, while also seeking the acceptance of members currently in that field. Clients wrestle cognitively to retain their sense of individuality during this process. Tiedeman and O'Hara referred to this process as *differentiation* and *integration.*

This cognitive decision-making schema has similarities to Erik Erikson's psychological development stages (especially the trust vs. mistrust stage) and to other decision-making models. Therefore, Tiedeman and O'Hara's theory is also listed below under Decision-Making Theories.

*Major Concepts.* Key concepts associated with this theory include:

*Differentiation:* clients become unique and different based on their biology and environment.

*Integration:* while retaining individuality, clients attempt to become cognitively integrated into a career.

*Ego development:* the development of ego is a key component of the career decision process.

*Developmental Process.* The three-step developmental process in this model is:

*Step 1. Problem Condition:* problems are formulated, and solutions are used.

*Step 2. Psychological States:* clients explore, clarify, and accommodate.

*Step 3. Self-Comprehension:* learning about, doing, and doing with awareness.

**Crites's Developmental Theory.** John Crites's (1981) developmental model is associated with the study of *vocational maturity*. It is a continuous process (like Super's) that moves clients through a series of stages and tasks. In this comprehensive model of career counseling, the counselor's role is to assess the following three areas through use of a Career Maturity Inventory.

*Differential:* "What are the problems?"

*Dynamic:* "Why have the problems happened?"

*Decisional:* "In what manner are the problems being dealt?"

After diagnosis Crites believed the role of the counselor was to

- use a client-centered approach with a developmental focus,

- move on to psychodynamic techniques (e.g., interpretation), and finally,

- use trait-factor and behavioral techniques to affect change.

**Gottfredson's Development Theory.** Linda Gottfredson's (1981) developmental approach is known as the *Circumscription and Compromise Theory*, which holds that clients circumscribe and compromise on their occupational choices as they grow. Clients eventually develop a range of acceptable occupational alternatives in which they will take jobs because they are compatible with their *self-concept,* a key component of Gottfredson's theory.

*Stages of Development.* The four stages of circumscription and compromise are:

*Stage 1.* Begins orientation to size and power (age 3–5).

*Stage 2.* Begins orientation to sex roles (age 6–8).

*Stage 3.* Begins orientation to social values (age 8–13).

*Stage 4.* Begins orientation to internal self (age 14 and older).

Gottfredson believed people ruled out occupations through

*Sex typing:* "It's a job for the opposite sex!"

*Wrong social class:* "The status is too high or low for me."

*Inappropriate intelligence levels:* "I do not possess the ability to succeed there."

*Inappropriate interests:* "I am not interested in this. I have other interests."

**Ginzberg, Ginsburg, Axelrad, and Herma's Developmental Theory.** Ginzberg, Ginsburg, Axelrad, and Herma (1951) held that choices about jobs and careers are individual attempts to optimize the fit between *personal priority needs and desire,* and *work opportunities* and *constraints.* Vocational decision making was seen as a *lifelong process.*

In their theory, clients pass through three periods in making a career choice:

*Fantasy* (birth to 11 years): their choice of play becomes work oriented.

*Tentative* (11–17 years): they then pass through four stages—interest, capacity, value, and transition.

*Realistic* (17 years and older): they now pass through three final stages—exploration, crystallization, and specification.

### Needs Theories

**Roe's Needs Theory.** Ann Roe's (1956) theory holds that career directions are first determined by the home environment and "the patterning of early satisfactions and frustrations." Roe taught that a client's needs were determined by his or her genetic makeup, early childhood experiences, and parent–child relationships. Originally based on Maslow's *hierarchy of needs,* Roe's work, especially in identifying the levels and fields of careers (see below), led to the development of several career instruments, including the Vocational Interest Inventory, the Occupational Preference Inventory, and an interest instrument found in the fourth edition of the *Dictionary of Occupational Titles* (*DOT*). Roe believed that people chose careers to meet needs, and that employment sites are either person-centered or non-person-centered.

*Levels and Fields.* Roe classified occupations into six levels and eight fields. The six levels are professional and managerial (highest level), professional and managerial (regular), semiprofessional and managerial, skilled, semiskilled, and unskilled. The eight fields are person-centered fields: service, business contacts, managerial, general cultural, arts and entertainment; and non-person-centered: outdoor, science, technology.

**Hoppock's Needs Theory.**   Robert Hoppock's (1976) theory of career development holds that while occupations may not satisfy all of a client's needs, he or she still chooses an occupation to meet those needs. Hoppock identified several *physical needs* (similar to Maslow's *hierarchy of needs*) and *psychological needs* (such as the belief that a certain career will fulfill needs, and the need to be compensated properly) that lead to job choices. The better clients know what their needs are, the clearer and easier their career choice becomes.

## Social Learning Theories

**Mitchell and Krumboltz's Social Learning Theory.**   Mitchell and Krumboltz (1990) taught that the key determining factor in career selection was *life events*, or each client's unique *life/social experiences*. Other important influences included self-observation, task-approach skills, genetic inheritances, environmental conditions beyond the control of the client, world view, learning experiences, and honed skills (problem solving, work habits, cognitive and affective responses). Their theory has been praised for identifying specific factors that influence a client's choice of career, and as a model for career choices that encompass the life span.

**Sociological Approaches.**   Sociological, or situational, approaches are similar to social learning theories. They are based on situation-related influences such as status, racial and sexual barriers, social factors (e.g., class, family, aspirations), and environmental conditions (e.g., climate, community, resources, geography). These social, situational, and physical conditions influence

the issues of which clients are aware,

the clients' level of willingness to take risks,

the clients' work identity, and

the clients' career mobility.

Zunker (1994) said these factors are to be "considered beyond the control of an individual but are determinants in the process of selection" of a career (p. 57). In the seminal work of Blau, Gustad, Jessor, Parnes, and Wilcox (1956), individual characteristics that are responsible for choice are biologically determined and socially conditioned by social position and relations, family influences, and social role characteristics—with the client eventually reaching a hierarchy of job preferences from which to choose.

## Cognitive Approaches

Cognitive approaches concentrate on *how* clients make a career decision. Often they assist clients in processing information in order to make career decisions in their own best interests.

**Peterson, Sampson, and Reardon's Cognitive Theory.** Researchers Peterson, Sampson, and Reardon (1991) were the original developers of the cognitive information processing (CIP) approach to career counseling. Their focus is on *how* clients make a career decision, and *how they use information* in solving their career concerns. The career counselor's role is to create learning opportunities so that clients enhance their ability to make effective career decisions.

**Gelatt's Cognitive Theory.** H. B. Gelatt (1989) developed a continuous, cyclical cognitive decision-making model with specific decision-making steps. This theory can also be classified as a decision-making theory. The steps are:

*Step 1.* Client acknowledges that a decision needs to be made.

*Step 2.* Client collects data and examines alternative courses of action.

*Step 3.* Client estimates possible outcomes through use of his or her value system.

*Step 4.* Client makes a decision. It could be to just investigate or to wholeheartedly pursue action.

**Knefelkamp and Slepitza's Cognitive Theory.** Knefelkamp and Slepitza (1976) were early cognitive stage theorists who focused on college-age students. They viewed career development as evolving from a simple view of occupations to an in-depth and broad view of careers. Their stages are:

*Dualism:* Student is externally oriented with little evidence of self-processing; thinking is focused on one right career; simple and dichotomous thinking.

*Multiplicity:* Recognition of more career possibilities emerges, but with many important variables still missing.

*Relativism:* Thinking shifts from an external to an internal view, with a primary focus on making a decision about a career.

*Commitment and relativism:* Greater responsibility is assumed, and a challenge to be committed to his or her values, purpose, and goals emerges.

## Decision-Making Models

The ability to make effective decisions can be viewed as a learned skill. Therefore, the need for clients to learn decision-making skills is paramount. Counselors should explore areas that can affect a client's ability to make appropriate decisions such as risk-taking style, personal values, investment (amount of time, money, and ability to delay gratification), and self-efficacy (the belief that they can perform necessary behaviors). Decision-making career counselors focus on *generating alternatives.*

A typical decision-making model might move clients through the following process:

1.  Identifying the problem (Is it only career related?).

2.  Generating alternatives to pursue.

3.  Gathering information on the alternatives.

4.  Processing the gathered information.

5.  Setting goals with deadlines (subgoals, too).

6.  Making plans that move toward subgoals and major goals.

7.  Implementing the plans.

8.  Returning and reporting (evaluating the progress).

**Tiedeman and O'Hara's Decision-Making Theory.**  In 1963, these researchers created a process that is both a decision-making model and a developmental model. Clients move through a three step development process (problem condition, psychological states, and self-comprehension) with an emphasis on making decisions. *Ego development* is a key component of the career decision-making process.

## CAREER TESTING AND ASSESSMENT

Listed below are the more prominent tests and assessment tools used to evaluate clients in career counseling. For a more complete list of tests, see Chapter 6.

**Aptitude.** These tests measure specific skills or the potential to acquire skill proficiencies.

Armed Services Vocational Aptitude Battery (ASVAB)

Career Ability Placement Survey (CAPS)

Differential Aptitude Tests (DAT)

General Aptitude Test Battery (GATB)

Flanagan Aptitude Classification Tests (FACT)

**Interest.** These tests measure likes and dislikes. They also show if others in a specific field have similar interests and job satisfaction.

Strong-Campbell Interest Inventory (SII)

Self-Directed Search (SDS)

Kuder Preference Inventory

Career Assessment Inventory (CAI)

California Occupational Preference Survey (COPS)

McGinley Interest Inventory

**Personality.** These tests measure personality with an eye toward matching the client's personality to a career that fits his or her characteristics.

California Test of Personality

Edwards Personal Preference Schedule (EPPS)

Guilford-Zimmerman Temperament Survey

Sixteen Personality Factors (16PF)

Myers-Briggs Type Indicator (MBTI)

**Values.** These tests measure the client's beliefs and values and can be used to evaluate if a job fits with a client's core beliefs.

Career Orientation Placement and Evaluation Survey (COPES)

Minnesota Importance Questionnaire

Study of Values

The Values Scale

Work Value Inventory (WVI)

# CAREER EDUCATION IN SCHOOLS

Career education bridges school and work. Hansen (1977) defined career education thus:

> It is an effort by educators, parent-business-industry-labor-government personnel to systematically promote the career development of all persons by creating experiences to help them learn academic, vocational, and basic skills, achieve a sense of agency in making informed career decisions, and master the developmental tasks facing them at various life stages through curriculum, counseling, and community. (p. 39)

## Levels of Career Education

From kindergarten to college, career education is now a major part of a school counselor's workload. A successful career education program, according to Hansen (1977), involves a systematic effort of both school counselors and teachers to "increase one's knowledge of self, occupations, training paths, lifestyles, labor market trends, and employability skills." They must also increase their knowledge of the "career decision-making process . . . which helps the individual gain self-direction through purposefully and consciously integrating work, family, leisure, and community roles" (p. 39). In sum, effective career development must be a joint effort of school counselors and others (teachers, community, etc.) to teach career skills in a manner appropriate to grade levels.

**Elementary School Level.**   Use activities, media presentations, parents, and community resources to increase students' self-knowledge and self-concept. Invite parents into class to discuss their jobs, read books and stories that describe job duties, watch videos that illustrate the variety of jobs available.

**Middle School Level.**   Focus on the skills and educational levels needed to obtain specific jobs. Continue to emphasize self-knowledge. Expose students to people in community occupations. Hold career fairs, take field trips to industries and businesses, and use computer-assisted programs. Interviewing people about their jobs as a class assignment also has proved successful.

**High School Level.** Emphasize how work influences lifestyle and the importance of social interaction skills on the job. Hold activities that demonstrate the interrelatedness of life's roles. Provide guest speakers, encourage job shadowing, take field trips to colleges and technical schools, and emphasize self-knowledge through various self-assessment instruments.

**Role of the School Counselor**

Career development counselor roles include teacher, trainer, monitor, consultant, liaison, and referral resource. The counselor helps students to achieve the following hierarchy of goals in regard to their career progression: awareness, exploration, orientation, and preparation.

## COMPUTER-ASSISTED CAREER GUIDANCE

Prominent computer systems used for career exploration include Coordinate Occupational Information Network (COIN), CHOICES, System of Interactive Guidance and Information (SIGI PLUS), DISCOVER, Guidance Information System (GIS), Computer-Linked Exploration of Careers and Training (C-LECT), KANSAS CAREERS, and Career Information Delivery Systems (CIDS).

The two most popularly used applications are SIGI PLUS and DISCOVER. These two measure skills, values, and interests, and can be updated with the latest career information and research. DISCOVER is a computer-based career development and counselor support system. It is mostly used in secondary schools but can be applied to college students and adults also. Published by the American College Testing Foundation (1984), this colorful computer program allows clients to explore the following modules at their own pace:

1.  Beginning the Career Journey

2.  Learning about the World of Work

3.  Learning about Yourself

4.  Locating Occupations

5.  Learning about Specific Occupations

6.  Making Educational Choices

7.  Planning the Next Steps

8.  Planning Your Career

9.  Making Transitions

# CAREER RESOURCES

**Professional Career Organizations**

The following are both divisions of the American Counseling Association:

•  National Career Development Association

•  National Employment Counseling Association

**Publications**

*Dictionary of Occupational Titles.* The *DOT* contains specific information on over 22,000 job titles. This highly technical manual lists the specific tasks and skills required of occupations, the purpose of specific occupations, the tools and machine skills needed, the materials used on the job, the service or product made, the industries associated with the occupation, workers' duties, the physical location of job (e.g., indoors, on water), etc. The *DOT*, first published in 1939 by the U.S. Department of Labor, classifies information by codes.

*The Guide for Occupational Exploration.* The *GOE* is a supplement that simplifies the *DOT* for counselor use.

*Occupational Outlook Handbook.* The *OOH* shows occupational trends and projections. It is nontechnical (unlike the *DOT*) and is written in narrative form. Updated every two years by the Department of Labor, this handbook allows clients to gain an appreciation of the vast variety of occupations from which they can choose. It shows national job prospects, long-term occupation forecasts, industry statuses, job descriptions, and a helpful index of the *DOT* codes by job title.

*Military Career Guide.* This guide details the career paths for each branch of the military service. It also uses the *DOT* codes and shows parallel civilian occupations.

*What Color Is Your Parachute?* This user-friendly self-help book (Bolles, 1993) has been a bestseller for many years. It offers practical suggestions for resume writing, finding jobs, and interviewing, and it provides self-assessment tools related to the world of work.

**Internet**

http://seamonkey.ed.asu.edu/~gail/career.htm

http://www.jobweb.org/occhandb.html (for *Occupational Outlook Handbook*)

# Chapter 10

# LIFESPAN ISSUES

Each of us develops in ways that are like all other individuals, like some other individuals, and like no other individuals. Most of the time, our attention is directed to an individual's uniqueness. But psychologists who study life-study development are drawn to our shared as well as our unique characteristics. (John W. Santrock, 1992, p. 13)

Outlined below are several theories that attempt to explain the human condition throughout the life span: from birth through adult development, from cradle to crypt. The chapter begins with current information on human growth and development over the life span. It concludes with information relevant to older adults, including death and dying. While the chapter is not all-inclusive, it includes issues along the life span that should be useful to counselors.

## By the Year 2050

Predicted changes in the US population by the year 2050 include

| Group | 1996 | 2050 |
|---|---|---|
| White | 73% | 53% |
| Black | 12% | 14% |
| Hispanic | 10% | 25% (will surpass Blacks) |
| Asian | 3% | 8% |
| American Indian | — | (no change) |

**Baby Boomers**

Baby boomers (born 1946–1954) form a unique subculture, a large cohort moving through society causing many changes. The first turned 50 on January 1, 1996.

Many are now experiencing the death of a parent—one of the more traumatic events people experience during their lifetime. This loss will require them to deal with housing the remaining parent. They may choose to relocate their employment to be near ailing parents. The loss will also awaken them to a greater sense of their own mortality.

Baby boomers are beginning to experience serious illnesses. Arthritis, high blood pressure, hearing, vision, AIDS, and heart disease will be common ailments. They will increase their spending on healthcare, and may become consumers of quick fixes and magical cures.

One-third of baby boomers say they would quit working if they had enough money to live comfortably for the rest of their lives. They seek ways to escape boredom.

Seventy percent of baby boomers believe extramarital sex is "always wrong."

This educational levels of this cohort are 87% high school graduates, 25% college graduates, and over 50% have had some college experience.

Baby boomers reentering college need academic counseling to help focus their motivation "and operationalize it into some behavioral or tactical change" (Austin, 1992, p. 85).

# LIFESPAN THEORIES

**Heredity/Environmental Theories**

Some believe that both genes and environment are necessary for a person to exist, and that they interact to form a person's IQ, temperament, height, weight, abilities, and interests (Santrock, 1992).

Early behaviorists, such as John Watson (1913) and B. F. Skinner (1953), suggested that the environment manipulates our biological and psychological drives as well as our needs, which results in our growth and development as we continually respond to the rewards and punishments of nature (our natural experiences). More recently, behaviorism has taken the life-long view that people are neutral at birth, capable of ill or good, and become products of their experience, with maladaptive behaviors being learned behaviors. People are considered the same as animals, except the human response to stimuli is more complex, less instinctual, and on a higher level of conceptualization.

### Basic Needs Theories

Psychoanalytic and psychosexual development approaches teach that there is an interaction between a client's basic internal needs, or forces, and his or her environment.

Sigmund Freud combined basic needs with biological factors in his five-stage development model:

1.  Oral        (0–18 months)   Gratification needs are met through feeding and the organs connected with that function (mouth, lips, tongue).

2.  Anal        (2–3 years)     Gratification needs are met through activities connected with the anus and retaining and passing feces (smelling, touching, playing with feces).

3.  Phallic     (3–5 years)     Gratification needs of both boys and girls are met through acknowledgment of, curiosity about, and experimenting with their genitals. Anatomical differences in the sexes are discovered.

4.  Latency     (6–12 years)    The child represses interest in sexuality and develops intellectual and social skills. Sexual fantasies occur, with uncontrolled expression of some instinctual sexual impulses causing guilt and perhaps unfavorable consequences for the child.

5.  Genital     (12–19 years)   Needs emerge as sexual reawakening. Sexual gratification moves to someone outside the family.

The phallic stage includes the Oedipus complex (son's attraction to mother) and the Electra complex (daughter's attraction to father). These are conflicting times for the child. *Fixation* occurs when incomplete or inhibited development happens during one of the above five stages.

Freud also described the *libido* as the basic energy or force of life, consisting of life instincts and death instincts. Two libido drives that Freud identified as never being satisfied are *sex* and *aggression*. This theory views adolescence as a period of storm and stress, which Anna Freud (1946) termed "developmental disturbance." As the adult emerges from adolescence, a genital drive develops creating an imbalance among the id, ego, and superego.

Others, such as Abraham Maslow (1987) and William Glasser (1965) have also identified *needs* as essential motivations throughout the life span. Descriptions of these are found elsewhere in this book.

## Growth Theories

> All the world's a *stage*
> And all the men and women merely players;
> They have their exits and their entrances;
> And one man in his time plays many parts.
> (William Shakespeare, *As You Like It*, Act II, scene 7)

**Growth Through Developmental Stages.** In developmental stage growth, important life-span changes and challenges occur in a "fixed sequence and are roughly related to chronological age," requiring "successful resolution of periodic crises" (Zunker, 1994, p. 318). Vaillant (1977) said adults still change as they reach middle age, often dramatically, and that one stage of life is not superior to another, as a person's current stage of development "could rarely be achieved until the previous one was mastered" (p. 207).

For instance, Robert Havighurst's (1953) developmental stage tasks require that in early adulthood people address such tasks as selecting a mate, establishing a home, raising children, starting a career, involving themselves in community activities, and establishing themselves in social relationships. In middle age, the tasks include obtaining a stable economic status, balancing the relationship with the spouse, preparing teens for adulthood, adjusting to changes in their bodies, and developing social interests (hobbies, activities). All these tasks also are potential problem areas in a person's life, requiring adjustment and completion, or life satisfaction is not obtained.

**Growth Through Psychosocial Stages.** Erik H. Erikson (1968) saw life as constantly changing, and the social context of change as crucial in the development of the personality. Erikson identified eight stages in which a person confronts a psychosocial crisis (a developmental task) that must be addressed and resolved. The more successfully each stage's crisis is resolved, the healthier an individual's development will be. Erickson's psychosocial growth stages are

1. *Trust vs. Distrust* (birth to 1½ years): If basic needs are met, newborns develop trust; if not, they develop distrust.

2. *Autonomy vs. Shame and Self-Doubt* (1½–3 years): If allowed to assert themselves, infants develop independence; if not, they develop shame and self-doubt.

3. *Initiative vs. Guilt* (3–6 years): Young children assume responsibility and meet challenges; if not, guilt occurs.

4. *Industriousness vs. Inferiority* (6–11 years): Children conquer academic and social skills; if not, a sense of inferiority develops.

5. *Identity vs. Role Confusion* (adolescence): Adolescents obtain social identity; if not, confusion about adult roles sets in.

6. *Intimacy vs. Isolation* (early adulthood): The new adult obtains intimate relationships; if not, he or she becomes lonely and isolated.

7. *Generativity vs. Stagnation* (middle adulthood): The adult needs to feel valuable and contributory: if not, a sense of stagnation occurs.

8. *Integrity vs. Despair* (later adulthood): The elderly need to view their life as meaningful and making a contribution (generativity); if not, regrets and despair develop.

**Growth Through Cognitive Development.** Jean Piaget, the Swiss developmental psychologist, studied cognitive development (intelligence), focusing on *how* children got their answers rather than *what* answer they got. He examined the development of thinking skills in young children and in 1954 identified four stages of cognitive development.

1. *Sensorimotor* (birth to 2 years): Child differentiates self from objects, seeks stimulation, and will think of objects that are not present.

2. *Preoperational* (2–7 years): Child's language develops, but finds it hard to take another person's viewpoint.

3. *Concrete operational* (7–11 years): Child starts logical thinking, can understand conversations, and can sort or place items in different orders (e.g., biggest to smallest).

4. *Formal operational* (11–15 years): Child begins abstract thinking, tests hypotheses, and can solve problems using logic.

Piaget's ideas that can be used in counseling to help develop a client's thinking skills include

- waiting a long time in silence after a question is asked,

- having clients explain their answers in detail,

- having clients debate their ideas (Piaget said if they debate long enough they will come to the truth), and,

- when counseling children, allowing them to manipulate things (as in play therapy).

**Growth Through Overcoming Unconscious Anxiety.** Sigmund Freud believed that growth occurs as people overcome anxiety and conflict and conquer their unconscious. Blocking the way to successful maturation is the neurotic use of *defense mechanisms*, which people use to protect themselves from life's painful emotions and experiences. Defense mechanisms that are fruitful areas for counselors to explore include:

*Repression:* rejecting from *conscious thought* (through suppression, denial, forgetting) thoughts or ideas that provoke anxiety.

*Fixation:* remaining at the level of emotional development that existed when trauma was encountered at some earlier point in life.

*Projection:* avoiding the conflict within oneself by ascribing one's own ideas or motives to someone else.

*Reaction formation:* expressing an attitude, motive, or behavior that is contrary or opposite to one's true feelings.

*Intellectualization:* avoiding becoming aware of feelings through use of abstract vocabulary, being philosophic, thinking, etc.

*Rationalization:* justifying unacceptable attitudes, beliefs, or behavior by supplying a reason that conceals the true motive or thinking.

*Displacement:* transferring or substituting a different object or goal for the true impulse or motive.

*Introjection:* identifying via fantasy the expression of impulses or motives.

*Regression:* retreating to earlier childlike or more primitive forms of behavior.

*Denial:* refusing to see or blocking out something that is real or true.

**Growth Through Moral Development.**   Lawrence Kohlberg's (1958, 1976, 1986) studies in moral development led to the belief that morality unfolds in stages, through the development of thinking and reasoning skills. From Kohlberg studies of people's responses to structured situations or moral dilemmas, three major stages of moral judgment or reasoning were developed:

1. *Preconventional level:* Children obey parents to avoid being punished. Later, they still look out for themselves first (egocentric) but are aware of other people's interests.

2. *Conventional level:* Children's moral development is measured by their cooperation with peers, a belief in the Golden Rule, and a higher sense of others' interests.

3. *Postconventional level:* Adults realize that laws are necessary and that society's laws and values are somewhat arbitrary and particular to cultures. Fewer than 25% of adults attain this level of moral reasoning. Adults who develop even further choose ethical principles based on abstract concepts such as justice and the equity and value of human rights, being willing to disobey laws for the sake of "justice."

   Counselors who see moral development as being crucial to life-span development believe it offers the guidelines and rules clients should use in interactions with others and self. These guidelines determine feelings, reasonings, and behaviors when confronted with ethical dilemmas. Developing decision-making skills in clients is a common topic in counseling, and making judgments that are moral implies that clients will have values above and beyond emotions. Therefore, when people are in a position to choose between an act of convenience and an act of conviction, it is this choice that defines their happiness. It is this choice that defines their character (Schlessinger, 1997).

**Growth Through Intellectual and Ethical Development.** William Perry (1970) focused his work on the way in which young adults think differently from adolescents. According to Perry, adolescents tend to see the world in a *dualistic way of polarities* (right/wrong, good/bad, we/them, etc.). As adolescents move into their young adult years, they reach the stage of *multiple thinking* (seeing multiple perspectives and a diversity of opinions), rather than remaining dualistic thinkers. Later, they reach the *relative subordinate thinking stage*, in which they take an analytic and evaluative approach to new information that is actively and consciously pursued. Finally, in full adulthood, they shift to *full relativism*, wherein they comprehend that the truth is relative (the meaning of an event is related to the context in which it occurs). It is here that the adult recognizes that relativism permeates all aspects of life.

**Growth Through Faith Development.** James Fowler (1976) developed a stage theory of how faith develops. His concept of faith is not limited to religious faith but includes faith in others. Fowler's stages are:

1. *Undifferentiated Faith* (0–4 years): Primal faith develops (similar to Erickson's infantile trust vs. mistrust crisis). Trust precedes the ability to exercise faith.

2. *Intuitive–Projective Faith* (2–7 years): Intuitive or imaginative faith develops into concrete operational thinking (Piagetian logic).

3. *Mythical–Literal Faith* (childhood and beyond): Personal meaning is now found in stories and dramas. Reflection on contradictions and conflicts occurs, with clear differentiation of facts from fantasy. Concrete operations are performed.

4. *Synthetic–Conventional Faith* (adolescence): Authority is looked to with faith when facts conflict. Commitments, attitudes, and beliefs begin to develop into a personal lifestyle.

5. *Individuated–Reflective Faith* (young adulthood and beyond): Values and beliefs are carefully scrutinized and the opinions of others are often rejected. There is a conflict between group identification and self-actualization. Vocational decisions are considered.

6. *Conjunctive Faith* (mid-thirties and beyond): There is a reworking of the past, with a commitment to justice that goes beyond community, religion, or nation.

7. *Universalizing Faith* (midlife to death): Life is focused on overcoming division, oppression, and brutality. Fowler (1976) believed that few people attain this stage, which is similar to Maslow's self-actualization.

**Growth Through Ecological Adaptation.** Uri Brofenbrenner's (1986) adaptation of ecology to human development examined the many levels and systems that affect people's growth. For example, a troubled adolescent is a part of several systems at the same time: family, school, peers, community, etc. Counselors need to be sensitive to the influences of all these various systems. Brofenbrenner called the systems:

*Microsystem:* The system in which the client lives (home, family, school, job, peers, neighborhood).

*Mesosystem:* The relationship between elements found in the microsystem (e.g., how experiences on the job affect home experiences).

*Exosystem:* When a new system not found in the microsystem affects the client (e.g., the government condemns the client's home).

*Macrosystem:* A person's culture, including behavior patterns, values, beliefs, and traditions passed on through family genealogy.

*Chronosystem:* The patterning of life's transitions and environmental events over the course of a lifetime (e.g., the consequences of actions taken now will affect the client's system later; examples include the long-term effects of an abortion, an accident that will lead to job difficulties later, or the effects of divorce on children).

**Growth Through Social Learning.** Social learning theory combines social environments with cognitive factors. It goes beyond behaviorism's stimulus–response paradigm to the belief that people can, by themselves, do something important (self-efficacy). Albert Bandura's (1989) cognitive social learning theory postulates that people learn by observing what others do. Through *observational learning* (also called *modeling* or *imitation*), people recognize the behaviors of others and then adopt those behaviors themselves.

**Growth Through Frankl's Existentialism.** While a prisoner in the Nazi German concentration camps during World War II, Viktor Frankl (1959) observed that some prisoners soon gave up and died, while others seemed to have a deeper *will to live.* Frankl felt that finding a *meaning in living* allowed some to endure horrible circumstances. Frankl attributed their ability to endure and transcend circumstances to their searching for and finding a deeper meaning to life. He concluded that society is generally characterized by a search for meaning, or *ultimacy*. Those who find meaning focus on what is ultimate in life, not simply on themselves.

Frankl believed that mental and emotional illnesses are really symptoms of an underlying sense of meaninglessness or emptiness, and that the counseling process should attempt to eliminate that emptiness by helping individuals detect their unique meaning or mission in life. His approach is called Logotherapy.

**Growth Through Spiritual or Religious Development.**   Clients may develop and progress toward a better self and more effective goals as they adhere to their spiritual values or religious doctrines. Progression depends on the degree to which clients align their behavior with their moral beliefs. Counselors can assist clients in measuring personal growth through exploring clients' core values and monitoring clients' commitment and sacrifice for those principles.

## ADULT STAGES OF LIFE

Numerous theories have been developed describing stages of adult life. A few are listed below.

Kenniston (1970) said that as youth transition into young adulthood, they enter a period of economic and personal temporariness as they struggle between *self-autonomy* and *becoming socially involved*. The two criteria for successful transition into young adulthood are economic *independence* and *independent decision-making*, while *change* and *continuity* epitomize the transition.

Daniel Levinson (1978) identified major transitions or tasks occurring at different age stages of adulthood. Two key stages are early and middle adulthood:

> *Early adulthood:* At ages 17–22, two key tasks are addressed: exploring the possibilities for adult living and developing a stable life structure. A successful transition is found in forming a dream of adulthood that is desired (especially in terms of marriage and a career). At ages 28–33, the task is to satisfy the desired dream.

*Middle adulthood:* At ages 40–45, four tasks are to be resolved: being young vs. being old; being destructive vs. being constructive; being masculine or feminine; and being attached to others vs. being separated.

*Later adulthood:* At ages 46 years and older, the tasks are to create, modify, and enhance personal life structures; and to form specific personal life structures (such as vocation, love, marriage, having a mentor, relationships with family).

Levinson's tasks have been criticized for containing no statistical analysis, for being dated, and for studying only males. Others say the quality and quantity of his biographies are outstanding, and in the true clinical tradition (Santrock, 1982).

Roger Gould (1978), a psychiatrist examining the attitudes and life histories of over 520 men and women, which led to his theory of transformations in adult development, believed that a linking of stages and crises led to developmental transformations. Gould's transformations are:

*16–18 years:* desires to escape parental control

*18–22 years:* leaves the family, adjusts to a new peer group

*22–28 years:* develops independence, commits to a family and career

*29–34 years:* questions self, has role confusion, adjusts to marriage and career

*35–43 years:* feels an urgency to attain goals, is aware of time limits, realigns goals

*43–53 years:* settles down, accepts one's life

*53–60 years:* increases tolerance, accepts one's past, is less negative

Gail Sheehy's (1976) book *Passages: Predictable Crises of Adult Life* was widely read in the 1980s and was on the New York Times best-seller for 27 weeks. Sheehy's premise was that adults pass through chronological stages in which they solve problems before progressing to the next stage. It is the periods between stages, which Sheehy called "passages," that provide opportunities for growth. She found that happier adults are those who

- may feel miserable but confront themselves,

- set goals,

- appraise weaknesses,

- seek independence, and

- know their strengths.

Terms Sheehy used to describe these stages include "trying twenties," "catch-thirty," "deadline decade" (between ages 35 and 45), and the "age forty crucible." Each passage earns a person his or her own *authentic identity*, which is constructed through one's own strenuous efforts. Those who *fully experience life's issues* and examine themselves in light of those issues will find true personal identity and thrive.

## OLDER ADULTS

When working with mature clients, counselors should study the developmental models of aging. Gerontology counseling has grown in recent years, and there is extensive new information.

Santrock (1992) lists the following factors associated with late adulthood:

- Some disease or illness can be expected (arthritis first, perhaps followed by hypertension, heart disease, cancer, or stroke).

- Consuming medications is common.

- Males' sexual performance declines more than females'.

- Physical exercise is still needed (although at a reduced rate).

- Overweight individuals have an increased mortality rate.

- There is a decrease in vision, hearing, teeth, taste, and smell.

- Sensitivity to pain increases.

- Heart rate and blood pressure rise.

- Reflexes and stamina decrease.

## Elderly Workers

Recent research indicates that older workers (age 40 and over) who continue to seek work:

- seek and find increased amounts of part-time employment;

- tend to have longer periods of unemployment than younger people;

- have a persistent and progressive decline on tasks requiring speed;

- have unimpaired, but slower intellectual functioning, due to filtering new stimuli through the lens of their life experiences;

- find their overall job satisfaction to be age related; and

- feel an increased need for security and social affiliation.

## Counseling Older Adults

In working with older adults counselors need to

- build and maintain positive attitudes about their worth and dignity;

- use problem-solving approaches that deal with specific and immediate problems;

- use a life review process in order to integrate the past and prepare for the future;

- help them feel a sense of accomplishment in their life (leaving a legacy, making a contribution, etc.); and

- educate society and advocate for a change in attitudes about the elderly.

## Theory of Margin

Michael Day (1983) holds that personal empowerment comes as adults address and balance load and power. The more successfully they balance these two factors, the more margin (empowerment) they have. *Load* is defined as the demands self and society make on individuals to maintain a minimal level of autonomy. *Power* is defined as the resources and abilities that individuals can command to cope with load.

Elderly clients increase their margin by consciously decreasing their load or by increasing their power. In the elderly there is often a debilitating shift in the margin equation due to the erosion of their power (e.g., the death of a spouse, loss of job, reductions in income, health deterioration, changes in residence). Elderly clients are overcome by change (load). They tend to insulate themselves in an effort to preserve some control over their lives, often withdrawing more and more from life's activities.

When clients are helped to increase their positive resources and capture greater control over their choices, they gain excess margin (a power surplus). Then they are better able to deal with the life changes associated with aging. The ability of elderly clients to deal successfully with these changes is an important contributor to their life satisfaction.

# GRIEF AND DYING

It should be noted that death and separation are not the only losses clients experience. Losses of tangible (e.g., property, pets, personal belongings, body parts) and intangible (e.g., friendships, safety, marital status) items all involve a grieving process. Even the *way* in which death occurs (e.g., drawn out, traumatic, homicide) affects those who survive the deceased (Muxen, 1995).

Grief includes the emotional numbness, disbelief, separation anxiety, despair, sadness, and loneliness that accompany a loss. When clients lose someone they love, they generally proceed through stages toward recovery.

## Stages of Grief

**Averill's Stages of Grief.**   Averill (1968) wrote that stages toward recovery follow the following pattern:

*Shock* (1–3 days): feels disbelief, weeps, becomes easily agitated.

*Despair* (4 weeks is peak, but may last several months): a painful longing for the dead, memories of the dead, may bargain for the return of the dead, remains irritable.

*Recovery* (about one year after death): resumes ordinary activities, recalls pleasant memories of dead, establishes new relationships.

**Parkes' Stages of Grief.** Parkes' (1972) dimensions, or stages, of grief are

- Numbness

- Pining

- Depression

- Recovery

## Sensory Centration Saturation

Sensory Centration Saturation (SCS) is the cognitive condition of a person immediately following the death of a close friend or relative, or a major emotional shock. Clients in this brief crisis state (1–4 days) are tender and emotionally impressionable. They perceive all incoming stimuli through the filter of their loss. External stimulation, such as an innocent comment, lyrics of a radio song, etc., are first filtered through the lens of connection to the loss. SCS is also called the *Jerry Garcia Syndrome* after the grieving followers of the Grateful Dead guitarist, who continued to experience the world from a Dead Head perspective long after the 1995 death of Garcia.

## Grief in the Family

According to Marla Muxen (1995), the affect of a loss or death on a family will depend on the following four factors and how the family deals with them:

1. *The manner of the loss or death:* Was it sudden, lingering, ambiguous, violent, intentional, or chronic?

2. *The family's processes and internal and social network at the time of the loss:* Key factors to evaluate include family cohesion, family flexibility, open communication vs. secrecy, family rules about emotions, availability of extended family, use of social and economic resources, the prior role of the deceased member within the family, and conflict or strained relationships at time of loss.

3. *Timing of the loss:* Key factors to evaluate include untimeliness or prematurity of the loss, concurrent multiple losses, the family's stage in the developmental life cycle, and each individual's place in the developmental life cycle.

4. *The sociocultural context of death for the family:* What are the ethnic, religious, philosophical and sociopolitical family background and beliefs? What is the historical context of the loss? How do gender roles influence or restrict family members?

## Stages of Dying

**Kubler-Ross's Stages of Dying.** Elisabeth Kubler-Ross (1969) divided the behavior and cognition of dying persons into five stages. Later (1974) she said that the stages are not in invariant sequence. Research on her stages of dying has yet to confirm the validity of her widely accepted five stages:

1. *Denial and isolation:* They deny this is happening to them.

2. *Anger:* They ask, "Why me?" and may resent others such as physicians or family members, especially healthy persons.

3. *Bargaining:* They hope that death can be postponed or delayed, and even bargain with God through repentance or promises.

4. *Depression:* They accept the certainty of death, and may disconnect from others. (Kubler-Ross said counselors should not try to cheer them up because they have a need to contemplate their own impending death.)

5. *Acceptance:* A sense of peace develops. They may want to be left alone. There is an absence of feelings and physical pain.

# Chapter 11

# HUMAN SEXUALITY

## SEX COUNSELING

Sex counseling is different from sex therapy. In sex therapy, the counselor focuses on sexual dysfunctions, which are identified later in this chapter. In sex counseling, the counselor provides sexual information. The moral obligation of sex counselors is to be prepared to provide timely and accurate data. Counselors must first be comfortable with their own sexuality. They must have the confidence and openness to discuss sexual issues candidly, and they must be willing to be direct with clients.

### Counselor's Professional Attributes

Counselors who see clients or couples with sexual concerns must

- be up-to-date on the research on sexual dysfunctions (i.e., primary and secondary impotence, premature ejaculation, delayed ejaculation, vaginismus, and orgasmic dysfunction);

- know the terminology related to male and female anatomy;

- be familiar with sexual life-span issues, transitions, and age-related physical changes;

- be conversant on sexually transmitted diseases, contraception, birth control methods, abortion, adoption, homosexuality, rape, sexual abuse, gay and lesbian issues, and sexual techniques;

- respect the rights of clients, not imposing values or unduly influencing a client's decision in sexual matters;

- know appropriate community resources for referrals of sexual matters that need immediate attention; and

- know the laws related to sexual abuse, rape, and incest.

### Goals of Sex Counseling

Sex counseling follows a pattern similar to other types of counseling. Therefore, the goals of sex counseling are to move clients toward:

- self-exploration,

- self-knowledge, and

- behavior change.

### Guiding Principles

Today sex counselors generally adhere to certain guiding principles, such as those listed below:

Sexual activities should be pleasant for both partners.

Sexual activities that degrade, or to which a partner objects, are inappropriate and should be stopped.

Sexual activities are enjoyed most when they are aligned with a client's value system.

Clients should be responsible sex partners, protecting themselves and others from sexually transmitted diseases (STDs).

Clients should inform sex partners in advance of any STDs they may have.

Clients should be educated where necessary about proper sexual functioning.

Clients should be sensitive to the sexual needs and preferences of their partners.

Clients may need to be told directly how to satisfy a partner's needs.

# TERMS FOR SEXUAL BEHAVIORS

*Ejaculation:* expulsion of semen from the penis

*Exhibitionism:* compulsive public exposure of the genitals to strangers

*Fetishism:* attraction to an object or nonsexual part of the body

*Frigidity:* inability to experience orgasm during intercourse, or persistently adverse to sexual intercourse

*Frotteurism:* the fantasy of touching nonconsenting persons

*Functional dyspareunia:* pain experienced during sexual intercourse

*Functional vaginismus:* painful contractions of the muscles around the vagina

*Gender identity disorder:* persistent discomfort with one's gender; desire to be, or insistence that one is, of the other sex

*Impotence:* failure of the male to achieve or maintain an erection during sexual intercourse

*Libido:* Freud's term for sexual drive or sexual desire

*Masochism:* being sexually excited by emotional or physical pain during sex

*Paraphilias:* recurrent and intense sexual fantasies involving nonhuman objects, or suffering or humiliation of one's sex partner

*Pedophilia:* sexual preference for prepubescent children

*Premature ejaculation:* expulsion of semen from the penis involuntarily

*Promiscuity:* indiscriminate frequency and choice of sexual partners

*Sadism:* being sexually excited by inflicting emotional or physical pain on another person

*Sexual addiction:* habitual and overly frequent seeking of sexual gratification

*Transsexualism:* a strong desire to be a member of the opposite sex

*Transvestism:* being sexually aroused by dressing like a member of the opposite sex (cross-dressing)

*Vaginismus:* involuntary contraction of the vaginal muscles

*Voyeurism:* finding sexual excitement in watching others undress or make love

## Common Female Sexual Dysfunctions

- Lack of sexual desire (low libido)

- Inability to achieve orgasm (primary orgasmic dysfunction)

- Inability to control constrictions of the vagina (vaginismus)

## Common Male Sexual Dysfunctions

- Sexual apathy, loss of interest (low libido)

- Inability to achieve and maintain an erection (impotence)

- Inability to delay ejaculation (premature ejaculation)

- Inability to ejaculate at all (ejaculatory incompetence)

# GENDER ISSUES

Every individual has both male and female characteristics, referred to by the Chinese as the *yin* and *yang*. Androgynous and gender sensitive counseling helps clients find or uncover both their male and female characteristics and find the balance in their masculine and feminine parts.

## Gender Imbalance

Couples may experience imbalances in their relationship based on gender differences. When this is suspected by the counselor, or raised by one of the partners (in individual, couples, or family counseling), the counselor may wish to explore the following areas in search of the difficulty:

- communication patterns,

- privacy issues,

- shifting tasks in the family,

- power and control,

- attempts to relabel deviance,

- economic imbalance,

- generational differences, and

- adjustment issues related to a partner's unemployment.

### Gender-Sensitive Counseling

As the counselor begins to explore the presenting problem with a couple, each person's view of their gender role can be addressed. How did they arrive at their current gender roles? Counselors also can explore the following areas:

differences in how they grew up female and male,

duties or roles that their parents assumed and that the clients have now brought unwittingly to their current relationship,

behaviors in their current relationship they find uncomfortable and would like to renegotiate,

aspects of their partner's role they find uncomfortable, and

current traditions and practices they wish to change.

### Important Issues for Men

Men are more often able to be sensitive to women's issues when the counselor structures the session to allow the woman time to fully explain her feelings and concerns. Often she has not been heard at home, and the counselor can facilitate time so the man can more fully appreciate her point of view.

Key issues for men as they interact with women are often power and control, according to Susan Chamberlain-Hayman (1998). These issues include

- men's feelings that they are entitled to women's sexual compliance,

- men's physical power over women,

- men's control over women's reproductive rights (impregnating women, planting seeds),

- men's sense of ownership of women ("my wife," marking their territory), and

- men's power and control over other men (competitiveness).

In working with men, counselors may find the old adage, "Men need to be appreciated; women need to be listened to," helpful.

## A Woman's Perspective

Building on work by Perry (1970), Belenky, Clenchy, Goldberger, and Torule's (1986) research revealed that women view reality from five different perspectives, and that their *self-concepts* and *ways of knowing* are intertwined. The five perspectives are listed below:

*Silence.* Women experience themselves as subject to external forces or authority, without a voice, opinionless.

*Received knowledge.* Women believe that they are capable of being educated and obtaining knowledge.

*Subjective knowledge.* Women perceive themselves as capable of understanding information from a personal perspective (subjectively or by intuition).

*Procedural knowledge.* Women are personally active in learning and pursuing knowledge, both obtaining and communicating information.

*Constructed knowledge.* Women see knowledge in context and create knowledge of their own.

## Influences on Gender Roles

There are many forces that teach and keep women and men in stereotypical gender roles. In examining the various areas of influence in this section counselors should keep these points in mind:

- clients can be made aware of these influences and can reexamine the gender roles they have chosen, and

• clients may prefer to adhere to traditional roles, with it being unethical to pursue changes they do not desire.

**Cognitive Influence.** Based on Kohlberg's (1966) cognitive development theory, current cognitive theorists believe that children's behavior and attention are directed by an internal motivation to conform to gender-specific sociocultural standards and stereotypes. This theory holds that in early childhood, a concept of gender is developed through repeatedly conceiving of oneself as either male or female. "Gender consistency" solidifies through the following age stages:

> *Preschool-aged children:* Children believe they can change their gender but do not have the cognitive processes necessary to see gender as adults do.

> *Ages 6 to 7 years* (Concrete Operational Stage): Children understand that gender remains consistent, and that outside appearances (short hair, dress, etc.) do not change gender identity.

> *After 7 years:* When gender consistency is fully developed, children imitate the behavior of same-sex role models and receive rewards from others for gender consistency.

**Parental Influence.** Masculine and feminine behaviors and attitudes are developed through children's relationships with their parents. Fathers influence children's gender identity through playful interactions and ensuring conformity to social norms (Santrock, 1992). Fathers are more involved in socializing sons than daughters (Lamb, 1986), and are more likely than mothers to treat sons and daughters differently and create clear gender distinctions (Huston, 1983). Mothers influence gender roles through nurturing and physical care (Santrock, 1992).

Two theories on parental influences on gender roles are described:

1. *Identification theory:* This theory of gender development stems from the Freudian observation that preschool-age children develop a sexual attraction to the opposite-sex parent. At age five or six, the child renounces the attraction because of anxiety and shifts the affection on to the same-sex parent, adopting that parent's gender characteristics.

2. *Social learning theory:* This theory holds that children's gender development occurs through observation and imitation of the gender behavior of parents and others. In addition, punishments received from par-

ents and peers for inappropriate gender role behaviors enforce gender stereotypes. Critics of this theory say it is too passive and that cognitive views of gender development are more accurate because children actively construct their own ideas about gender identity.

**Biological Influence.** From Freud's early assumptions comes the belief that sexuality is essentially unlearned and instinctual. Erik Erikson defended this position and claimed that the psychological differences between males and females stem from anatomical differences. Because of "genital structure," males are more intrusive and aggressive (penetrating), whereas females are inclusive, accommodating, and passive (receptive). This is sometimes called "anatomy as destiny."

Because of genetic, biochemical, and anatomical differences, boys and girls are treated differently. The key issue to address, according to Huston (1983), is not the biological differences, but rather the "directness" or "indirectness" of their effects on social behavior.

**Peer Influence.** While parents provide early influences on gender roles, peer influence increases during adolescence. Peer pressure to conform to gender roles begins in elementary school (called "gender school" by Luria and Herzog, 1985, because of the strong influence it has on the development of gender roles), increases through middle school, and hits an apex in high school. Adolescent peers openly reward those who participate in gender-appropriate games and who demonstrate they prefer being with those of the same sex (Maccoby, 1989).

**School and Teacher Influences.** Research supports the notion that boys and girls are treated differently throughout their educational experiences. Gender bias is found in many areas of the educational system: in teacher-student interactions, on the athletic field, in praise and attention received, in curricula, in textbooks, in influence toward class choices, in encouragement to attend college, etc. (Santrock, 1992; Ormrod, 1998).

The amount of time spent in schools, the constant exposure to adult role models, and peer reinforcement during this crucial developmental phase of gender identity all reinforce stereotypical male and female roles in society.

**Language Influence.** The daily language to which children are exposed carries heavy sexist overtones and influences gender identity formation. DeLoache, Cassidy, and Carpenter (1987) revealed that 95% of all characters in storybooks that were of indeterminate gender (e.g., Baby Bear of "The Three Bears") were identified by mothers as being male.

The use of "he" and "him" to refer to any person whose sex is not specified has been traditional in English grammar, but can have an adverse effect on females' sense of self-worth. Current preference is to avoid "sex-specific references" and to use language that is "gender neutral." While this may seem difficult and awkward to those trained by the old rules, counselors should nevertheless sensitize themselves to the effects of the words "his" and "her" on clients in counseling sessions.

**Media Influence.** The average American home has the television set turned on just under seven hours per day. TV and its commercials are therefore important influences on gender roles. TV reinforces what is appropriate gender role behavior. TV, radio, magazines, and newspapers not only determine the roles, but present an ideal image of what men and women should look like, feel like, and purchase in order to be more "male" or "female."

The depiction of women's and men's roles in the home, workplace, and family has changed over the years, but they still tend to be based on gender stereotypes and sexual attractiveness. In the fields of athletics and media (movies, radio, TV) gender distinctions have narrowed somewhat, and women are now afforded greater recognition, exposure, and admiration for stepping out of traditional roles.

# FEMINISM

Feminism is not a set of counseling techniques, nor is it a set of conclusions. Rather, it is a lens through which different realities are viewed and understood (Chapman, Condie, & Helgeson, 1995). Feminism begins with the recognition that women have an inferior status in our society and proceeds to analyze the specific forms and causes of that inequality. Feminism also recommends strategies of change, and eventually leads to a recognition and validation of women's realities, women's interpretations, and women's contributions.

## Goals of Feminist Counseling

Feminist counseling:

* seeks to counteract the injurious effects of traditional socialization;

* rejects traditional personality theory, the medical model, and the use of diagnostic labels;

- stresses the social context in which people exist as the prime determinant of behavior;

- abandons the hierarchical relationship between counselor and client;

- defines the personal as political;

- views women's experience as shared by every women, not as one woman's crisis;

- assesses client change in ways that are observable, concrete, verifiable, and behaviorally defined;

- seeks for client insight and increased understanding;

- focuses on changing the individual through increased competence and control; and

- changes society through increasing women's ability to affect political change.

**Feminist Techniques**

The feminist counselor does the following:

- actively uses reframing and relabeling techniques,

- uses modeling in an overt manner, models instrumentality and competence in order to promote self-mastery and control of resources,

- highlights the historical and social nature of past events that shape present behaviors, and

- emphasizes the here-and-now.

Chapman, Condie, and Helgeson (1995) listed the following eight ways of empowering female clients:

1. Enhance self-esteem by focusing on their unique and positive contributions.

2. Underscore their competence and inner resources.

3. Support decision-making abilities and encourage assertive behavior.

4. Encourage development of their own social support network rather than relying on male partners for support.

5. Assist them to identify and deal with their patterns of dependency.

6. Support competence in both their traditional and nontraditional roles.

7. Help them negotiate for their own personal space and time, in or outside of the home.

8. Help them differentiate between internal and external sources of distress.

# WOMEN AND DIVORCE

Key issues for women facing divorce center around a loss of security. This could include fear of, or actual loss of income, loss of relationship, loss of family unit, loss of support, or loss of community status (Chamberlain-Hayman, 1998). Counselors should be aware that recently divorced women are at risk of psychological and physical difficulties (Combs, 1991) and have higher rates of psychiatric disturbances, alcoholism, clinical depression, psychosomatic problems (such as sleep disturbances), and increased psychiatric hospital admissions (Santrock, 1992).

Common issues that counselors address with newly divorced women include child-care needs, re-education, knowledge concerning community resources, restoration of confidence in decision-making skills, and interactions with extended family members and in-laws. In addition, many women will need support as they must continue to interact with their former husbands (e.g., in court, at child visitation, resolving finances).

## Women and Career Counseling

The traditional feminine socialization of women has limited their opportunities to seek, find, and enjoy success in the workplace. Since career decisions are often made in high school, counseling should take place at the elementary and high school levels and should emphasize developing positive self-concepts by females toward traditionally male-dominated occupations such as mathematics and science, where higher paying careers are usually found.

Chusmir (1983) found that women in male-dominated careers were likely to possess many of the personality characteristics and motivations commonly attributed to men, even though they retained a pro-feminist attitude and wanted to maintain their femininity and identity as a woman.

Not only do families and other institutions socialize women into traditionally female careers, counselors too have brought sex bias into their work (Schlossberg & Pietrofesa, 1978). It is important that counselors be aware of their own sexist attitudes and the effects these may have on women. In career exploration, counselors should implement activities that develop attitudes, aptitudes, and skills that increase women's career options and decrease job stereotyping. Approaches that have proven successful with women in career counseling include teaching behavioral skills and using simulation to promote "self-discovery."

# Chapter 12

# MULTICULTURAL COUNSELING

> Every person is like all other human beings in some ways, like others in other respects, and finally, like no one else. (Kluckholn & Murray, cited in Lee, 1984, p. 594)

Multicultural, or cross-cultural, counseling is any counseling relationship in which counselors and clients differ in cultural background, values, and lifestyle (Peterson and Nisenholz, 1995). Recent developments in the base of knowledge (research, theories, texts, interventions, etc.) about different cultures and their distinguishing features has highlighted the need for more effective cross-cultural counseling skills.

## ROLE OF THE COUNSELOR

### Responsibilities of Counselors

The amount of information now available on the topic of multicultural counseling is overwhelming, perhaps inviting the idea that a counselor "must possess the wisdom of Solomon and the patience of Job if he or she is ever to establish a cross-cultural relationship" (Helms, 1984, p. 153). However, counselors will find their way if they remember "the true meaning of multi-

**221**

culturalism—respect for differences" (Bowman, 1996, p. 16). Learning about themselves is an important prerequisite to embracing multiculturalism, which is a lifelong endeavor.

Personal responsibilities of successful multicultural counselors include a willingness to

confront their own biases and stereotypes;

understand the appropriate place for their values in a counseling session;

educate themselves in differing cultures, views, values, attitudes, etc.;

develop culturally sensitive intervention techniques, which include recognition of

- historical events that influence current opinion,

- social-environmental conditions that persist today,

- distinguishing cultural differences, attitudes and practices that may inflame others.

- past successful intervention skills; and

ask clients for clarification about and the significance of cultural issues that are unclear or unknown to the counselor.

### Skills Needed by Counselors

Counselors must be able to articulate the problem. This may be difficult if the counselor and the client come from two culturally different perspectives.

Counselors must be able to recognize resistances and deal with them as they relate to cultural differences between the counselor and client.

Counselors must be able to diminish defensiveness. When clients feel the session is directionless, they may become unsure or use defensive behaviors.

Counselors must possess recovery skills. They must be able to get out of trouble and recover from an innocent mistake, and thereby increase rather than diminish rapport (Pederson, 1991).

**Assessing Cultural Factors**

Counselors may use the following questions, adapted from Hanna and Brown (1995), to assess the effects of culture on a client:

How does your culture (or race) make you feel different from others?

Compared to others in your cultural group, in what ways are you different?

What are the specific values in your culture that you identify as being important?

At this particular time in your life, what are the issues related to your heritage that are being questioned by others? By whom and why?

What is the hardest part about being a minority in this culture?

What do you see as the main differences in living in America compared to the country of your heritage?

What lessons have you learned about your culture? Other cultures?

What are people from your culture really against?

What might I, or any outsider, not understand about your culture?

# TYPES OF CULTURES

There are many different types of cultural distinctions. Cultures can be:

*Universal:* People are similar in biology, and have the same basic needs.

*Ecological:* People are influenced by climate, terrain, food, geography, housing, etc.

*Racial:* People are identified by physical features (skin color, size, facial features, etc.).

*Religious:* People join together to share religious or spiritual values and practices.

*National:* People from the same country usually speak the same language and share attitudes and biases based on its laws, government, level of freedom, educational system, etc.

*Regional:* People may form a subculture within a nation or other large culture based on the distinct attitudes, dress, and accents of their region.

## Subcultures

Some clients who appear to be mainstream may belong to a subculture that affects their behavior and family life. The disabled or those with certain disorders (e.g., those who have been sexually abused, anorexics, AA members, etc.) can be considered subcultures with their own language, sense of isolation, and experience of discrimination. These subcultures can have a strong influence on the counseling process. Two prominent subcultures are listed below.

**Military Personnel.**   Characteristics of these people may include:

- a high degree of patriotism;

- mobility and frequent relocation, which affect friendships, schooling, etc.;

- issues of confidentiality in counseling due to security clearances;

- repression of expression of emotions to officers (the bosses) for fear of reprisal;

- the importance of the "mission of the Base" to the exclusion of other relationships;

- the difficulty of the transition back into civilian life;

- issues of control due to strong male domination in families;

- resentment of authority in general, combined with respect for military authority; and

- the influence of differences in rank outside military life (e.g., in civic organizations, churches, socializing).

**Religious Clients.** Characteristics of these people may include

- a history of persecution, which may alienate them from the dominant religion in the area; geographic distances from others of the same religion, which may cause feelings of isolation;

- practices, dress, behaviors, and language that may draw attention to them and the differences of their religion; and

- their "relationship to God," which may influence matters related to death, divorce, abortion, interdenominational marriages, sexual abuse, and how these clients respond to life's inconsistencies.

## Cultural Generalities

Andrew Helwig (1992) offered the following broad observations on cultures:

All minority group members may be subject to discrimination and stereotyping.

A culture's expectations for women may be different from the expectations for men, and women may be treated differently than men.

Language barriers may exist between different cultures.

Nonverbal behavior may be different in each group and have its own meaning.

Counselors should not stereotype clients into preconceived ideas of what they should be like, even if they are basing their counseling on what they have read or experienced with one or two clients. According to Axelson (1985), generalizing can lead to patronizing of clients, being insensitive to clients' individuality, and misunderstanding of clients' verbal and nonverbal communications. Counselors should investigate the degree to which their clients may embody culturally unique characteristics and tap into clients' strengths.

## Common Values Across Cultures

Stephen Covey (1990) wrote that there are certain "natural laws that are woven into the fabric of every civilized society throughout history and comprise the roots of every family and institution that has endured and prospered"

(p. 33). Covey believed these are part of the human condition, part of the human consciousness, part of the human conscious. He called them the Lighthouse Principles. Covey's principles, which seem to exist in all cultures regardless of social conditioning, can be drawn on by counselors to establish links to clients of other cultures. They are∧

*Fairness:* the basis of our sense of equity and justice.

*Integrity and honesty:* the foundation of trust from which cooperation and personal and interpersonal growth occur.

*Human dignity:* the respect due all people since we are all created equal and are entitled to life, liberty, and the pursuit of happiness.

*Service:* the idea that all people want to make a contribution.

*Quality:* the idea that people move toward and seek excellence.

*Potential:* the idea that we can grow and continue to develop.

*Growth:* the process of developing our talents.

# ETHICAL CODES

The American Counseling Association Code of Ethics (ACA, 1995) says, "Counselors do not condone or engage in discrimination based on age, color, culture, race, religion, seal orientation, marital status, or socioeconomic status." In addition, "Counselors will actively attempt to understand the diverse cultural backgrounds of the clients with whom they work. This includes, but is not limited to, learning how the counselor's own cultural/ethnic/racial identity impacts her/his values and beliefs about the counseling process."

# MODELS OF MULTICULTURAL COUNSELING

### Identity Development Model

In the racial/cultural identity development model, counselors understand that cultural differences (attitudes and behaviors) have significant implications in counseling. This model attempts to address broad differences through five stages of development:

1. *Confirming:* The minority client begins to identify with the majority.

2. *Dissonance:* The conflict with self vs. majority results in a challenge to the minority client's self-image.

3. *Resistance and immersion:* The client accepts his or her own views and values and rejects the majority's culture.

4. *Introspection:* The client increases his or her own positive self-image.

5. *Integrative awareness:* The minority client now can incorporate and enjoy his or her own culture and appreciate the good in the majority culture.

### Pederson's Triad Model for Training

Paul Pederson's (1991) training model involves interactions among the triad of client, counselor, and the client's concern (as expressed from the client's point of view). Pederson's "culture in general" approach, as opposed to a culture-specific method, teaches principles that apply to all multicultural contacts, wherever they may occur. This approach emphasizes self-understanding, flexibility, and tolerance for cultural differences.

# MULTICULTURAL TERMS

The following terms associated with multicultural counseling are defined in Chapter 18: career counseling in multicultural settings, culture, cultural encapsulation, cultural norms, cultural pluralism, emic, ethnic, ethnocentrism, etic, minority, prejudice, racism, social class, and world view.

# Chapter 13

# SPIRITUALITY
# AND RELIGION

Though religious and spiritual issues may be difficult to deal with, that's all the more reason we need to deal with them. This doesn't have to be at the top of the agenda, but we should give it the attention that it needs as a potential critical issue in the lives of clients. (Eugene Kelly, 1995)

## DEFINITIONS

### Spirituality

The word *spirituality* is derived from the Latin word *spiritualis*, meaning *breath* or *air*. Elkins, Hedstrom, Hughes, Leaf, and Saunders (1988) described spirituality as "a way of being and experiencing that comes through awareness of a transcendent dimension and that is characterized by certain identifiable values in regard to self, others, nature, life, and whatever one considers to be the Ultimate" (p. 10).

Shafranske and Gorsuch (1984) described spirituality as "the courage to look within and to trust. What is seen and trusted appears to a deeper sense of belonging, of wholeness, of connectedness, and of openness to the infinite" (p. 233).

## Spiritual Well-Being

Kelly (1995) defined spiritual well-being as "a securely held set of meta-empirical and natural beliefs and values giving rise to an inner hopefulness about the ultimate meaning and purpose in life, a deep peace that is a source of joy in living as well as courage to confront suffering forthrightly, and an actively benevolent connection with others and the universe" (p. 167).

## Spiritual Distress

*The Handbook of Nursing Diagnosis* defined spiritual distress as "the state in which an individual or group experiences or is at risk of experiencing a disturbance in the belief or value system that provides strength, hope and meaning" (Carpenito, 1993, p. 301).

*The Diagnostic and Statistical Manual of Mental Disorders* (*DSM-IV*) defined spiritual distress as "distressing experiences that involve loss or questioning of faith, problems associated with conversion to a new faith, or questioning spiritual values that may not necessarily be related to an organized church or religious institution" (American Psychiatric Association, 1994, p. 685).

## Religion

Religion in its fuller meaning embraces spirituality, but also generally signifies specific systems of belief and practice that are often institutionalized in creeds, rituals, and moral codes (Kelly, 1995). Corbett (1990) defined religion as an "integrated system of belief, lifestyle, ritual activities, and institutions by which individuals give meaning to (or find meaning in) their lives by orienting them to what is taken to be sacred, holy, or the highest value" (p. 2).

Albanese (1992) wrote that religion influences "customs, laws, beliefs, institutions, morality of the culture of which it is a part" (p. 6).

Many clients derive a sense of spirituality from their religious practices. McConkie (1995) has said, "religion is more than theology, more than a knowledge of Deity and the system of salvation revealed by him; it is the actual practice of the revealed precepts. Religious people are 'doers of the word, not hearers only'" (p. 626).

## Difficulty with Definitions

Albanese (1992) warned, "A definition means an end or a limit—a boundary. A definition tells us where some reality ends; it separates the world into what is and what is not that reality. Religion cannot be defined very easily because it thrives both within and outside of boundaries. The boundaries of religion are different from the logical boundaries of good definitions. In the end, religion is a feature that encompasses all of human life" (p. 3).

Sheridan, Bullis, Adcock, Berlin, and Miller (1992) believed that a commitment to the true definition of diversity entailed developing effective practices and strategies that recognize the significance of religion in people's lives and the role religion and spirituality play in the evolution of society. Thus we see that a definition of diversity needs to encompass both spirituality and religion.

### Distinguishing Between Spirituality and Religion

Counselors should take caution when distinguishing between the areas of spirituality and religion. Religious clients may falsely be seen as rigid, hypocritical, overly ritualistic in their religious practices, conservative, simplistic, or lacking in spiritual depth or human caring. Kelly (1995) said that these misperceptions of religious clients may prevent counselors from recognizing the positive and deeply spiritual involvement that many people have within organized religion. In turn, spiritual clients may falsely be seen as mystical, eclectic, selfish, ethereal, liberal, suspicious, or without direction. These misperceptions of spiritual clients, according to Kelly (1995), may prevent counselors from understanding the deeply religious, humane, and benevolent attitudes toward others and the universe that these "nonaffiliated but spiritually committed" clients hold.

Spirituality and religion are often blended. In a national study of people in small groups, Wuthnow (1994) found that 55% of those polled *strongly agreed* that one's spirituality does not depend on being active in a religious organization.

Therefore, honoring a broad definition of religion and spirituality seems to be important in building a strong client–counselor relationship.

# ROLE OF THE COUNSELOR IN ADDRESSING SPIRITUAL ISSUES

The role of the counselor, according to Albanese (1992), is to strive to understand the meanings clients attach to their specific beliefs and practice, particularly as they fit into the larger understanding of their own religion.

## Counselor Goals

The goal in working with spiritual and religious clients is to help them expand their personal awareness of their own beliefs, and make developmentally positive decisions based on their clarified religious values (Albanese, 1992). In seeking to help clients apply their personal beliefs, the counselor is careful to allow clients to express their own religion or spirituality so as to better develop a greater sense of wellness.

Kelly (1995) suggested that the role of the counselor in clarifying and applying clients' religious and spiritual beliefs should be enhancing personal development, facilitating personal problem solving, and overcoming emotional and mental distress.

## Counselor Characteristics

Besides the qualities that have proven successful with a wide array of clientele, counselors working with religious and spiritual clients should also:

Be objective toward religious or spiritual beliefs that may differ from their own. If not, they refer them to another counselor.

Have broad-based knowledge of major religions and their spiritual traditions, including the cultural aspects of those religions.

Ask for needed information, and seek clarification on all matters related to the idiosyncrasies of specific denominations.

## Reasons Counselors Avoid Issues of Spirituality and Religiosity

**Lack of Training.**   Most traditional counseling approaches do not address the needs of the religious client, leaving counselors-in-training without models for successful intervention. Sheridan et al. (1992) found that few counselors had received any training in spiritual issues, but, more significantly, that the topic received little attention in the curricula of their graduate counseling programs. They also found that professional groups support the need for clinicians to receive formal education, clinical supervision, and training in the area of religion and spirituality. However, 79% of all clinicians surveyed (LPCs, LCSWs, and psychologists) stated that religious or spiritual issues were rarely or never addressed during the course of their graduate education and clinical training.

**Anti-Religious Tradition.**   There is a long tradition among psychologists and psychiatrists, rooted in Freud's anti-religious position, of viewing religion

as antithetical to psychological and emotional health (Genia, 1990). Many clinicians automatically assume, without critical examination of the specific dynamics involved, that ministers and other religious leaders, can best deal with
the client's spiritual dimensions. When clients present dominant religious themes
and concerns in counseling, these issues are often ignored, challenged as inadequate and irrational, or analyzed as symbolic representations of neurotic fears,
wishes, impulses, or conflicts (Genia, 1990). For example, Ellis (1980) said,
"Religiosity is in many respects equivalent to irrational thinking and emotional
disturbance . . . [and] the elegant therapeutic solution to emotional problems is
to be quite unreligious . . . the less religious they are, the more emotionally
healthy they will be" (p. 637).

Kelly (1995) suggested that counselors may feel hesitant to address issues
of spirituality due to the following six reasons:

1.  Fears of crossing ethical boundaries and inappropriately influencing
    a client's values.

2.  Strong opinions about the privacy of clients and their religious be-
    liefs.

3.  Belief that a publicly funded setting may be an inappropriate site to
    discuss religion, or religious issues.

4.  Lack of knowledge about spirituality and religion.

5.  Uncertainty about the importance or relevance of religion to the
    client's current problem.

6.  Feeling ill at ease with their own spirituality.

**Assessing a Client's Spiritual and Religious Beliefs**

Counselors can ask clients the following questions to better assess and
understand their spiritual and religious culture.

What role does spirituality or religion play in your life?

What are the specific spiritual or religious values in your culture that you
would identify as important?

What are the religious or spiritual values with which your current behavior is not aligned?

How do your religious or spiritual beliefs make you feel different from others? In what way?

At this particular time in your life, what are the issues related to your religion that are being questioned by you or others? Why?

In what areas do people of your faith conflict with society? In school? At work?

What is the hardest part about being a religious minority in this culture?

What might I, or another outsider, not understand about your culture?

## Interventions

Counselors should explore the religious life of a client with an attitude of "accepting inquisitiveness." Kelly (1995) said that counselors should enter into the world of clients' personal spiritual belief systems and then help clients clarify and apply their beliefs in ways that allow them to express their own religion or spirituality. Albanese (1992) believed that successful interventions help clients expand their personal awareness and make developmentally positive decisions based on clarified religious values.

Drawing on the client's responses to the eight questions above, counselors have some understanding of the client's spiritual and religious beliefs, and can make appropriate interventions, one of which may be to explore how a client can learn to live in a counterculture in the midst of the larger culture. Clients may need to recognize the difference between appropriate guilt responses and dysfunctional shame responses. Cognitive therapy techniques may also be useful in helping clients to realize that while they have made a mistake or transgressed, it does not necessarily mean that they are bad, damned, or flawed. Other useful techniques include meditation, prayer, journaling, being of service to others, and participation in the rituals of one's denomination. Repentance and restitution may also be within a client's value system and prove to be effective intervention strategies.

# RELIGIOUS AND SPIRITUAL BELIEFS

## Of Counselors and Psychologists

Kelly's (1995) survey of counselors and an earlier survey of psychologists by Shafranske and Malony (1990) revealed:

- 64% of counselors surveyed believed in a personal God.

- 70% are affiliated with an organized religion.

- 85% "seek a spiritual understanding of the universe and their place in it" (69% highly agreed with this statement).

- 80% sought "inner wholeness and strength through communication with a higher power" (62% highly agreed with this statement).

- 89% of counselors believed in some transcendent or divine dimension to reality (psychologists were at 70%).

- 30% of surveyed psychologists believed "religious and/or spiritual notions are illusory products of human imagination" (only 5% of counselors agreed with that statement).

**Of the US Population**

Gallup and Castelli (1989) found that

- 94% of the US population believed in God,

- 90% pray, and

- more than 75% report that religious involvement has been a positive experience in their lives.

**Of Christians**

There are many types of Christians. The three categories below were originally derived from the works of Corbett (1990). They can be used by counselors to gauge clients' flexibility toward change, and gain insights into their value system and how they perceive their world.

**Fundamentalists (40% to 50%).** This population maintains a strict, literal adherence to orthodox, traditional formulations of beliefs. They interpret the Bible as being without error, to be understood literally, with every word being the unerring word of God. The Bible is an infallible guide for knowing and living. They feel strong incompatibility with human secularism, liberalism, modernism, liberal social issues, and scientific or rational interpretations. They see sharp differences between those who have "been saved" and those who have not. They view nonfundamentalists as too accommodating with the world. Some fundamentalists may view counseling as evil or anti-religious. The following denominations may typify this group: Assembly of God, Liberty Baptist Fellowship (Kelly, 1995).

**Conservatives (40%).** This population consists of moderates who hold a close and firm belief in traditional teaching and doctrine. They interpret the Bible as being the inspired word of God, and God's word as the standard of practice. They do not interpret the Bible literally. They are cautious about innovations in belief, practices, and ethics, and leery of counseling. The following denominations may typify this group: Roman Catholic, Latter-Day Saints (Mormons), Lutherans.

**Liberals (10% to 15%).** This population takes a flexible stand in interpreting traditional belief and practice according to human advances in science, rational enlightenment, and contemporary lifestyles. They interpret the Bible as a collection of human writings, ethical teachings that contain valuable lessons. The Bible is interpreted in light of human scholarship, science, and rational inquiry. They see the combination of faith and reason as a guiding principle, and the Golden Rule as a priority that moves people toward a more humanitarian world, a global brotherhood. They are tolerant and open to the beliefs and practices of other religions and philosophies that move people toward unity and peace. Women play a larger role in their organizational hierarchies. The following denominations may typify this group: Universalists, Unitarians (Kelly, 1995).

# Chapter 14

# A BRIEF HISTORY OF COUNSELING

## VOCATIONAL GUIDANCE MOVEMENT

Jesse Davis is credited with being the first American to begin formal work in the vocational guidance field. In 1898, Davis was working in Detroit, Michigan, helping high school students with their educational and vocational needs, and emphasized the moral value of hard work (Zunker, 1994).

It was Frank Parsons, however, who was given the name "Father of Guidance" (Shertzer & Stone, 1980). Parsons founded a vocation bureau in Boston, Massachusetts, in 1908, when he began offering guidance services to Boston school children. This resulted in an alignment of counseling services with educational institutions. Parsons also wrote a seminal text, *Choosing a Vocation* (1909), which offered a cognitive career-counseling theory postulating a single desirable occupation for each person. By 1913 Parsons' vocation bureau evolved into the National Vocational Guidance Association.

### Vocational Legislation

In 1917, the Smith-Hughes Act allocated federal funds for vocational guidance programs. One year later, the Vocational Rehabilitation Act extended vocational guidance to veterans, but it was not until 1927, when Edward K.

Strong, Jr., printed the first copy of his *Vocational Interest Blank* (1974) that most Americans recognized the usefulness of career counseling in a broad educational context. Later, Williamson's book *How to Counsel Students* (1939) firmly established career assessment as a vital function of public schools.

The Vocational Rehabilitation Legislation of 1954 expanded the 1918 version by allocating funds for specific training of rehabilitation counselors who would commit to work with disabled persons. Another key piece of legislation, the National Defense Education Act (NDEA) of 1958, established school counseling programs and training of school counselors. The early influence of career legislation eased the way for the public to accept broad-based counseling services in the future.

# MENTAL HEALTH COUNSELING MOVEMENT

The development of the mental health movement in America was born out of Clifford Beers' 1908 book, *A Mind That Found Itself*, which chronicled his personal mistreatment in a mental sanatorium, and resulted in an awakening of the public to a greater concern for the individual. Beers, in company with the National Committee for Mental Hygiene, led the charge in America to reform legislation and establish free mental health clinics.

The early work of G. Stanley Hall in promoting interests and well-being of children, coupled with an increased publication of articles by others on this topic during the 1920s and 1930s, focused greater attention on stages of children's mental health. Hall introduced Freudian concepts of child growth into the American consciousness, fostering acceptance of other theories regarding stages in the mental health of children. Later, Carl Rogers' (1942) classic work, *Counseling and Psychotherapy*, provided an essential framework for all counselors, especially those employed during the post World War II era. Rogers' text helped meet the recently recognized and accepted needs of veterans returning from the war.

## The 1960s

The cultural focus of the 1960s was on the individual. This, coupled with the affluence of America in the 1960s, led to new research into how to deal with the complexity of the human mind and spirit. Many new theories and therapists emerged during this time. New approaches, such as behavioral techniques, encounter groups, reality therapy, gestalt models, weekend retreats, sex therapy, and rational emotive therapy, became firmly established in US culture.

The first state to formally license counselors was Virginia, in 1978. Both licensure and certification of counselors were adopted by a significant number of states during the 1980s.

Originally formed in 1951 as the American Personnel and Guidance Association, in 1983 the APGA changed its name to the American Association for Counseling and Development (AACD) and expanded its branches to every state in the US. By 1992, the AACD again changed its name, this time to the American Counseling Association (ACA), which it retains today.

As early as the 1970s, the Association for Counselor Education and Supervision (ACES), one of the many subdivisions of the ACA, had envisioned a uniform standard of training for counselors in America. That standardization was realized in 1981 when the Council for the Accreditation of Counseling and Related Educational Programs (CACREP) was formed. CACREP began promoting the professional competence of counseling practitioners through the development of preparation standards for counseling, encouragement of excellence, and accreditation of counseling and preparation programs.

The 1980s and 1990s have seen the proliferation of self-help books, new theories, and important texts in the mental health field. Included are books that have broken new ground for counselors: Cloe Mandanes' (1981) *Strategic Family Therapy*, Carol Gilligan's (1982) *In a Different Voice*, Irwin Yalom's (1985) *Theory and Practice of Group Psychology*, Eugene Kelly's (1995) *Spirituality and Religion in Counseling and Psychotherapy*, to name a few.

## HANDICAPPED EDUCATION MOVEMENT

When the vocational rehabilitation laws of 1954 passed, many people were trained through federal funds to work with disabled persons, drastically increasing the number of counselors nationwide. With the passage of Public Law PL94-142 in 1975 (also called the All Handicapped Children's Act), every state integrated physically challenged students into the mainstream of US classrooms and allowed them access to individualized educational program. Specifically the law assured

- free appropriate public education to all children ages three through 21 years,

- that each handicapped individual would be placed in the least restrictive environment, and

- that each child would receive an individualized educational plan.

# HISTORICAL TIME LINE

1800 — Johann Christian August Heinroth (1773–1843) published books in German; he was the first to use the term "psychosomatic."

1879 — Wilhelm Wundt created the first psychological lab.

1890 — Freud practiced psychoanalysis.

1898 — Jesse Davis commenced work in Detroit high schools.

1906 — Eli Weaver wrote *Choosing a Career.*

1908 — Frank Parsons started guidance services in Boston schools.

1908 — Clifford Beers wrote *A Mind That Found Itself.*

1909 — Frank Parsons wrote *Choosing a Vocation.*

1913 — National Vocation Guidance Association was formed.

1917 — Smith Hughes Act allocated federal funds for vocational guidance counseling.

1927 — Strong printed the *Vocational Interest Blank.*

1939 — E. G. Williamson published *How to Counsel Students.*

1942 — Carl Rogers wrote *Counseling and Psychotherapy.*

1945 — Returning World War II veterans heightened the need for counseling.

1952 — The American Personnel and Guidance Association (APGA) was established (forerunner to ACA).

1954 — Vocational Rehabilitation Legislation created funds for training of rehabilitation counselors.

1958 — National Defense Education Act (NDEA) established school counseling programs and counselor training.

1962 — Gilbert Wrenn wrote *The Counselor in a Changing World.*

1971 — Joseph Hollis and Richard Wantz published the first edition of *Counselor Preparation Handbook.*

1973 — APGA chartered the subdivision Association for Specialists in Group Work.

1974 — APGA chartered the subdivision Association for Spiritual, Ethical, and Religious Values in Counseling.

1975 — Public Law PL94-142 (the All Handicapped Children's Act) mainstreamed physically challenged students and created individualized educational programs (IEP).

1978 — Virginia was the first state to license counselors.

1978 — APGA chartered the subdivision American Mental Health Counselors Association.

1979 — APGA relocated its head office to Falls Church, Virginia.

1981 — The Council for Accreditation of Counseling and Related Education Program (CACREP) was formed.

1982 — The National Board for Certified Counselors (NBCC) was formed.

1983 — APGA changed its name to the American Association for Counseling and Development (AACD).

1983 — AACD relocated its offices to Alexandria, Virginia.

1992 — AACD changed its name to the American Counseling Association (ACA).

1992 — The ACPA was disaffiliated as a subdivision of the ACA.

1994 — *Guidepost* (the ACA newspaper) changed its name to *Counseling Today.*

1994 — Forty-one states had adopted state licensure or certification.

1994 — Counseling Awareness Month was established (April).

1994 — Elementary School Counseling Demonstration Act, proposed by ACA, was signed into law by the US President.

1995 — NBCC appointed the WebCounseling Task Force to examine the practice of on-line counseling.

1998 — Managed Health Care began to influence counseling.

# Chapter 15

# CONSULTATION

In the 1970s counselors began to ply their trade outside of schools and therapy sessions, using their skills to help individuals and groups define and solve work-related problems or problems with their clients.

In the 1980s and 1990s, the concept of consultation by counselors was broadened, and the term took on a new definition. Currently, consultation is defined as a voluntary or paid relationship, which counselors enter into with a person or persons, school, group of people, or institution in need of their expertise in human relations (for example, solving problems, increasing efficiency, strengthening relationships, motivating people, or thwarting potential problems).

In recent years, counselors have been moving away from simply trying to remediate their clients' personal, emotional, and psychological problems, and toward trying to change institutions, organizations, systems, and communities that contribute to people's problems. Instead of simply assisting clients to adjust and adapt to their individual environments, counselors are now encouraging their clients to work systematically to change those environments.

Generally consultation by counselors focuses on improving the mental health of individuals or the functioning of systems.

## MENTAL HEALTH COUNSELORS AS CONSULTANTS

Counselors in private settings often do consulting work. Sometimes they act as outside experts to schools, but most often they consult in private enterprise or with social service agencies. Some counselors assist with Employee Assistant Programs (EAPs).

Because counselors have expertise in human nature, are strong motivators, know group skills, and understand the complexities of human interactions, they are often needed by businesses, clubs, and corporations. Consultants seek to increase effectiveness within these groups. Many of the same talents that are used in interpersonal counseling are used in consulting, but the context, role, and function differ. Consultation is often workplace related, with an emphasis on correcting work-related problems.

Mental health consultants usually work as part of a triad (the counselor works with another professional to help others). The duration of the relationship is usually short term. For example, a counselor might be paid to test, assess, and then deliver a day-long workshop on team-building skills to a local fire department that is having personality conflicts. The counselor could also be hired later to provide follow-up and continued training.

## SCHOOL COUNSELORS AS CONSULTANTS

In 1966 the American School Counselors Association, in conjunction with the Association for Counselor Education and Supervision (both subdivisions of ACA), acknowledged consultation as being within the purview of school counselors. They stated that the three primary responsibilities of school counselors were counseling, coordination, and consultation. Since that time, school counselors have often taken on the formal consultant role within the school system in collaboration with school administrators, teachers, parents, and community resources.

Consulting, for school counselors, is different than it is for mental health counselors. For school counselors, consulting often takes the form of unpaid work. It usually involves collaborating or correlating current school counseling efforts with parents or community members, rather than working independently as an outside expert.

### School Counselor as Change Agent

When school counselors take on the role of consultant, the following process can give direction to their work:

1.  *Establish the need for change* through the use of assessments, tests, research, information gathered from outside sources, and the concerns of individuals or community groups.

2.  *Collect allies* by gathering support from groups, leaders, the administration, and especially parent groups.

3.  *Identify concerns* through brainstorming, purposing alternatives, surveying, etc.

4.  *Insure that everyone involved has ownership* of the plan.

5.  *Identify specific goals* and set a timeline for both major and incremental goals. Assign responsibility to certain people or groups. Get a public commitment from them. Also, be sure to set future dates to refine and adjust the plan.

6.  *Commence the work.*

7.  *Monitor progress* toward goals. Encourage. Share success stories. Fine tune the plan.

## CONSULTANT SKILLS

Often the consultant is required to negotiate conflicts and use problem-solving skills within small groups of people. Therefore, bargaining, negotiating, and mediating are core skills for the consultant.

The effective consultant is conscious of psychological dynamics, humans motivations, and the purposes of human behavior. A knowledge of the psychological dynamics of individuals and groups, and an ability to deal with them in the here-and-now are vital. Additional traits such as spontaneity, creativity, imagination, flexibility, and willingness to manage a plethora of expectations are needed.

For in-school consulting, being able to balance a principal's need for order and structure, a student's need for input and participation, and a parent's need for a sense of fair play is no easy task. Therefore, a consultant needs the ability to balance, manage, and achieve results. The role is demanding and requires many talents.

A counselor's ability to remain objective and unfettered by political influence also can be challenged when acting as a consultant. Ethical conduct must prevail. Common questions that confront consultants include:

How much information that I obtain can or should be shared with management without violating confidentiality?

Who is the designated client?

Are the goals of the group or institution congruent with my values?

## TYPES OF CONSULTATION

Consultation may be content-oriented or process-oriented.

### Content-Oriented

This type of consultation focuses attention on the transfer of knowledge or information from the consultant to the consultee. It is a pragmatic and eclectic approach geared toward organizing people and events. The consultant has skills and assumes the role of expert. Goals are predetermined. The consultant acts as a problem solver and usually possesses a high proficiency in a certain technical area.

### Process-Oriented

This type of consultation focuses on the process. The consultant attempts to answer the questions how and why while focusing on rectifying present concerns. The consultant may use communication theory, attribution, change or motivation theory while getting clients to "own" the problem. The consultant teaches that clients have the skills within themselves to solve their problems. Process-oriented consulting works at making clients more aware of events in their environment and how these events affect work and attitudes.

## WHY CONSULTANTS ARE HIRED

- Consultants are experts in human relations or in content topics.

- Consultants are agents for change.

- Consultants can be mandated by the government.

- Consultants can be hired to prove a point.

• Consultants may confirm a previous decision or a future recommendation.

• Consultants may perform an independent study.

• Consultants may provide an outside objective opinion.

• Consultants can solve problems.

• Consultants can create Employee Assistant Programs (EAPs).

• Consultants can resolve conflict management issues.

**Employee Assistant Programs**

Some consultants are hired by large businesses or corporations to oversee or participate in Employee Assistance Programs. EAPs help corporations keep absenteeism low and morale and efficiency high. Typical programs include conducting seminars/workshops, employee exit help, child care, relocation assistance, wellness programs, etc.

# CONSULTING MODELS

### Program-Centered Administrative Model

This model focuses on "working with a specific program's organizational structure and not on the consultee's difficulties with the program or structure" (Peterson & Nisenholz, 1995). In addressing the "organizational development" (OD) of the system, the consultant may act as a diagnostician, facilitator, action-researcher, or instructor.

### Edgar Schein's Model

This process model has been called by different names: *purchase model, purchase of expertise, doctor-patient,* and *process consultation model* (Rockwood, 1993). It centers on the purchase of the consultant's expertise. In conjunction with the hirer, the consultant identifies "intervention strategies" (Schein, 1978) while following four stages:

1. Entry into their system

2. Diagnosis of the situation

3.  Intervention designs and implementation

4.  Evaluation

**Stephen Covey's Model**

This model is based on teaching correct principles of living (Covey, 1990) rather than playing a role or adapting techniques to solve problems. Here the consultant embodies and teaches effective intrapersonal principles based on Covey's (1990) book, *The Seven Habits of Highly Effective People*. Covey's seven habits include the following:

Habit 1.  Be Proactive (you have choices, so act, don't react).

Habit 2.  Begin with the End in Mind (start with a clear understanding of your destination).

Habit 3.  Put First Things First (organize priorities).

Habit 4.  Think Win/Win (not your way, or my way; but the better way).

Habit 5.  Seek First to Understand, Then to Be Understood (listen to understand people).

Habit 6.  Synergize (combining efforts/differences to create alternatives).

Habit 7.  Sharpen the Saw ("recharge your batteries" through personal renewal in the following areas: physical, mental, social/emotional, and spiritual).

**Caplan's Model**

This still popular mental health consultation model was developed by Caplan in 1970. It emphasizes a consultant/client relationship that can address any of the following:

1.  the consultant and the client,

2.  the client,

3.  the institution (family, school, etc.), or

4.  the management and consultant.

## Kurpius, Fuqua, and Rozecki's Model

This 1993 triadic process seeks collaboration to solve problems. The emphasis is on behavioral or structural change. The consultant works with clients in order to benefit another person or group. The process is as follows:

1.  Prior to Entry: plan and know your role as the consultant.

2.  Enter: establish rapport, set ground rules, focus the group.

3.  Accumulate Information: gather information by direct observation, interviewing, reviewing written records, testing, outsiders' observations, questionnaires, surveys, polling, psychodrama, sociograms, or focus groups, etc.

4.  Define the Problem: analyze the situation from many angles.

5.  Select Alternatives: synthesize.

6.  State Objectives: set goals, and enlist clients' commitment.

7.  Implement the Plan: begin action.

8.  Evaluate: follow up on outcomes.

9.  Terminate: end the relationship, make follow-up available.

## Behavioral Model

This model emphasizes verbal interactions. It focuses on behaviors that are causing concern and determines what has created these behaviors. It can be used with individuals or organizations. The counseling consultant also examines the consequences if problems are not rectified. The four stages of this process are

1.  Identification of the problem,

2.  Analysis of the problem,

3.  Implementation of the plan, and

4.  Evaluation of the program.

# Chapter 16

# TAKING EXAMINATIONS

## TEST ANXIETY

Test anxiety is normal. In fact, a moderate amount of anxiety improves learning and performance (Shipman & Shipman, 1985). It helps focus attention on doing well. Too much anxiety, however, is not helpful. Some students score lower on tests because they are nervous. Some become physically upset, sweat, or have difficulty breathing.

If you have test anxiety, learn procedures that will help you control it. Wasting time worrying about it is a self-defeating behavior. Keep your anxiety at a level that will help you do well on the test.

### Controlling Anxiety

The following suggestions may help to lower high anxiety:

Allow yourself plenty of time to get to the test, find a seat, and get settled. Don't rush. If possible, visit the test room before the exam.

Anxiety is easily spread, so limit your talking to others before the test.

Have a plan for the test. This chapter will give you suggestions on how to prepare. You will feel confident about the test if you have a plan.

Don't try to cram. Cramming at the last minute can make you very tense.

Get a good night's rest before the test.

Have a protein-filled dinner the night before the test. Have a meal high in carbohydrates such as pasta right before the test. Caffeine and sugar-filled snacks before and during the test can increase your anxiety, so eat fruit instead.

Avoid significant others before the test. You will be volatile, and any disagreement can weaken your concentration.

Relax by taking several slow, deep breaths. Exhale, as you let your shoulders drop slowly. Another relaxation exercise is to turn your head slowly in a circle—right ear to right shoulder, head back, left ear to left shoulder, head forward, and vice versa.

Some students use test anxiety as an excuse not to prepare. Since they believe their anxiety will keep them from doing well on the test, they figure, why study? This is irrational thinking! If you prepare well, you will be able to pay attention to the test and do better.

## STUDY METHODS

### Preparing for the Exam

**Know What to Expect on the Test.**   Get all the information you can about the test before you begin studying. Find out what type of test it will be (multiple choice, essay, short answer, etc.) and what material it will cover. Know how specific the test will be (a general concept test, or one looking for particular names, dates, and numbers). Are there sample tests from which to study?

**Review Frequently.**   Reviewing class notes often is better than cramming at the last minute. Reread your notes right after you've written them. Make sure you understand the concepts you've written down.

**Exam Review.**   If you have a large amount of material to cover, try dividing it into smaller parts and study the most difficult sections first. Practice recalling the information aloud or explain it to someone else. Use memorizing schemes (pegword system, linking, phonetic alphabet, etc.).

**Study for Main Ideas.** Learn main ideas and principles first. Prepare as if the test requires short answers and you have to explain your answer.

**Get Rest.** Don't stay up all night cramming. Learning diminishes with fatigue. If you do stay up late, give yourself frequent breaks to keep your mind alert.

## Study Groups

**Set Ground Rules for Study Groups.** Discuss the format or process that your group will follow. Stick to it. Bring study materials (texts, class notes, previous exams). Limit the group to three or four people.

**Have the Proper Attitude.** Allow no negative comments or expressions of fear. (Talk specifically about this in the beginning.) Studying is easier and more productive with positive attitudes (J. King, personal communication, June 28, 1995). Approach studying as a serious event, not as a socializing time. Party later.

## Know Your Theory

For an oral or written examination on your personal theory of counseling (one of the major theories or a self-generated theory), the following suggestions will help bring cohesion to your thinking and greater integration of material when responding to questions.

First, just assume your theory is correct; that it has worked and will work.

Test your theory by applying it daily in all situations you encounter. Retain these real-life examples to support your responses. These form an important databank of experience you can use if you lack actual on-the-job experience.

In your study group, increase each other's base of experience by quizzing each person on how their theory applies in different settings and situations. For instance, when a person mentions a construct of their theory ask, "OK, now give us an illustration to prove it," or "Tell us how that would apply to an adolescent" (or a single mother of three, or a Native American, etc.).

## The SQ3R Method

The SQ3R is a very effective study method. It helps you to better understand and retain material. The method involves five major steps:

*Survey:* When you gather your study materials, scan through the material on which you will be tested. This enables you to get a broad view of the content areas covered and provides a framework in which to categorize details or supporting ideas.

*Question:* Generate questions to focus your studying. Write exam questions that you think are important. Asking questions helps to prepare you by raising your curiosity and involvement with the material. Exam questions often ask you to think about information in several ways:

- to *evaluate* the information,

- to *integrate* one concept with another,

- to *analyze* information, and

- to *apply concepts* to different situations.

*Read.* Look through all the materials, including class notes, text chapters, sample exams. Pay special attention to any underlined sections you may have marked.

*Recite or recall.* This vital part of studying asks that you memorize as much pertinent information as you can. Close the study materials and summarize the main points. Practice recalling important concepts and definitions, especially in bed before you fall asleep.

*Review.* Go back and review all the material again. This will fix the information in your long-term memory. Now you should be able to answer all the questions you posed to yourself. If you can't, review again. Make sure you understand the concepts. Don't just memorize names and details.

# ESSAY QUESTIONS

## Computer or Hand Written?

Some people think and compose differently writing on a computer than writing long hand. Ascertain which way you write and think better. With a computer, your paper or test will look neater, and a spell checker helps prevent misspelled words. Also, rearranging paragraphs and inserting and omitting sentences is easier on a computer. Cleaner-looking papers give an appearance of professionalism and speak to your ability to use new technology.

However, using a computer depends on electricity. You could have a power outage. If a glitch occurs, a disk goes bad, or you encounter a printing problem, you may be in big trouble. If any of these technical difficulties happen, will accommodations be made for you? Also, editing papers on a computer takes more time than most people think. There is a tendency to worry about appearances, which can cost you valuable composing time. If you decide to use a computer for taking an exam, arrive early, hook it all up, and run through a blank piece of paper. During the test, print out every answer when you complete it. Don't wait until the very end to print your responses.

## Test Preparation

You are likely to do well on an essay question if you plan and prepare for it. Not only will you know the material, you will feel confident. When you are prepared you will not fear! You will be able to put your time and energy into answering the question. You won't spend time worrying.

Prepare yourself for the kinds of questions you will get. If you are well prepared, you are likely to succeed. Remember:

Essay questions ask you to organize information, evaluate evidence, draw conclusions, compare, or contrast.

Essay questions ask for details and examples.

Essay tests ask if you know the details and can reason and organize information.

Use erasable ink pens. Bring two or three with you to the exam.

## Taking Notes

You can prepare best if you listen well in class, read your textbooks carefully, have sample exams, and make good, readable notes. Students who take notes in class learn more material from a lecture than students who don't take notes (Kiewra, 1989).

**Review Your Notes for Questions.** Review your notes and study guides, and begin thinking of possible questions. Thinking of possible questions is a vital component of test preparation. Look for common themes and main ideas.

How was the material organized in the book or lectures (from most important to least important, by events through time, etc.)? What are the main ideas or principles? Are there questions at the end of the section or the chapter?

**Review Your Notes for Answers.** After you have thought of possible test questions and reviewed your notes, write each question at the top of a sheet of paper. Review your notes again. When you find information that will help you answer a question, write it on that sheet of paper.

**Organize the Information You Noted.** Organize your notes for each question. Look at the main ideas and the details and examples that support them. You can organize information in many ways (when things happened, where things happened, what was most important and the least important, etc.). You can also make an outline or draw a diagram.

### Getting Started on an Essay Examination

When you receive your examination paper, follow these simple rules:

1. Read the directions carefully and completely. What is really being asked?

2. Budget your time. Give the most time to the questions that are worth the most points. Answer the "easy" questions first.

3. If you are not sure of the answer to a question, skip it. Go back to it later.

### How to Answer an Essay Question

*Read the question carefully.* Make sure you answer the question asked.

*Make an outline.* List all the specific points you want to mention. Jot down names, dates, statistics. This will organize your thoughts and help make your essay smooth. If more than one essay question is asked, start the second question, and all other questions, at the top of a new page. This allows you to go back and add more pages to any question without disrupting other questions. Don't number your pages until you are completely through.

*Write clearly.* An essay test examines not just what you know, but how you say it. Be concise. Give personal or professional examples to support your main ideas.

*Organize your first paragraph.* It should include the key points upon which you will elaborate in the essay.

*Organize the body of the essay.* Talk about one key idea in each paragraph. Support your main ideas with details, facts, and personal examples. Include authors' names, book titles, and research to add credibility to your paper. Quote others!

*Write a concluding paragraph.* Summarize the key points again. Be sure to state clearly your beliefs and the professional beliefs of others.

*Review your essay.* Make sure the conclusion you reach is supported by the information in your essay. Your introduction should either be a question that the conclusion answers, or a statement that the conclusion backs up. If they don't jive, do some rewriting. Use the questions below to help you review your answer. You should be able to answer these questions.

- Did you answer the question? Make sure you answered the question you were asked.

- Does every sentence in the essay add to the answer? Do they all relate to the question you were asked?

- Are there any grammar or spelling errors?

- Is there a strong introduction and conclusion?

- Did you use examples from the classroom, books, personal experiences, etc.?

*Make corrections.* Reread. Insert additions only at the end of each question if possible. Lastly, number your pages.

# NON-ESSAY QUESTIONS

## Objective Tests

The category of non-essay or objective tests includes multiple choice, true/false, fill-in-the-blank, short answer, and matching questions. Objective test questions ask you to recognize information. An objective test looks for your knowledge of details and your ability to reason.

**Studying for Objective Tests.** Begin studying for an objective test the same way you do for an essay test. Some people find it helpful to make a study guide by outlining each possible test topic. Highlight key words or phrases. Recite the main points.

**Taking an Objective Test.** To begin an objective test do the following:

1. Read the directions carefully and completely.

2. Budget your time for each question. Set your watch to beep at regular intervals. Give the most time to the questions that are worth the most points. Answer the easiest questions first. This enables you to finish the ones you know before you run out of time. It will also raise your confidence.

3. Skip difficult questions. You can go back to them later.

**Multiple Choice Exams**

Go through the entire exam before you begin and underline instruction words on the test (e.g., "compare," "contrast"). Answer all the questions you know best first. On multiple choice exams, generally two answers are correct, one is doubtful, and one is flat out wrong. Your choice should be the best option as you see it.

As you go through the test, mark the harder questions, so you know to go back to them. When you do return, try to use any information you may have gleaned from the other questions to help you. In order to answer multiple choice questions, do the following:

1. Read the directions carefully. They will tell you whether to mark the *right answer*, the *best answer*, or *all correct answers*.

2. When first reading a question, try to figure out the right answer before you read all the choices given.

3. Watch for clues in the choices that may help you eliminate incorrect answers. For instance,

   *Absolutes.* An absolute is a word such as *always, never, every, all,* or *none.* Answer choices that contain these words often are incorrect.

*Grammar Clues.* Singular subjects require singular verbs, plural subjects require plural verbs.

*All of the Above.* This choice for an answer is often correct, especially if at least two of the choices are correct.

## True/False Exams

Approach true/false questions in the following manner:

1. Check each part of the true/false sentence. If any part of the sentence is false, the entire statement is false.

2. Statements that contain a qualifier may be true. A qualifier is a word such as *some, most, many,* or *usually.*

3. Again, questions that contain absolutes (see above) are often false.

## Fill-in-the-Blank Exams

On fill-in-the-blank questions, no choices are given. You are asked to write in a correct answer on the blank line. For these types of questions:

1. Read the statement carefully. Information in the statement may help trigger your memory.

2. Pay attention to grammar clues (e.g., plural subjects, plural verbs).

3. Sometimes you can explain your answer by writing a brief justification in the margin.

## Matching Exams

Matching questions usually are columns of words or phrases that have to be matched with an item in another column. For this type of exam:

1. Read each list all the way through before you begin to match.

2. The first time through, mark only those answers you know well.

3. Grammar clues can tell you some of the answers. Remember, singular subjects require singular verbs; plural subjects require plural verbs.

# ORAL EXAMINATIONS

Oral examinations come in many forms. The ideas below will be helpful for a formal presentation, or an oral exam.

## The Right Attitude

You need to find an effective frame of mind if you are asked to give an oral presentation. One suggestion is to take a "salesperson's approach" (J. King, personal communication, June 28, 1995), in which you sell both yourself and your material. The product you are selling is your practitioner skills, knowledge-base, personal experience, ideas, philosophy, theory, integration ability, and professionalism.

You can also take a "teaching approach" (J. King, personal communication, June 28, 1995). Imagine you are informing the committee or group about your subject matter. You can use overheads and handouts. You can ask the examiners to think back into their own past and draw on examples familiar to them, etc., in an attempt to engage them in your material in a personal way. They may then be less likely to spend time thinking of critical questions to ask. Your material should be interesting, perhaps new, and presented so as to engage your listeners.

## Responding to the Exam Committee's Questions

Keep yourself separate from your material. Discuss the issues, not any personal attachment to the material. How?

Don't overly personalize your responses.

Keep the discussion within the arena of the mental health field, not on your personal preferences.

Personal experiences are OK to illustrate a point, but personal reactions may indicate that you are not aware of the professional and academic research that addresses this issue.

Cite others. Instead of saying, "Well I think . . . ," you might say, "Well, according to Hollis . . . . " This can keep you from feeling defensive. If questions are directed at you in response to a personal statement, you may feel as if you are being attacked.

If responding personally, keep the ownership professional by saying, "It is my opinion that . . . " or "It is my judgment that . . . " or "From my experience . . . . "

Draw on your internship or practicum experiences with real clients to demonstrate that your theory actually works with clients.

For each of your statements, ask yourself, "What evidence (personal and academic) do I have to substantiate this?" If you are challenged on a statement, can you defend yourself?

You have permission to say, "I don't know" or "I'll have to think more about that."

Avoid "red-flag" words, words that might be perceived as off-color, politically incorrect, biased, or that might raise questions in your examiners' minds.

Use gender-neutral language (e.g., "he or she" instead of "he").

## The Litmus Test on Oral Exams

Overall, what is an oral examination committee looking for in a master's degree candidate? Expertise? Perhaps, but only if you have demonstrated a competency or personal interest in a specific topic. The attributes sought by most committees include the following:

Do you *speak the language?* Do you *know the terms* of the discipline? Can you use them effortlessly?

Do you *know the literature?* Are you familiar with the major theorists and important studies?

Can you *synthesize information* into a rational response when confronted with hypothetical questions? Remember, keep the focus of the response within your professional field, and not on yourself.

*Is your theory tight?* When challenged to provide specific examples of its effectiveness with diverse populations or in special situations, you must be able to respond.

# EXAMINATION VOCABULARY

Knowing what written or oral questions are "really" asking is vital. Many essay questions have key words that tell you what kind of answer the question is seeking. Be sure you understand all of the following terms:

*Account for:* give reasons, justify, give an explanation.

*Analyze:* separate into parts to determine the nature of the whole.

*Articulate:* describe or pronounce clearly and distinctly, fit together in a coherent whole.

*Compare:* discuss similarities and differences.

*Contrast:* discuss differences.

*Criticize:* judge the merits, find fault with.

*Critique:* review critically.

*Define:* give a clear, short definition or explanation, show how an idea differs from similar ideas.

*Demonstrate:* prove a point, give evidence, examples, or facts to back up your conclusion.

*Describe:* give a clear, detailed, statement.

*Discuss:* analyze and explain in detail.

*Diagram:* draw a picture, map, chart, or table, to demonstrate the idea.

*Enumerate:* name one by one, count out.

*Evaluate:* ascertain or fix the value or worth, appraise.

*Explain why:* give causes, use examples.

*Explain what:* give a definition or description, use examples.

*Explain how:* describe how something happens, or how to do something, use examples.

*Extrapolate:* infer by extending or projecting known information.

*Illustrate:* show the idea, explain, give examples.

*List:* give a list of items, explain each briefly.

*Relate:* show how ideas are connected.

*State:* give main ideas briefly.

*Summarize:* state all ideas briefly, leave out the details.

*Trace:* follow something from beginning to end, describe the main points.

# Chapter 17

# RESEARCH PAPERS

For research papers, many academic departments and professional journals insist that the format and style of papers presented conform to standards outlined in the *Publication Manual of the American Psychological Association*, 4th edition (APA, 1994).

## GENERAL RULES

**Writing Papers**

Use standard-size paper (8 1/2 x 11 inches).

Always make a copy of your paper.

Do not use folders. Staple the final copy in the top left corner.

Double-space between all lines of the manuscript.

Do not hyphenate words at the end of lines.

Do not use contractions.

If you are using a word processing program, do not justify the right margin or you will have trouble with word spacing.

Do not use a word processor to create italic, bold, or other special fonts. Instead, use underlining to indicate italics.

Leave uniform margins (at least one inch) at the top, bottom, right, and left.

Indent five to seven spaces for the first line of every new paragraph. The only exceptions to this are in the cases of block quotations, titles and headings, abstracts, table titles, and figure captions.

## Order of Manuscript Pages

Number all pages consecutively, except pages that have figures or tables. Arrange the pages of the manuscript as follows:

Title page (separate page, numbered 1)

Abstract (separate page, numbered 2)

Body of paper (start on new page, numbered 3)

References (start on new page)

Appendices (start on new page)

Tables (start on new page, each on a separate page)

Figure captions (start on a new page)

Figures (place each on a separate page)

## Manuscript Page Header and Running Head

Pages can get separated, so identify each page of your paper by typing the first two or three words from the title in the upper right-hand corner above, or five spaces to the left, of the page number. This is the page header. It should not be confused with the running head, which goes only on the title page (one double space below the page header) and appears in the printed article. The running head is limited to 50 spaces.

## Headings

Headings indicate the organization of a paper and establish the importance of each topic. Topics of equal importance are positioned consistently in the same style and size throughout the paper. A centered main heading is used to separate and identify the primary topic areas of the paper. Subheadings set flush with the left-side margin and indented paragraph headings are used when you wish to break a section into two or more distinct topic areas.

## Listing Items within a Paragraph

When you want to list items within a paragraph or sentence, use numbers with one parenthesis as follows: 1) . . . , 2) . . . , 3) . . . . Or use lower case letters in parentheses as follows: (a) . . . , (b) . . . , (c) . . . . When you want to list whole paragraphs, such as itemized conclusions or successive steps in a procedure, number each paragraph or sentence with an Arabic numeral (i.e., 1, 2, 3 . . .) followed by a period as follows:

1. Begin with paragraph indention. Type second and succeeding lines flush with the left margin.

## Spacing with Punctuation

Leave a space after punctuation marks:

after commas, colons, and semicolons;

after periods ending sentences;

after periods separating parts of a reference citation; and

after periods used in initials of personal names (exception: no space after internal periods in abbreviations, like a.m. or I.B.M.).

## Hyphens, Dashes, and Minus Signs

Hyphen: no space before or after (e.g., day-by-day).

Dash (or em-dash): type as two hyphens with no space before or after (e.g., Essays—published and unpublished—are . . . ).

Minus sign (or en-dash): type as a hyphen with space on both sides (e.g., b – c).

## Numbers and Percentages

Generally, numbers one through nine (1–9) in sentences are to be spelled out in letters ("nine"). Numbers 10 and greater should be typed as numerals ("173"), except where they begin a sentence ("Two thousand stripling warriors went . . . "). Use the symbol for percent (%) only when it is preceded by a Arabic numeral (68%). Use the word "percentage" when a number is not given ("It was a higher percentage than . . . ").

## Nonsexist and Ethnically Unbiased Language

Use gender neutral language. Choose nouns, pronouns, and adjectives to eliminate the possibility of ambiguity in sex identity. Formal research writing should be free of implied or irrelevant evaluation of the sexes (e.g., "The researcher goes to great lengths to verify his or her sources.")

## Abbreviations

Do not abbreviate, except for those formally accepted abbreviations such as Dr., Mr., Ms., Mrs., L.P.C., Ed.D., U.S.A., etc.

## Quotations

Quotations amplify or support the content of your paper. They should be used sparingly. There are two types of quotations: short quotations of less than 40 words, and longer quotations, which are usually set in block form.

Short quotes are typed within the sentence and set in double quotation marks ("___"). Longer quotes are put into block form, which has an indented margin, but the opening paragraph is not indented.

If there is a quotation within a quotation, which is set within quotation marks, put the secondary quotation in single quote marks ( e.g., "You are 'numero uno' as a school counselor.").

The punctuation mark at the end of a quote may be changed to fit the position of the quote within your sentence. Do not change any part of the quote that may change the context of the original material.

If you are consciously omitting some words from a quote, use three ellipsis points (. . .) with a space at each end to indicate parts of the original quote are missing. Use four ellipsis points (. . . .) with no space on the left side to show omissions between two adjoining sentences within the material you are quoting.

Brackets [ ] are used to enclose insertions in quotations. These additions may be transitional words not included in the material quoted or other grammatical forms to make the quotation conform to your sentence.

## Commonly Misspelled or Misused Words

For spelling and usage, look in the dictionary when in doubt. Remember, computer spell checkers may not distinguish between words that sound alike or look alike.

### Misused Words:

accept (to receive) and except (other than)

there (at or in that place) and their (possessive of them)

complement (to make complete) and compliment (to praise)

who's (contraction of who is) and whose (possessive of who)

its (possessive of it) and it's (contraction of it is)

your (possessive of you) and you're (contraction of you are)

affect (as a verb, to have an impact on; as a noun, an emotion) and effect (as a verb, to cause; as a noun, a result)

### Misspelled Words:

| | | |
|---|---|---|
| a lot | independent | potpourri |
| accommodation | judgment | privilege |
| aggression | knowledge | questionnaire |
| commitment | maintenance | receive |
| data (is plural) | obsessive | recommendation |
| definitely | occurrence | separate |
| ellipsis | occurred | vacuum |

### Misunderstood Abbreviations:

| | |
|---|---|
| cf. (compare) | e.g. (for example) |
| et al. (and others) | i.e. (that is) |
| viz. (namely) | |

# CITATIONS

Each quotation must be given a reference. The reference must be clearly cited so readers can access the quoted material in its original context. The citation within the text must include the last name of the author, the year of publication, and the page number.

## Text Citation

The purpose of listing a reference within the text is to make it easy for the reader to identify the source of an idea and to find it in the reference list at the end of the paper. The last name of the author and the year of publication are inserted in the narrative at the appropriate point. No page number is required unless you are citing a quotation. For example,

> The empty chair technique (Perls, 1969) can be used to great advantage with affective clients.

If you want to cite a source that you did not read in the original, but in a secondary source, use the following method:

> Conatser (1997, as cited by Seelye, 1998) found that affective clients with low self-esteem . . .

**Incorporating Citations into the Text.**    There are four ways to incorporate citations within a paper:

1.  The author(s) name(s) can be used within the context of your sentence with the year in parentheses. Be sure to remember to spell out the word "and" when the authors names are not in parentheses. For example,

    Hinckley and Monson (1998) studied . . .

2.  The author(s) name(s) and the year can be set in parentheses after the material used. Replace "and" with an ampersand (&). For example,

    Others found this result, too (Hinckley & Monson, 1998).

3.  When there are three to five authors, the term "et al." is used after all of the author's names have been listed the first time in the regular text. For example, in the first mention of a source in the text:

In a follow-up article, Hinckley, Monson, Faust, and Packer (1998) found that levels of gratitude in men are . . .

Any following citations should read:

Hinckley et al. (1998) found that gratitude was . . .

4. When there are six or more authors, each citation includes only the surname of the first author followed by "et al." Also include the year. For example,

Kirkpatrick et al. (1998) has several reasons . . .

When citing a series of studies, put the author's names in alphabetical order, then cite the study's dates in chronological order. For example,

(Lloyd, 1991; McLaws, 1982, 1989; Policky, 1983; Sargeant, 1959, 1964)

Remember, an ampersand (&) is used with multiple authors when they are listed within parentheses; the word "and" is used outside parentheses. Examples:

Renkoski and Belcher (1996) found that social isolation is not always a negative experience.

Social isolation is not always a negative experience (Renkoski & Belcher, 1992).

## Reference Lists

The reference list consists of the sources that were used (cited) in the paper or article. It is placed at the end of the paper or article. It includes only references cited within the body of the paper.

(A bibliography, if used, contains sources for more information on the topic, which were not cited within the text). References are listed alphabetically by author. The format is: first author's last name, initials, additional authors' last names and initials, date, title, city of publication, publisher (see examples below).

In reference lists capitalize only the first letter of the first word, proper nouns, and the first letter of the first word following a colon in titles of books, chapters, articles, etc. Do not indent the first line, but indent every line thereafter five to seven spaces.

**Reference Examples:**

Book (one author):

Odahlen, D. E. (1996). *Counselor's delight: Just dough it (4th ed.)*. Rapid City, SD: Holyoak Press.

Book (two authors):

Hamby, T. O., & Gough, R. L. (1995). *Hilti management schemes as applied to men's religious groups (3rd ed.)*. New York: McGraw-Hill.

Book (edited):

Barnes, R. P., Slack, W. V., & Fisher, P. M. (Eds.). (1993). *Team management for youth counselors (4th ed.)*. Kamus, WA: Moriancumer Publications.

Journal article (one author):

Kubler, W. E. (1989). Public monuments on private land. *Journal of Redwood Roads, 63,* 213–218.

Journal articles (two authors):

Kilness, P. G., & Messick, J. L. (1995). School counselor's Christmas: Holiday techniques. *Journal of Counseling and Development, 26,* 66–83.

Article in an edited book:

Forbyn, J. (1994). Ouch: Headaches from hell. In K. Belcher, M. Sorenson, & J. Miller (Eds.), *Jann's neuron pains* (pp. 89–102). Alpine, UT: Thanksgiving Point Press.

**Electronic Citations**

*The Publication Manual of the American Psychological Association (4th edition)* includes a section on electronic media and on-line sources. It gives the following guidelines: "as with any published reference, the goals of an electronic reference are to credit the author and to enable the reader to find the material" (APA, 1994, p. 218). Electronic citations should be arranged as follows:

Author's Last Name, First Name. [author's internet address, if available]. "Title of Work" or "title line of message." In "Title of Complete Work" or title of list/site as appropriate. [internet address]. Date, if available.

**Listserv Messages:**

Truhe, Joann. [Jtruhe@colo.sp.com]. "REPLY: Chronic pain and spirituality." In *C-CHRONIC*. [ccronic@nmsu.edu]. 24 October 1996.

**World Wide Web:**

Allen, Douglas. "Counseling in Melbourne." [http://douglas.ray/archives/damien-5.html]. April 1991.

**FTP Site:**

Rambo, Lorene. [690123.289@aol.com]. "Shorty Joab, Kaynus, and Uncle Thug." [ftp.br.ucla.wv/pub/day/FAQ/home/gen/allen.txt]. December 1966.

**Gopher Site:**

"Rural Psychopathology, 1993." [farmer.ranch.com SDSU Online Library/Country & Rural Demographics of the Midwest] 2 May 1983.

Kjerengtroen, Lidvin. "The Last Great Viking at SDSM&T." [gopher.usd.eduTheEd/Acute/R- Net/P-SLC (Salt Lake City)/Pursuit of Norway's Leader]. 30 June 1890.

**Usenet Group Messages:**

Hayman, Susan. [Hayman@pauls.chinook.com]. "Myths/Man." In [abc.myths.eternal]. 23 May 1994.

**E-Mail Messages:**

Pratt, Gene. [pratt@uwyo.larami-wy-pt.edu]. "The Sacred Grove: An Advisor's Dilemma." Private e-mail message to Florence Womeldorpf, [flojoe@wall.sd.com]. 2 May 1983.

# DISSERTATIONS

A typical Table of Contents for long formal research papers, such as a dissertation, may include

Introduction

Statement of the Problem

Importance of the Problem

Definition of Terms (all the terms that may be unique to your study)

Limitations of the Study

Review of the Literature

Literature that is relevant to this study

Summary of the Literature Review

Methods and Procedures

Hypothesis

Population and Sampling

Content Analysis or other Methodology used

Presentation and Analysis of Data (how the data is presented; graphs, charts, etc.)

Summary

Discussion of the Findings

Conclusions

Recommendations

References

Appendices (copies of forms, letters, instruments, etc., used in the study)

# Chapter 18

# GLOSSARY

Common psychotherapy and counseling terms used throughout this book are listed below. Many of the terms below are also defined within the context of the chapters.

**Abreaction:** an emotional release resulting from recalling and reliving painful and repressed experiences (associated with psychoanalytic psychology).

**Accreditation:** a process through which public recognition is granted to a college or university or specialized program of study that meets certain established qualifications or standards; applies to programs of study, not to individuals.

**Accurate empathy:** ability to accurately sense the inner world of clients and their subjective experiences so as to communicate back to them an understanding of their felt world.

**Active listening:** paying total attention, especially to group members; being sensitive to verbal and nonverbal cues; being attuned to underlying messages (such as body posture, style of speech, gestures, mannerisms).

**Acupressure:** this ancient Chinese body technique involves the use of finger pressure (not needles) on specific points on the body to treat ailments such as tension, stress, arthritis, aches/pains, and menstrual cramps.

**Acupuncture:** small fine needles are inserted at specific pressure points to stimulate and disperse the flow of "chi" (vital energy) and restore a healthy energy balance.

**Affect:** feeling or emotions.

**Affective counseling theories:** gestalt, client-centered, existential, and holistic.

**Altruism:** in group therapy, through sharing and "giving of self," group members gain a sense of contribution, value, and self-worth (associated with Irwin Yalom's curative factors).

**Anal stage:** second stage of Freud's psychosexual development, at which time pleasure is derived from retaining and expelling feces.

**Analogue study:** a study similar (analogous) to studies that were conducted under actual and similar conditions and circumstances. Typically analogue studies take the form of simulating or recreating natural conditions within a laboratory setting.

**Analytical psychology:** the system of psychology and psychotherapy as developed by Carl Gustav Jung, also known as Jungian therapy.

**Anchoring:** this technique occurs when a counselor accesses a client's emotional state with a specific stimulus such as touch, sound, facial expression, posture change (often associated with NLP).

**ANCOVA** (analysis of covariance): similar to ANOVA, but the influence of one or more independent variables on the dependent variable is controlled.

**Anima** (the yin): the feminine component of the male personality (associated with Jung).

**Animus** (the yang): the masculine component of the female personality (associated with Jung).

**Anna O:** an early case study by Freud and Breuer of a female client with hysteria, which today is considered the first client case to be chronicled by counselors.

**Anorexia nervosa:** a disorder involving excessive fear of weight gain, overdieting, profound weight loss, and malnutrition.

**ANOVA** (analysis of variance): a more general form of the t-test. This kind of analysis determines if the mean scores on three or more factors differ from or interact significantly with one another. Performing an ANOVA results in an F value, or a value of significance. This determines if significant differences are present. ANOVAs also are used in Trend Analysis to test for trends or patterns. If a new variable is introduced, will the groups support a statistically significant trend? If there is more than one dependent variable, a MANOVA is used.

**Archetypes:** hidden symbols in one's individual unconscious, which are derived from the collective unconscious; innate predispositions derived from the cumulative experiences of the race; the contents of the collective unconscious—e.g., birth, death, magic, the hero, God, sun, and child; a response pattern occurring universally in the human experience; contains two archetypes: the animal (female traits) and anomies (male traits) (associated with Jung).

**Architects of the family:** the parents.

**Aromatherapy:** The use of oils distilled from plants to treat emotional disorders like stress and anxiety; oil is massaged into the skin, inhaled, or placed in baths; often used in conjunction with massage therapy, acupuncture, reflexology, herbology, chiropractic, and other holistic treatments.

**Art therapy:** the use of drawing, painting, sculpting, etc., as a means of reconciling emotional conflicts and increasing self-awareness and personal growth. The therapist observes and analyzes art objects with the client, examines art produced by a client, and discusses it with the client.

**Assertiveness training:** training in the ability to express all manner of emotion, the capacity to express one's rights without denying the rights of others.

**Assessment:** there are two types of assessment: criterion-referenced (compares a person's achievement to a predetermined criterion), and norm-referenced (compares a person's achievement to others who have previously taken the test/instrument).

**Association:** the process of remembering something by mentally putting yourself back into the experience or projecting yourself into a future situation; clients benefit by making successful associations (connections) between stimulus (a precipitating event) and their response to that stimulus.

**Attending:** counselor behaviors used to pay attention to the client (listening, reflecting, engaging in eye contact, observing body language, being psychologically present, etc.).

**Bandaiding:** in group therapy, prematurely rescuing group members from working things out with each other.

**Bell-shaped curve:** also known as the "normal curve." One of the shapes made by plotting statistics on a graph. The example in Figure 18.1 shows six equal amounts (scores or individuals), with three parts above the average (the mean) and three below.

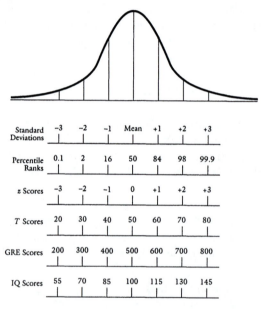

| Standard Deviations | -3 | -2 | -1 | Mean | +1 | +2 | +3 |
|---|---|---|---|---|---|---|---|
| Percentile Ranks | 0.1 | 2 | 16 | 50 | 84 | 98 | 99.9 |
| z Scores | -3 | -2 | -1 | 0 | +1 | +2 | +3 |
| T Scores | 20 | 30 | 40 | 50 | 60 | 70 | 80 |
| GRE Scores | 200 | 300 | 400 | 500 | 600 | 700 | 800 |
| IQ Scores | 55 | 70 | 85 | 100 | 115 | 130 | 145 |

**Figure 18.1**

**Biofeedback:** a technique for stress-related conditions such as asthma, high blood pressure, migraines, and insomnia; a way of monitoring metabolic changes in the body (temperature changes, heart rate, muscle tension). Through visualizing, relaxing, or imagining while observing light, sound, or metered feedback, clients are taught subtle physical adjustments to move toward a more balanced internal state.

**Bird walking:** in group therapy, when a member gets verbally off track or strays from the subject; when group members interrupt their own story to tell a substory (a term credited to Myron Basom at the University of Wyoming).

**Blocking:** in group therapy, a leader's intervention to prevent or stop unproductive behaviors such as scapegoating, storytelling, bird walking, or gossiping.

**Borderline personality:** a disorder characterized by instability, irritability, self-destructive acts, impulsiveness, and extreme mood shifts; a personality type that lacks a sense of their own identity and has a shallow understanding of others.

**Bulimia:** excessive eating (bingeing) followed by self-induced vomiting (purging).

**Career:** vocations, occupations, and jobs (and related activities) that form a sequence throughout a client's life span.

**Career counseling:** "all counseling activities associated with career choice over a life span. In the career-counseling process, all aspects of individual needs (including family, work, and leisure) are recognized as integral parts of career-decision and planning" (Zunker, 1994, p. 3); giving advice about career information gathering and the process of effective decision making.

**Career counseling in multicultural settings:** career counseling with multicultural clients; each client is treated as an individual, with his or her own idiosyncratic personal and cultural background and current environment.

**Career development:** involves decision-making throughout the life span, especially through work experience and further education; a model of counseling that sets up objectives and encompasses such areas as knowledge of self and the situation, personal values, resources and information, interests, knowledge of the world of work, and skills.

**Career guidance:** services that help clients develop effective decision-making skills in regard to the world of work, educational needs and opportunities, leisure, and self-knowledge.

**Catastrophizing:** overly imagining something terrible will happen; thinking of the absolute worst scenario for a situation (associated with Albert Ellis).

**Catharsis:** a burst of emotions that appears suddenly during new insights; an "Ah ha" moment (according to Rogers); an emotional release of pent-up feelings that can facilitate trust and bonding; more than mere expression of emotions, for without proper processing, catharsis may be harmful to clients or group members.

**Certification:** a process through which recognition is granted to an individual who has met certain predetermined qualifications; frequently offered by a professional organization composed of persons who hold similar credentials; credentials awarded by state governments upon completion of legally mandated requirements; an indication of skill and ability.

**Chiropractic:** a belief that the spine is the "backbone of human health"; misalignments of the vertebrae cause pressure on the spinal cord, which leads to diminished function and perhaps illnesses.

**Chiropractor:** a professional who tries to analyze and correct misalignments through spinal adjustment techniques.

**Chunking:** breaking a task down into small chunks (task analysis) and addressing them singly (associated with NLP).

**Circular questioning:** asking each family member the same question about a situation to ascertain each individual's perceptions.

**Clarification:** helping clients to rephrase their communications so the counselor can better understand what they are intending to say; rephrasing statements so the meaning is more clear.

**Classical conditioning** (respondent): using a stimulus to elicit a response (sweating, salivation, flinching, etc.).

**Closed-ended questions:** questions that structure the response; they usually begin with the word "is," "are," "do," or "did," and elicit one-word or short answers.

**Coalitions:** in family therapy, groupings or alliances formed between certain family members.

**Cognition:** thinking, the process of knowing, rational knowledge and awareness.

**Cognitive-behavioral counseling theories:** REBT, reality therapy, TA, trait-factor analysis, hypnotherapy, NLP, cognitive therapy, behavioral therapy, family systems therapy.

**Cognitive behavior modification:** techniques that seek to change maladaptive thinking in order to change maladaptive behaviors.

**Cognitive dissonance:** mental discomfort associated with being confronted with new information that requires a decision or that does not fit with old beliefs; a counselor's attempt to reduce dissonance by using it to motivate clients to change (associated with Leon Festinger); similar to disequalibrium.

**Cognitive restructuring:** an active attempt to alter maladaptive thought patterns and to replace them with more adaptive cognitions (associated with REBT).

**Cohesiveness:** in group therapy, bonding between members; when members have a sense of belonging, working together, enjoying the group process, and trusting each other.

**Collective unconscious:** Jungian term for "the gift" or "consciousness" we each innately and vicariously possess as a result of the experiences others have had throughout human history; a type of unconscious consisting of archetypes and innate predispositions derived from the cumulative experiences of the race; inherited from human's ancestral past; instincts and the archetypes together form its contents and exercise a preformed pattern for personal behavior to follow from the day the person is born.

**Colon therapy:** the cleansing of the large intestine with purified warm water; colonic treatment similar to enemas in removing toxic debris from the colon.

**Communality:** feeling a similarity to others and a communion when interacting with others (associated with Adler).

**Compensation:** the process by which clients overcome their innate feelings of inferiority; encourages clients to excel in areas in which they were most weak or deficient as children; when clients mask their weaknesses or positive traits to make up for their limitations; a Freudian defense mechanism.

**Complementary transaction** (Adult to Adult): interaction that leads to good communication; one of the three communication modes in Transactional Analysis.

**Computer analysis of data:** information is input (recorded) into a computer and later analyzed through such programs as the Statistical Package for the Social Sciences.

**Concreteness:** the addressing of concerns in specific terms rather than in broad or vague generalities.

**Conflict resolution:** a method of resolving conflict through meditation, through new methods, or through a third party.

**Confrontation:** a technique counselors employ to point out discrepancies between clients' words and actions, or thoughts and actions (oftentimes by saying, "On one hand . . . , yet on the other hand . . . ") (associated with gestalt therapy).

**Congruence:** agreement between a client's behavior and his or her values and beliefs.

**Conjoint counseling:** counseling two or more family members at the same time.

**Consciousness:** awareness; that of which one is aware and for which one can be held accountable.

**Control group:** the norm or standard group from which data is collected, which is eventually compared to data collected from an experimental group.

**Core conditions:** the three vital components of successful counseling: empathic understanding, genuineness, and unconditional positive regard (associated with Carl Rogers).

**Correlation coefficient:** a statistical index that shows the relationship between two groups of numbers but does not give information regarding the cause or effect of those groups of scores. It can range from 1 to 1.0 and gives information about the relationship between groups.

**Counseling:** the application of principles of effective living, human development, learning theory, group dynamics, etc., acquired from multiple disciplines and human experience; the application of research to individuals, couples, families, and groups, for the purpose of alleviating problems and psychopathology, and increasing mental stability and effective living; the practice of diagnosing and treating mental, emotional, social, and behavioral disorders, teaching psychoeducational techniques to prevent disorders, consulting to individuals, couples, families, groups, and organizations, and doing research to more effectively apply psychotherapeutic techniques; a "growing, evolving, continually changing concept, responsive to a nexus of interlocking pressures and concerns" (Belkin, 1988, p. 20).

**Counselor:** a person trained specifically in the practice of counseling, whose training is in helping individuals and families solve problems; a professional usually employed in nonmedical settings (schools, agencies, private practice); a profession with proficiency in conducting groups and delivering seminars and workshops.

**Countertransference:** a counselor's unconscious emotional responses to a client that interfere with the counselor's objectivity; unresolved conflicts of the counselor that are projected on to the client.

**Criterion-referenced:** also called "domain referenced"; an assessment that compares a client's performance on a test to some predetermined criteria.

**Crossed transactions** (Adult to Child, Child to Parent): interactions that produce barriers in communication; one of the three communication modes found in Transactional Analysis.

**Cultural empathy:** the ability to relate to the impact of a client's cultural background, race difference, gender issues, religious concerns, etc.

**Cultural norms:** representations of a group's basic interpretation of life; the standards values set for living and lifestyles within a particular culture.

**Cultural pluralism:** an appreciation of cultural, racial, ethnic, gender, religious diversity; and appreciation of differences in lifestyles, family configuration, age, health, etc.

**Culture:** learned behaviors shared and transmitted by the members of a particular society.

**Data** (the plural of datum): items of information that researchers obtain from or about the subjects of their research.

**Deductive reasoning:** the process of collecting and combing data and then drawing conclusions from the facts.

**Defense mechanism:** unconscious mental processes designed to protect the ego from thoughts or feelings that might cause anxiety, lowered self-esteem, or total mental collapse (associated with Freud).

**Degree of freedom:** in inferential statistics, this refers to the number of scores in a frequency distribution that are "free to vary"—that is, that are not fixed and can have multiple values until the researcher affixes a specific value to them.

**Demand characteristics:** all of the various cues, information, knowledge, and even rumors that subjects have heard about the proposed experiment and that are likely to influence their performance on it or perceptions of it.

**Denial:** refusing to see or blocking out something that is real or true; a self-defense mechanism of distorting what one thinks/feels/perceives in a traumatic situation; a defense against anxiety by denying the reality that something is threatening (associated with psychoanalysis).

**Development of excellence:** in E. G. Williams' *Trait-Factor Theory*, this was the purpose, the end result, the goal of all aspects of life.

**Diagnosis:** "the attribution of a name and cause, implying illness, to specific psychological states and behavioral patterns" (Belkin, 1988, p. 559).

**Directive counseling:** a term originally used in place of vocational counseling and trait-factor counseling.

**Disassociation:** the process of experiencing or remembering something as if by watching it from the outside; a thinking style resulting in objectivity that facilitates planing and comparing.

**Disorders:** see Major Personality Disorders in Chapter 5.

**Displacement:** a Freudian term meaning the transferring or substituting of a different object or goal for the impulse or motive that is truly felt of desired; the direction of energy toward another person when the desired object or person is not available.

**Double-blind study:** a study in which neither the subjects in the study nor the researchers know whether the subjects are actually receiving a treatment or being given a placebo.

**Ear candling** (ear coning): putting of the narrow end of a hollow candle (professionally designed) at the opening of the ear canal and lighting the opposite end to remove earwax buildup, help ear and sinus infections, and alleviate hearing problems.

**Eclectic counseling:** counseling that selects or uses many different pieces of various theories and techniques.

**Ego:** the part of the personality that mediates between external reality and inner demands; the part of the personality that exhibits consciousness and keeps in contact with reality (a Freudian term).

**Ego-defense mechanisms:** intrapsychic processes that operate unconsciously to protect clients from threatening (anxiety-producing) thoughts, feelings, and impulses (associated with psychoanalysis).

**Ego psychology:** the psychosocial approach of Erik Erikson, which emphasizes the development of the self (ego) at various stages of life.

**Electra complex:** unconscious sexual desires of the female child for the father, with accompanying feelings of hostility toward the mother (associated with psychoanalysis).

**Emic:** one of two classic views of the world (the other is etic), which proffers that people need to understand and help a group from that group's perspectives, from within that culture.

**Empathic understanding:** immersion into another person's feeling world so as to experience that world as that person feels it; the ability to emotionally relate and resonate with a client's experience as if it were the counselor's very own experience; one of three core conditions for effective counseling by Carl Rogers.

**Empty chair:** a gestalt technique often called the "two chairs," where an empty chair is placed in front of a client and the client communicates with a person imagined to be sitting there.

**Environment:** the physical world (geography, architecture, flora, etc.) in which an individual lives and which influences his or her self development.

**Epistemology:** the study or theory of the origin, nature, and limits of knowledge; the underlying rationale for counseling interventions.

**Error types:** in statistical analysis, there are two main types of error. Type I errors occur when the null hypothesis is rejected (believing that there is a difference) when in fact, it is correct. Type II errors occur when the null hypothesis is not rejected (believing that there is no difference) when in fact, there is a difference.

**Esalen Institute:** an institute in Big Sur, California, during the 1970s, which helped increase the visibility of gestalt counseling.

**Ethnic:** designating groups with commonly held practices, attire, rituals, knowledge, and lifestyles.

**Ethnocentrism:** the belief that one's group, usually the dominant culture, is the center of everything, is more important, and sets the standard.

**Ethnography:** a close-up analytical description of an intact culture (e.g., living with the Amish for a year).

**Etic:** one of two classic views of the world (the other is emic), which holds a global view of humanity, a belief that people are more similar than different; focuses on similarities rather than differences.

**Ex post facto:** a Latin term for "after the fact." Research that attempts to determine the cause for, or consequences of, existing differences in groups of individuals; also referred to as "causal-comparative" research.

**Existential factors:** in group therapy, the recognition of universal life factors, such as life can be unfair, life is faced alone, and pain and death are a part of life, can be curative (associated with Irwin Yalom).

**Existential theories:** see Humanistic theories.

**Experimental group:** the group that is tested directly (e.g., given some treatment) and from which data is collected by the researcher.

**Explosive layer:** the fourth layer of gestalt neurosis; after first passing through the "implosive layer" where clients let go of phony roles and release pent-up energy that they have been holding back by pretending to be who they are not, they address the explosive layer; the vital layer of authenticity, which may be felt as an explosion into pain and joy.

**External locus of control:** the belief that events occur independently of our own actions and that the future is determined by chance, luck, and forces outside themselves; low levels of self-responsibility.

**External validity:** the degree to which results are generalizable, or applicable, to groups and environments outside the research setting. Threats to external validity include selection of subjects and subject reactions (including Hawthorne effect, demand characteristics, Pygmalion effect, placebo).(See also Validity and Internal Validity.)

**Extinction:** the process of eliminating an undesirable behavior.

**Factor analysis:** the statistical method used when determining if a set of variables can be reduced to a smaller number of factors.

**Faith in others:** having social interest in all people, recognizing their good traits (associated with Adler).

**Family alignment:** the coalitions family members form: the manner in which the family members join together or oppose each other.

**Family constellation:** the number, sequencing, and other characteristics of family members; an important determinant of lifestyle (associated with Adler).

**Family reenactment:** in group therapy, experiences or behaviors of members ignite memories and interaction styles that are similar to the member's family of origin, thus raising old issues but creating an opportunity in group to better understand those relationships.

**Family rituals:** established patterns or ways of doing things as a family.

**Family sculpture:** placing "family members in physical positions in the room to represent the degree of emotional distance present with the family" (Hanna & Brown, 1995, p. 15).

**Feminist modeling:** modeling by a female counselor geared to help female clients learn healthier, less neurotic, more independent responses to the politics of life that women face.

**First order reality:** a real or factual situation.

**Fixation:** the condition of being "stuck" at a level of psychosexual development because of trauma encountered at some earlier point in life (associated with psychoanalysis).

**Focusing:** paying close attention to something; Eugene Gendlin's self-help technique based on imaging a person's own "felt senses" in the body and dealing with them as they arise within and from the body.

**Free association:** a Freudian term for spontaneous and uncensored verbalization of whatever comes into a person's mind, which gives clues to the nature of the person's unconscious thoughts and conflicts.

**Freudian slip:** a verbal slip of the tongue that exposes an unconscious thought or contains a hidden meaning.

**Front range:** according to Erving Goffman, the aspects of role presented to others within a defined social establishment.

**Games:** unproductive and superficial patterns of interaction for the purpose of concealing real meaning; complementary ulterior transactions leading to a payoff (associated with Transactional Analysis).

**Genital stage:** the final stage of Freudian psychosexual development, usually attained at adolescence, in which heterosexual interests and activities are predominant.

**Genogram:** a family map; a diagram that identifies each family member for three or more generations. It shows births, marriages, divorces, deaths, and can be used to trace generational links to diseases, alcoholism, etc.

**Genuineness** (being congruent): being fully present to the client, transparent, while the counselor is reading his or her own inner experiencing and allowing the quality of that inner experiencing to be apparent in the therapeutic relationship; "the most basic of the three [core] conditions" (Rogers, 1959, p.184).

**Gestalt:** means "whole" (associated with Fritz Perls).

**Giving feedback:** verbal reactions of what is observed; as a therapeutic technique, the reactions should be specific and descriptive rather than global or judgmental.

**Goal setting in groups:** group leaders help members select and clarify their own specific goals as they relate to the group's purpose; a technique that can prevent aimless and unproductive sessions.

**Gossiping in groups:** when a member talks about another member in the group without addressing him or her directly.

**Grief:** the emotional numbness, disbelief, anxiety, despair, sadness, and loneliness that accompany the loss of someone or something that is loved or has significant meaning.

**Group norms:** the rules of group conduct that provide parameters to members for acceptable behavior; may include formal and informal rules, spoken and unspoken ones.

**Groupthink:** "the forcing of group opinion on all members of the group" (Peterson & Nisenholz, 1995, p. 256).

**Guided imagery:** the use of "mental images" to promote physical healing or changes in attitudes and behavior; guiding clients through a relaxing visualization experience; used to alleviate stress and stress-related conditions; has been successfully used with cancer, AIDS, chronic fatigue syndrome; involves boosting the immune system.

**Halo effect:** the influence on a subject's later observations of a researcher's own preconceived impressions. This can create either a positive or a negative bias.

**Hawthorne effect:** the influence that receiving special attention or knowing that they are participating in an experiment has on subjects. They may perform or react differently because of this special treatment.

**Here-and-now:** in gestalt therapy now "starts with the present awareness of the patient" and "refers to this moment" (Simkin & Yontef, 1984, p. 297 ); clients are not working in the here-and-now when they refer to their lives outside of the counseling sessions ("When I . . . ") or earlier in the hour ("Just a while ago I said . . . ") because the past is a memory and the future is a fantasy; clients become important only as they experience themselves in the present.

**Hidden job market:** jobs that are vacated then filled without the general public ever knowing of the vacancy; vacancies that are unadvertised or unknown to the public, which Helwig (1992) estimated to be about 80% of all filled jobs.

**Histrionic:** overly emotional.

**HIV therapies:** treatment of the human immunodeficiency virus, AIDS, and its symptoms.

**Homeostasis:** a state of physiological equilibrium.

**Humanistic theories:** theories that focus on the uniqueness of each person's internal perspective, which determines one's reality; a counseling style with emphasis on the here-and-now not on "what was" or "what will be"; a view typified in the work of Carl Rogers, Rollo May, Victor Frankl, Fritz Perls, Eric Fromm, Abraham Maslow, Gordon Allport, etc.

**Hypnosis:** an altered state of consciousness involving relaxation.

**Hypnotherapy:** sometimes referred to as hypnotism, this technique draws on a host of methods in an attempt to bypass the conscious mind and access the subconscious, where suppressed memories, repressed emotions, and forgotten events dwell; can facilitate behavioral, emotional, or attitudinal change; commonly used for weight loss and smoking cessation, and to treat phobias and stress (Segedin, 1994).

**Hypothesis:** a theory or conclusion from a deductive argument that postulates an expected relationship between two or more variables. It should be based on theory or evidence, be testable, and be as clearly and concisely stated as possible.

**Id:** a part of the personality, present at birth, that is blind, demanding, and insistent; functions to discharge tension and return to homeostasis (balance) (associated with psychoanalysis).

**Ideal self:** the self-concept a person would most like to possess, upon which he or she places the highest value for self.

**Identification:** part of the developmental process by which children learn sex role and other behaviors; can be a defensive reaction; a term used when clients feel inferior or insecure and seek to align themselves with more successful people or with causes in an effort to feel of greater self-worth (associated with psychoanalysis).

**Identified patient** (or client): the individual for whom therapy is sought (often used in marriage and family therapy).

**Identity crisis:** a developmental challenge, often occurring during adolescence, when a person seeks to establish a stable view of self and define a place in life (associated with Erik Erikson).

**Imitative behavior in groups:** in the spirit of Bandura's *Social Learning Theory,* members will model behaviors of both the leader and other group members.

**Immediacy:** a counselor's addressing an issue, an observation, or an impression at the very moment it occurs in the session; the term for the ability to explore with a client what is occurring in the counselor-client relationship immediately; the counselor's awareness of not only what the client is communicating in the moment but also what the counselor is communicating (associated with gestalt therapy and Fritz Perls).

**Implosive intention:** a behavioral term for when a counselor intentionally "floods" or induces anxiety in a client with the idea that with repeated inducement the client's anxiety will be gradually reduced.

**Implosive layer:** the third layer of gestalt neurosis; the place where clients must allow themselves to completely experience their deadness, rather than denying it; at this neurosis layer clients expose their defenses and start to make contact with their genuine self through peeling back this layer clients expose the next layer, their "explosive layer."

**Implosive therapy:** therapy that induces anxiety via presentation of vivid images or cues (flooding); a client's anxiety is expected to diminish (extinguish) through repeated exposure and the absence of any threat.

**Incongruence:** the discrepancy between the individual's experience and his or her distorted perception of the experience (associated with Carl Rogers and Fritz Perls).

**Individual psychology:** a system of psychoanalysis with a social orientation developed by Alfred Adler.

**Inductive reasoning:** inferring about the unknown through the basis of what is already known.

**Inferiority complex:** feelings of inadequacy and powerlessness; born helpless and dependent on others, we must grow and overcome feelings of inferiority all our life; what is overcome as we strive for superiority.

**Inner child:** the sense of childish vulnerability within us; a form of counseling where clients imagine their return to early childhood experiences (traumatic or normal) with the goal of healing and resolving present psychological problems.

**Instinct:** a biological urge (drive) that moves clients toward action.

**Instrumentation:** the development, choice, and use of instruments (e.g., tests); the entire process of collecting data in a study.

**Instruments:** assessment tools and other tests used in research (e.g., demographic questionnaires); any specific procedure or device for systematically collecting data.

**Integrative counseling** (integrationalism): another term for eclectic counseling. While pure "eclecticism tends to be technical and pragmatic . . . integrationalism tends to refer to a conceptual or theoretical creation beyond a blending of techniques" (Corey, 1991, p. 426).

**Intellectualization:** the process of keeping material or content on a cognitive level; in Freudian psychology it involves avoiding becoming aware of inferiority or other feelings through use of intellectual vocabulary, being philosophic, thinking, etc.

**Internal locus of control:** the belief that rewards and satisfaction are contingent on people's own actions and that they can shape their own fate; high levels of self-responsibility.

**Internal validity:** any observed relationship of two or more variables that is meaningful in its own right rather than being due to something else. For instance, the observed differences on the dependent variable should be directly related to the independent variable, and not due to some other unintended variable. Internal validity is established when external variables are controlled. Threats to internal validity include selection, instrumentation, maturation, mortality, and researcher-induced bias.

**Interpretation:** a counseling technique used to unmask true client meaning.

**Introjection:** identifying via fantasy the expression of impulses or motives; the process of a client taking on (introjecting) the beliefs, values, and standards of another person or group; can result in the development of positive or negative traits; an existential error, a defense mechanism (associated with psychoanalysis).

**Introjects:** imprints or memories from parents or others.

**Ipsative score interpretations:** see Normative and ipsative score interpretations.

**Irresponsibility:** in Reality Therapy, it means inadequate and unrealistic behavior and efforts to fulfill personal needs.

**Job:** a task or set of tasks; a position of employment.

**Job seeking skills:** a vital component of placement services; skills that help secure employment.

**Job Training Partnership Act** (JTPA): a federally mandated program that offers employment and job training programs to lower economic wage earners.

**John Henry effect:** procedures are discarded as ineffective because of a failure to obtain statistically significant results when, in fact, the procedures are highly effective. This effect usually occurs when an atypical performance is obtained from the control group (Marshall, 1995).

**Kurtosis:** one of the shapes formed by plotting statistics on a graph. The example in Figure 18.2 depicts a "degree of peak" in scores. It is shaped differently from a normal bell-shaped curve.

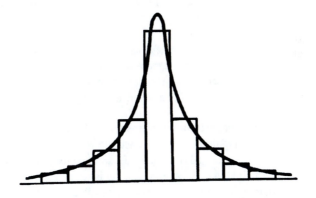

**Figure 18.2**

**Latency stage:** a Freudian term for the period of psychosexual development that follows the phallic stage and occurs before the adolescent genital stage.

**Law of effect:** Edward Thorndike formulated this behavioral law that states that when a stimulus-response connection is followed by a reward (reinforcement), that connection is strengthened; a behavior's consequences determine the probability of its being repeated according to this law.

**Levels of measurement:** the statistics used in interpreting data will largely be influenced by one of the following levels of measurement:

*Nominal:* this system organizes numbers or subjects by arranging them on a scale in order to better classify or identify them. The numbers represent variable categories, and the intervals are not equal. This is the simplest scale for arranging data, and the least precise of the four levels. Example: freshman, sophomores, juniors, seniors. Statistic: mode, number, or percent in each group.

*Ordinal:* this system organizes data or subjects by placing them in order on a scale according to their magnitude: 1st, 2nd, 3rd, etc. Intervals are not equal. This is the most commonly used level of measurement in counseling research. Example: class rank, percentile rank. Statistic median, quartile deviation; number or percent at each level.

*Interval:* this system organizes numbers or subjects on a scale according to equal intervals, having the same quantities with equal units between values. Often used on psychological tests and inventories such as achievement tests or aptitude tests. Statistic: mean, variance, standard deviation, number or percent at each level. For example, the distances between scores on most commercially available mathematics achievement tests usually are considered equal.

*Ratio:* this system organizes numbers or subjects by arranging them on a scale by their magnitude, with an absolute zero point, and equal intervals that can be added or divided. Example: physical characteristics such as height, weight, age, speed. Statistic: mean, variance, standard deviation, number or percent at each value.

**Levels of significance:** these levels are determined by the researcher. An obtained result that is significant at the .05 level could occur by chance only 5 times out of 100 times. At the .01 level, sometimes referred to as "practical certainty," only 1 time out of 100 times would this result occur by chance. Psychological research usually accepts the .05 level as significant. However, both levels correspond fairly well to 2 and 3 standard deviations from the mean in a normal probability distribution (bell-shaped curve).

**Libido:** the basic driving force of personality; the combination of the death instincts (thanatos) and life instincts (eros); a psychic energy usually sexual in nature; the instinctual drives of the Id and the source of psychic energy (associated with psychoanalysis).

**Life scripts:** programming that occurs from childhood through cultural and familial influences (scripting), which ultimately directs our behavior in the most important areas of our life (associated with Transactional Analysis).

**Lifestyle:** the characteristic way in which a client lives and pursues long-term goals; important personal components in career planning that include memberships in organizations, hobbies, home, family, pace of life, leisure activities, and religious affiliation.

**Life tasks:** an Adlerian term used for the basic challenges and obligations accompanying life; specifically, work, sex, and society; a term to which Dreikurs and Mosak added the components of "spiritual growth" and "self-identity."

**Lighthouse principles:** the natural laws that are woven into the fabric of every civilized society throughout history and comprise the roots of every family and institution, including fairness, integrity and honesty, human dignity, service, quality or excellence, potential, and growth (Covey, 1990).

**Likert scale:** a common rating scale used in measuring degrees, often used to measure attitudes. Information is rated or ranked on a continuum, usually 1–5, but the scale can be 1–7 or 1–9. Example:

"I am an optimistic person" (circle one)

| Never | Seldom | Sometimes | Usually | Always |
|-------|--------|-----------|---------|--------|
| 1 | 2 | 3 | 4 | 5 |

**Linking:** in group therapy, the leader's verbal connection (link) of common themes and issues observed in the discussion; enables members to work on each other's problems.

**Locus of control:** the idea that an individual's circumstances are controlled by an "internal locus of control" or an "external locus of control"; identifies where one's sense of control is located, internally (within themselves) or externally (by external forces or from others) (associated with Rotter, 1966).

**Logotherapy:** a concept developed by Victor Frankl, whereby mental and emotional illnesses are viewed as symptoms of an underlying sense of meaninglessness or emptiness concerning life; associated with existential thought; seeks to eliminate people's emptiness by helping the individual to detect life's unique meaning; finding a mission in life.

**Managed health care:** specific requirements mandated by insurance companies for diagnosis, treatment plan, record-keeping, and counselor qualifications before payment will be made to a health care provider (e.g., a counselor).

**Manic depressive:** a person who has radical mood swings (from elation and depression); a severe mental disorder, officially called bipolar disorder.

**MANOVA** (multivariate analysis of variance): this analysis is used if two or more dependent variables are used in analysis, rather than the ANOVA.

**Marriage and family counseling:** counseling a couple or an entire family, usually on relationships and interactional patterns.

**Massage:** the practice of kneading or otherwise manipulating a person's muscles and other soft tissue with the intent of improving a person's well-being or health; body work in such specialized areas as

> *Pregnancy* (a variety of used to relieve common complaints of pregnancy and to ease the labor process).

> *Infancy* (techniques designed to enhance the bonding between parent and baby; preventive therapy; can help strengthen and regulate a baby's respiratory, circulatory, and gastrointestinal functioning; used to relieve gas and colic while relaxing both parent and child).

> *On-Site* (techniques done at the client's location, typically at the workplace; client remains fully clothed while sitting in a specially designed massage chair).

**Maturation:** a primary goal of gestalt therapy; asks clients to "grow up" and to assume responsibility for themselves while living in the "now."

**Mean:** the average score (computed by adding raw scores and then dividing that total by the total entry of scores).

**Measures of central tendency:** when scores are symmetrical (distributed normally on a bell-shaped curve), the mean, median, and mode scores will all be found in the same spot.

**Measures of variability:** there are three types of measures of variability:

1. *Range:* found by subtracting the lowest score from the highest score, and adding 1.

2. *Standard deviation* (SD): the most stable measure of variability, SD takes into consideration each and every score in a distribution. SD describes the variability within a distribution of scores.

3.  *Variance:* the square of the standard deviation (see ANOVA). @xnl@

**Median:** the middle score in a distribution of scores.

**Medical model:** a model that determines a health care helper's role; involves medication, diagnosis, and prescriptions; does not view the counselor's role as vital in the client's/patient's change process; a general belief that outward behavioral difficulties are symptoms of deeper underlying causes; often viewed as opposed to a human growth and development model.

**Metacommunications:** the second level of communications, achieved by placing conditions on surface-level communications.

**Midlife crisis:** stress an individual encounters at various transitional stages in midlife; it may result in behavioral changes.

**Mind reading:** attempting to guess what another person is thinking.

**Minority:** a group of people, or a member of a group, who, because of physical or cultural characteristics or beliefs, are singled out from others in a society for differential or unequal treatment, and who, in consequence of that treatment, regard themselves as objects of a collective discrimination; some number less than half of the represented population.

**Modalities:** a Multimodal Therapy term for the various areas of a person's life that constitutes his or her holistic essence (i.e., sensations, behaviors, affects, cognitions).

**Modality:** an NLP term that describes the systems of seeing (visual), hearing (auditory), feeling (kinesthetic), tasting (gustatory), and smelling (olfactory).

**Mode:** the most frequent score in a distribution.

**Modeling:** teaching by direct personal example. Clients or group members often learn by observing the counselor's behavior.

**Moral dilemma:** a situation that requires a person to consider values of right and wrong.

**Morita therapy:** absolute bed rest; developed by physician and American author S. Wier Mitchell (1829–1914), but later Kengi Morita (a Japanese psychiatrist) applied the process to clients with nervous exhaustion; a process whereby clients go to bed for a week for complete rest with no TV, radio or reading; a technique where isolation is absolute, save meals, and a daily visit by the therapist to teach the client to let feelings flow, relax, and recognize that they cannot control everything.

**Morphogenesis:** a healthy family system that tends to growth and develop.

**Morphostasis:** a healthy family system that tends to stay stable.

**Multiple regression analysis:** a statistical method used for analyzing the contributions of two or more independent variables to predict a dependent variable or criterion.

**Music therapy:** use of music in a clinical setting in pursuit of therapeutic goals; offers clients creative expression, both nonverbal and verbal.

**Musturbation:** a term characterizing the behavior of clients who are absolutistic and inflexible in thinking, maintaining that they "must" not fail, "must" be exceptional, "must" be successful, etc.; hence, *mus*turbation (associated with REBT).

**Mutuality:** see Universality.

**Narcissism:** extreme self-love, as opposed to love of others; a personality disorder characterized by a grandiose and exaggerated sense of self-importance and an exploitative attitude toward others, which masks a poor self-concept.

**Needs assessment:** a measure of the discrepancies between current conditions and desired conditions. To assess current conditions accurately, sampling with an appropriate instrument (assessment tool) should be used to gather, analyze, and tabulate data.

**NLP:** abbreviation for neurolinguistic programming.

**Nonparametric tests:** in analyzing data when you cannot assume that your distribution of scores is going to be normal (i.e., they won't resemble a bell-shaped curve), or when you cannot assume that the variances of your samples are similar to each other, you must use nonparametric statistics to test the significance of scores. Specific types of nonparametric tests include

   *Chi-square test:* Used to determine data that are in categories. The Chi-square test is based on comparison of *expected frequencies* and *ac-*

*tual frequencies* obtained. If these two are similar, you can conclude that the two groups are not different. If there are considerable differences, you can conclude that t2here is a significant difference between the groups.

*Mann-Whitney U test:* Used to analyze data that is to be placed in *rank order.* The researcher intermingles the scores from two independent sample groups into one large ranked group that produces a value whose probability of occurrence is then checked in the appropriate statistical table.

*Sign test:* this test is used to analyze two related (as opposed to independent) samples. The researcher simply lines up the pairs of related subjects (e.g., IQ and age) and determines how many times the paired subjects in one group scored higher than those in the other group.

*Kruskal-Wallis test:* (a nonparametric one-way ANOVA). Used when you have more than two independent groups to rank. Like the Mann-Whitney U test, the scores are intermingled and the sum of each group is tallied and compared.

**Nonstandardized tests:** tests or instrument procedures that are administered with little or no formal instruction (just routine instructions) and are scored informally (e.g., preference tallies, checklists, Likert scales, etc.).

**Norm:** a standard, model, or pattern for a group. Norms may be local, regional, national, etc. Test results are based on the performance of, or normed to, a particular group. In other words, the person being tested is compared to the norms of the group. Norm-referenced assessment compares clients, or groups, to others who have taken the test previously.

**Normative and ipsative score interpretations:** interpretations of test or survey scores may be

*Ipsative:* compares the performance level of an individual to him- or herself (looks at test results of two or more of that client's scores).

*Normative:* compares the performance level of test scores to some other group's achievement.

**Nuclear family:** the immediate, traditional family consisting of husband, wife, and children living together.

**Null hypothesis:** the educated guess that there is no significant difference between the variables or groups that were evaluated. Null means "no effect." If what is observed in the sampling is consistent with the null hypothesis, we stay with "fail to reject" and accept the null hypothesis. If what is observed is not consistent with the null hypothesis, we reject the null hypothesis.

**Object:** a technical term that means "that with which a subject relates."

**Object relations theory:** a version of psychoanalytic thinking that focuses on predictable developmental sequences in which early experiences of self shift in relation to an expanding awareness of others; a theory that holds that individuals go through phases of autism, normal symbiosis, and separation and individuation, culminating in a state of integration.

**Observer bias:** occurs when researchers confirm their own convictions by hearing, recalling, feeling, and seeing what they what or expect.

**Occupation:** a job; group of similar job skills among which a person can transfer without difficulty.

**Occupational development:** see Career development.

**Oedipus complex:** unconscious sexual desires of the male child for the mother accompanied by feelings of hostility and fear toward the father (associated with psychoanalysis).

**Open-ended questions:** questions that elicit longer, personal or individual responses, and usually begin with the words "what," "why," "how," "could," or "would"; questions that cannot be answered "yes" or "no."

**Operant conditioning** (instrumental): the condition when a response is given in order to obtain an outcome that reinforces the individual; a model wherein a response is strengthened by being positively reinforced when it happens, or weakened by ignoring or punishing it (associated with behaviorism).

**Oral stage:** the initial stage of Freudian psychosexual development, in which the mouth is the primary source of personal gratification; the stage, according to Erik Erikson, where the infant is learning to trust or mistrust the world.

**Outplacement counseling:** counseling services provided by businesses or organizations that are laying off or terminating job positions to the people being let go; services may include exit interviews, retraining, job search assistance, competency testing, school information, etc.

**Pain management:** a broad spectrum of techniques (e.g., exercise, mental-health counseling, surgery, medication) for diminishing, ending, or coping with chronic pain.

**Paradigm:** a model, example, or pattern.

**Paradigm shift:** a major change in the way in which a situation or concept is viewed; new information, often generated from a seemingly opposite perspective, that changes a client's overall assumptions or general approach to life or to a specific situation.

**Paradoxical intention:** a therapeutic strategy in which the client is instructed to engage in and magnify the very behaviors of concern; giving clients permission to do an activity or think the thoughts that they most fear, in the belief that excess behaviors may diminish or totally stop the unwanted behavior.

**Parameter:** a constant used to determine variables; the estimated value for a population inferred from a sample statistic.

**Parametric tests:** a method of analyzing statistics that is used when accurate assumptions *can* be made about the variance of scores for a population (see Statistical analysis).

**Paraphrasing:** summarizing or restating the content of a client's comments so as to check the accuracy of perceptions, or to increase client's confidence in the counselor.

**Parroting:** a counselor's technique of verbally repeating back to a client the exact words the client just spoke in an effort to check for accurate listening.

**Percentile or percentage** (%): this is a value that other percentages will either be above or below. For example, if the percentile is 60% then it is higher than 59% of all scores, and lower than 40% of all scores.

**Peripheral consciousness:** in group therapy, the ability of the leader to monitor the verbal and nonverbal behaviors of all members simultaneously, as if with a "third eye"; when leaders exhibit with-it-ness and pick up reactions to comments made by group members and confront or direct the focus of the group to them if appropriate.

**Persona:** the mask or facade we exhibit publicly with the intention of presenting a favorable impression so that society will accept us; a Latin term denoting the wearing of masks (associated with Carl Jung).

**Personal cosmology:** Trait Factor's E. G. Williamson's term for a person's personal orientation to the universe: a) either the person is alone in an unfriendly universe or b) the universe is friendly and favorable to the person and his or her development.

**Personal unconscious:** one of two types of unconscious (the other is collective unconscious); it closely resembles Freud's version consisting of everything that has been repressed during a client's past development (associated with Jung).

**Personalization:** a technique of changing clients' impersonal comments beginning with "You . . . " to personal statements beginning with "I . . . "

**Phallic stage:** the third stage of Freudian psychosexual development during which the child gains maximum personal gratification through direct experience with the genitals.

**Phobia** (phobic reaction): a very intense, usually irrational, hysterical fear of a situation, object, or person.

**Phobic layer:** the gestalt second layer; the stage where clients attempt to avoid the emotional pain that is associated with seeing aspects of themselves that they may prefer to deny (associated with Fritz Perls).

**Pilot study:** a preliminary study or test of research techniques and analysis; often used to determine the need for a full research project or dissertation.

**Placebo:** a fake dose; a nonmedicated dose administered to a control group in place of the medication given to the experimental group.

**Population:** a complete collection of the subjects or other elements to be studied (e.g., all the people with schizophrenia in a given location).

**Power:** in family therapy, identification of who in the family has authority and responsibility.

**Power-based tests:** tests that have no time limits or that allow large amounts of time to complete.

**Praxis:** the unity of theory and practice (associated with Paulo Freire, 1985, of Brazil).

**Prejudice:** a preconceived judgment or opinion without just grounds or sufficient knowledge; a positive or negative bias; often an irrational attitude or behavior against an individual or group; often manifest in "isms" (racism, heightism, classism, ageism, sexism, etc.).

**Primary prevention:** refers to the efforts of mental health professionals who work with schools, children, or with adults in order to prevent a later need for counseling.

**Private logic:** for every behavior clients have their own private reasoning that makes that behavior meaningful in terms of achieving a goal; conscious or unconscious thoughts about the purpose or goal being sought at the time of the behavior; a person's logical assumptions and logical processes of reasoning (associated with Adler).

**Profession:** a vocation with an underlying body of theoretical and research knowledge, and a publicly declared, self-imposed set of behavioral guidelines.

**Professional development:** continuing professional growth, training, etc.; efforts to rejuvenate and reeducate to avoid or counteract burnout.

**Projection:** the avoidance of conflict within oneself by ascribing one's own ideas or motives to someone else; confusion of self that occurs when clients attribute something outside of themselves to their own self; a powerful technique used to encourage clients to associate with someone else that part of themselves that they are unwilling to own; a Freudian term for attributing to others one's own unacceptable personal thoughts, feelings, or behaviors; a defense mechanism.

**Protecting:** in group therapy, the leader safeguards (protects) members from unnecessary psychological and physical risks associated.

**Proxemics:** refers to the spatial features of the environment, such as positioning furniture, seating arrangements, etc., which have an impact on behavior; a person's personal space.

**Psychiatrist:** a physician (medical doctor) who has had additional training (a residency) in the specialty of psychiatry; follows a medical model, prescribes medications, often working in private practice or in-patient facilities.

**Psychic energy:** a Freudian term for the energy that comes from the instincts (Id), which is changed by the ego or superego into actions.

**Psychoanalysis:** a Freudian system of therapy (see Chapter 2).

**Psychoanalyst:** a therapist who has had intensive training in psychoanalysis.

**Psychoanalytic counseling theories:** these include Freudian, Adlerian, and the work of Karen Horney and Harry Stack Sullivan.

**Psychodrama:** a therapeutic use of drama that involves a variety of highly energetic actions and the enactment of fantasies; a process whereby clients enact a scene; a staged event that is interactive, requiring clients to simultaneously think, feel, and act in an effort to learn more about themselves.

**Psychodynamics:** the interplay of opposing forces and intrapsychic conflicts, providing a basis for understanding human motivation.

**Psychologist:** a person who has passed a state licensing exam and usually follows a medical model of psychotherapy emphasizing testing, diagnosis, and interpersonal therapy.

**Psychosexual stages:** the Freudian chronological phases of development; stages that begin in infancy, with each successive stage characterized by a primary way of gaining sensual and sexual gratification.

**Psychosis:** a loss of touch with reality; delusional; socially dysfunctional; a severe mental disorder.

**Psychosocial stages:** Erik Erikson's growth stages (from infancy through old age); stages that present psychological and social tasks/crises that must be resolved if maturation is to proceed in a healthy fashion.

**Psychotherapist:** any therapist, counselor, psychologist, psychiatrist, social worker, or others professional in the mental health field.

**Pygmalion effect:** the researcher's own expectations are the cause of the changes in the subject's behaviors or attitudes.

**Quality of life:** the goal of multimodal therapy; emotional and interpersonal balance in a person's life, which creates a stable and whole person.

**QUOID:** acronym for a client who is "Quiet, Ugly, Old, Indigent, Dissimilar" culturally (see also YAVIS).

**Racism:** the belief that some races are inherently superior or inferior to others; can be expressed as an individual, institutional, or cultural bias.

**Rapport:** the atmosphere in the counseling session that facilitates bonding and closeness between a client and counselor; a close working relationship of counselor and client; developed by the counselor exhibiting such characteristics as warmth, openness, nonjudgmental behavior, caring, and other genuine "getting along" behaviors (associated with Carl Rogers).

**Rationalization:** justifying unacceptable attitudes, beliefs, or behavior by supplying a reason that conceals the true motive or reasoning; a defense mechanism that enables clients to accept a failing or disappointment (associated with psychoanalysis).

**Reaction formation:** expressing an attitude, motive or behavior that is directly contrary or opposite to a client's true feelings; a defense mechanism against a threatening impulse, involving actively expressing the very opposite impulse (associated with psychoanalysis).

**Reality:** "the way things are" (Covey, 1990, p. 24).

**REBT:** abbreviation for Rational Emotive Behavior Therapy.

**Reciprocal inhibition:** developed by Joseph Wolpe, this principle/theory holds that a person can be both anxious and relaxed (even depressed) at the same time (associated with behaviorism).

**Reciprocity:** a process whereby one credentialing agency accepts the credential of another agency as equivalent to its own; in some states called "endorsement."

**Red-crossing** (same as "bandaiding"): in group therapy, a premature rescuing of members from working things out with each other.

**Referent power:** where the self is used as a point of identification to help clients in their own self-examination process.

**Reflection of feelings:** repeating what the client has stated with emphasis on the affective or feeling portion of the message; a technique whereby a counselor reflects emotionally what the client verbalizes; a Rogerian technique that serves two purposes: enabling the client to see how another is perceiving what he or she is saying, and helping clients feel that the counselor is accepting them.

**Reframing:** presenting a new interpretation or perspective on a situation or problem so the client sees the situation or problem in a way that offers alternatives or produces new options; often associated with NLP counseling, this technique is used by the counselor to help the client revisualize an unpleasant significant memory by changing the way the scene is viewed and interpreted.

**Regression:** when clients are faced with anxiety brought on by a crisis or stressful situation, they may choose to regress or revert back to more immature, inappropriate, or childlike behaviors; a Freudian defense mechanism (associated with psychoanalysis).

**Regression toward the mean score:** this term refers to the tendency for a high or low score to regress (move) toward the mean (average) score if the test is taken again.

**Rehabilitation counseling:** counseling that focuses on those who are mentally ill, retarded, epileptic; have orthopedic, visual, or hearing impairment; have circulatory problems, amputated limbs, multiple sclerosis, cerebral palsy; have transportation difficulties; need deaf interpretation; are immobile; or need assistance with prostheses.

**Reiki therapy:** an ancient Tibetan healing processes that uses light hand placements, which channel healing energies to the client; a technique and philosophy commonly used to treat emotional and mental distress as well as chronic and acute physical problems, and to assist the recipient in achieving spiritual focus and clarity; superseded by the more recent Reiki Plus developed by Reiki Master David Jarrell, which supplements traditional Reiki with newer psychotherapeutic skills (e.g., hand placements on the head are used to tap into the collective unconscious).

**Reliability:** consistency. Research that is reliable is replicable. The same results occur in a repeat test of the same subjects. The test gets the same results if administered again. (Tests can be reliable but not valid.) Three types of reliability are:

> *Stability:* called "test-retest," this form of reliability occurs when the same instrument (test) is used on all groups, or on repeated occasions.

Results of the administrations are then correlated. A correlation co-efficient range is calculated between -1.00 and +1.00, but it should be noted that the amount of time and new circumstances occurring between test administrations may skew the stability.

*Equivalence:* this reliability occurs when different forms of the same instrument (test) are given to the same group. Then, a correlation is determined between the two test scores. Just how equivalent (or comparable) the two forms of the tests are influences this type of reliability.

*Internal consistency:* the extent to which the items comprising the test measure the same thing.

**Representational systems:** an NLP term for the encompassing patterns a client uses in taking and storing experiences including seeing, hearing, and feeling.

**Repression:** the unconscious exclusion of painful thoughts from conscious-ness; rejecting from conscious thought (through suppression, denial, forget-ting) ideas that provokes anxiety; the ego-defense mechanism whereby threat-ening or painful thoughts or feelings are excluded, or repressed, from aware-ness (associated with psychoanalysis).

**Resistance:** reluctance to bring to awareness threatening unconscious material that has been repressed; a defense mechanism (associated with psy-choanalysis).

**Resourceful:** in NLP counseling, those moments when a client has access to all his or her highest strengths, abilities, and feelings of capability and well-being.

**Responsibility:** as defined in Reality Therapy, it means the ability to fulfill one's needs without depriving others of the ability to fulfill their needs.

**Restatement:** repeating what the client has just said so as to anchor that comment with the client, or repeating to get the client to consider that area further.

**Retirement counseling:** helping clients who are approaching retirement; information about good health, emotional aspects of retirement, financial es-tate planning, medical needs, part-time employment, relocation, inheritance; legal help with wills or property.

**Ritual and undoing:** when a client attempts to reduce anxiety by using a ritualistic tendency that may reduce his or her sense of guilt; a client behavior that often comes in the form of "righting a wrong"; a client attempting to perform a good deed (e.g., going to church) to please a parent or be of service to alleviate guilt.

**Rolfing:** Ida P. Rolf's technique that uses deep manipulation of the fascia (connective tissue) to restore the body's natural alignment, which may have become rigid through injury, emotional trauma, and inefficient movement habits; a process involving ten sessions, each focusing on a different part of the body.

**RUST statement:** the "Responsibilities of Users of Standardized Tests" statement is a proclamation endorsed by the American Counseling Association regarding guidelines for the selection and use of standardized tests.

**Scapegoating:** when several members in a counseling group "gang up" on a single group member.

**Scattergram:** a depiction of the relationship between two variables made by plotting data on a graph.

**Schema:** a cognitive network or structure that organizes perceptions.

**Scores:** types of scores include

*Raw scores:* the initial scores obtained on an instrument.

*Derived scores:* scores converted for ease of interpretation.

*Norm-referenced scores:* scores compared for interpretation to other scores on the test; normed group scores are important because of their relevance as a comparison group.

*Criterion-referenced scores:* scores compared to an absolute standard for interpretation; the content validity of the instrument is particularly important because an internal comparison is made.

**Second order reality:** the client's premises and perception (first and second levels of reality may or may not be congruent). (See First order reality.)

**Self** (the self): our sense of who we are; a Jungian archetype that does not appear until middle age; the organizing principle of the personality, central in the collective unconscious.

**Self-actualization:** the "inherent tendency of the organism to develop all its capacities in ways which serve to maintain or enhance the organism" (Rogers, 1959, p. 196); the basic propensity of men and women to function so as to preserve and increase self integration; a term Maslow (1971) used for people who are "involved in a cause outside their own skin . . . they are working at something which fate has called them to somehow and which they work at and which they love, so that the work-joy dichotomy in them disappears" (p. 43).

**Self-defeating behaviors:** negative actions or thoughts clients choose that do not serve their best interests and thwart their efforts to move toward a more productive life.

**Self-disclosure:** revealing information about oneself; appropriate self-disclosure by counselors is calculated, used sparingly; the counselor's sharing of a personal experience or emotions with the intent to increase rapport or support the client's position or emotions.

**Self-fulfilling prophecy:** the expectation that individuals will act in a certain way, which causes them to act in that way; a powerful attitude especially significant in its ability to influence school children's performance.

**Self-psychology:** closely akin to object relations theory and aligned with the works of Heinz Kohut, who investigated how early childhood relationships form the self; psychology with an emphasis on the self rather than on the Freudian ego, instincts, or self-representation.

**Sensory centration saturation:** new stimuli filtered through the emotions of a recent loss.

**Shadow** (the shadow): a mask, according to Carl Jung, that embodies all that we would like not to be; our dark side or unconscious opposite; a part of our self to which we are not sufficiently well-related.

**Shaping:** changing behavior through successive approximations (shaping); changing behavior by identifying incremental steps to a goal, called "successive approximations."

**Silence:** a technique counselor's use to allow the client time to process information or generate solutions to concerns; also called "wait time."

**Skew:** a shape made by plotting statistics on a graph. Figure 18.3 shows a positive skew (on the left) and a negative skew (on the right). Both illustrate degrees to which a score may be skewed from the normal bell-shaped curve.

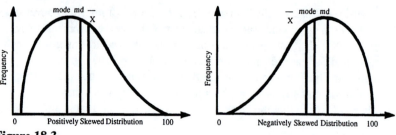

**Figure 18.3**

**Social class:** level of material possessions or economic advantages including assets and money; involves values, language, interpersonal relationship style, world view, level of opportunity, material possessions, respect and influence; the concept that people are a product of their cultures; a key component for consideration in cross-cultural counseling, where the behaviors, thoughts, and values of clients must be viewed from that culture's perspective.

**Social desirability:** the tendency for test takers to respond in ways that are perceived to be desirable to the test giver, to a particular group, or to society in general.

**Social interest** (*gemeinschaftsgefuhl*): a combination of concerns for others and appreciation of one's own role in the larger social order (associated with Adler).

**Social worker:** a mental health professional whose focus is on the social antecedents and consequences of emotional disabilities; professionals employed in social service agencies who tend to approach their work through casework, group work, and community/social welfare organizations.

**Sociogram:** an instrument used to measure the structure and organization of social groups, school classes, employee leaders, etc. The final product is a diagram/graph that shows the relationships of members within the group.

**Sociometry:** a method of identifying group members who are "exceptional" (isolated, popular, rejected, distant, highly social, leaders, etc.).

**Solomon four-group design:** a design used when studying the actual effect of the pretest on the experimental treatment.

**Speed-based tests:** tests that are timed, or tests that measure speed and accuracy.

**Spitting in the client's soup:** a phrase referring to when the counselor exposes the client's intentions in such a way as to make them unpalatable so the client can no longer maintain that current behavior with innocence.

**Splits:** a gestalt term (see Topdog/underdog).

**Splitting:** a term common to object relations theory; the defensive process whereby clients keep incompatible feelings apart and separate.

**Standard deviation** (SD or sd): takes into consideration each and every test score in a distribution and describes the variability within a distribution of scores.

**Standard error of measurement** (SEM): also known as "confidence limits" and "confidence band," a measure of reliability; an estimate of the standard deviation (SD) of the normal distribution of test scores that a client would theoretically obtain by taking the test innumerable times. This measurement helps determine the range into which a client's test score will most likely fall.

**Standardized scores:** scores that show the distance from the mean (average) score. Two common standardized scores are:

*Z score:* where the mean (average) is 0 and the standard deviation is 1 (the score minus mean, over standard deviation) (see Bell-shaped curve). The mean of the Z score will be zero with a standard deviation of 1. The Z score tells the number of standard deviations (SD) a person scored above (+) or below (–) the mean on the original scale.

*T score:* has no negative numbers; where the mean (average) is 50 and the standard deviation is 10 (see Figure 18.2).

**Standardized tests:** tests or instruments that are given through a formal or structured procedure (see Nonstandardized tests).

**Statistical analysis:** types of analyses of statistics include:

*Descriptive:* used to organize, summarize and present quantitative data collected from a sampled population (e.g., deviations, averages, standard deviations). Descriptive statistics can be presented in tables and graphs (which rearrange data and gives all of them back) or in summary statistics (which rearrange data and give back one number).

*Parametric:* used when accurate assumptions can be made about the variance of scores for a population, when scores are randomly drawn and normally distributed (bell-shaped curve).

*Nonparametric:* used when accurate assumptions cannot be made about the variance of scores for a population, when scores are not normally distributed.

*Inferential:* used when it is appropriate to infer from a small sample size to a more general population (e.g., t-test, ANOVA, ANCOVA).

**Storytelling:** in groups therapy, when a member strays into unproductive personal stories; a disruption in the group requiring the leader to intervene and ask how the story relates to the topic or to that person's present feelings.

**Stress inoculation:** associated with Albert Ellis, who taught coping skills to replace self-defeating statements (e.g., "What if I fail the test?" to "I will do my best."). It also refers to relaxation techniques such as deep breathing, and reframing exercises.

**Striving for superiority:** efforts to overcome our inferiority complex by striving for, and being motivated by, social power, recognition, and internal perfection; exemplified by healthy people striving for superiority in accord with the needs of society while embodying courage, wholesome ambition, independence, etc. (associated with Adler).

**Strokes:** behaviors of recognition, like saying "Hello" to someone; on a deep level strokes are a showing of concern or caring, like "giving someone a stroke; a need which if not received, may result in a "I'm not OK" position (associated with Transactional Analysis).

**Structural maps:** illustrations of the family's alliances, coalitions, boundaries, conflicts, patterns, etc.

**Structuring:** verbally defining with the client the counseling process (the limits, process, goals, roles expected, etc.).

**Sublimation:** when a client takes sexual energy and rechannels it into acceptable or creative behaviors (associated with psychoanalysis).

**Summarizing:** a technique where the counselor verbally synthesizes several client ideas or feelings; the pulling together of the important elements of an interaction or session, providing continuity and meaning.

**Sunday neurosis:** "that kind of depression which affects people who become aware of the lack of content in their lives when the rush of the busy week is over and the void within themselves becomes manifest" (Frankl, 1959, p. 129).

**Superego:** the aspect of personality that represents moral training; that which strives for perfection, not pleasure (associated with psychoanalysis).

**Supporting:** providing encouragement and reinforcement to an individual or group member when he or she displays desired behaviors. In groups, this leads to greater trust.

**Swedish massage:** the most common form of massage in Western countries; integrates ancient oriental techniques with modern principles of anatomy and physiology; a method where counselors rub, knead, pummel, brush, and tap the muscles.

**Systematic desensitization:** a form of classical conditioning in which anxiety-evoking situations are paired for inhibition responses; a "treatment package which includes relaxation training, construction of hierarchies of anxiety-eliciting stimuli via imagery with relaxation" (Unikel, 1973); a Joseph Wolpe (1958) technique that has been successful with clients who are afraid of flying, fear of heights, or have other fears that can be desensitized by addressing each escalating stage of fear that approaches the traumatic event.

**Systematic eclecticism:** a term associated with eclectic counseling referring to the appropriate way to harmoniously blend theoretical concepts and methods into a congruent framework; the "development of a comprehensive psychotherapy based on a unified and empirical body of work. It is the opportunity to construct a new integrative paradigm and, at the same time, to transcend more narrow 'schools' of therapy" (Norcross, 1986).

**t test:** a parametric test used to determine whether there is a significant difference between the means of two *matched samples* (t test for correlated means) or between the means of two *independent samples* (t test for independent means).

**TA:** abbreviation for Transactional Analysis counseling.

**Tabula rasa:** a term associated with Locke, who viewed children as not innately evil, but as a "blank tablet," or chalkboard, upon which their character will be written through life experiences.

**Tai chi:** a system of exercises used to improve physical fitness and promote mental and spiritual development; highly disciplined physical movements that unite the body and mind and bring balance to the individual's life; an external method (such as karate and judo) that stresses endurance and muscular strength, and an internal method (such as tai chi and aikido) that stresses relaxation and control; a treatment effective with back problems, ulcers, and stress.

**Theory:** a formulation of ideas about a topic, a systematic manner in which to view something; a hypothetical explanation for observed events; an educated guess; a prevailing concept that guides research; a set of interrelated propositions that define the relations among variables.

**Therapist:** a psychotherapist; any counselor, psychologist, psychiatrist, social worker, or other professional in the mental health field.

**Therapy:** William Glasser (1965) defines therapy as a "special kind of treatment which attempts to accomplish in a relatively short, intense period of time what should have been established during normal growing up" (p. 24).

**Third ear:** Theodore Reik (1952), a disciple of Freud, coined the phrase "listening with the third ear," a term for being cognizant of what the client is saying while at the same time allowing those words to stimulate ideas and hypotheses within the counselor's mind.

**Third party payments:** reimbursements of money to a counselor (provider) from a source other than the client (usually the client's insurance company or HMO).

**Thought-stopping:** a behavioral term for an intervention technique geared to inhibit recurring thoughts by purposefully stopping them when they appear; alternative thinking processes (singing songs, redirecting thoughts, etc.) are cognitively created so that unproductive thoughts can be better managed or stopped.

**Time series designs:** data that are collected over different periods of time and used primarily by behavioral counselors to track specific behavioral changes.

**Token economy:** a behavioral technique used to shape behavior through the use of an economy based on tokens (rewards or tokens that can purchase privileges, items, etc.).

**Topdog/underdog:** a gestalt term; "splits" that are disowned by the client but need to be retrieved and addressed (the topdog versus underdog is a common split, with both coexisting in one personality); a gestalt concept that holds that there is a topdog in each of us that knows what is best for us and is authoritarian, moralistic, perfectionistic (for which Fritz Perls used the symbol of a "super mouse") and an underdog in each of us that is apologetic and defensive.

**Transference:** in psychoanalysis, the client's unconscious and disproportionately emotional response to the counselor; the projection by the client of feelings he or she has toward others, or would like to have, onto the counselor.

**Transference neurosis:** that point in classical psychoanalysis when the client's fantasies about the counselor (both negative and positive) are at their peak and become the focus of counseling.

**Unconditional positive regard:** nonpossessive caring or acceptance of the client's individuality; acceptance; respecting the client regardless of differing values or views of the world; caring without condition, evaluation, or judgment; one of Carl Rogers' three core conditions for successful counseling.

**Unconscious:** that aspect of psychological functioning or of personality that houses experiences, wishes, impulses, and memories in an out-of-awareness state as a protection against anxiety.

**Unfinished business:** a gestalt term for issues or events from the past that still have current meanings and need addressing in order for a client to progress; a concept that holds that the past is valuable only as it affects the individual's present, and clients need to finish that which is unfinished.

**Universality** (or mutuality): a feeling of not being alone or isolated, and that other people (group members) have similar experiences or problems; in group therapy, the relief members feel upon discovering that others share similar issues or thoughts.

**Validity:** the degree to which the chosen instrument (test) actually measures what it is supposed to measure. Types of validity include:

*Face/Logical:* the test/instrument should look valid just on the face of it (e.g., does a test of family relationships ask about family members?).

*Content:* the test should contain items selected from the larger pool of items that could be included.

*Predictive* (criterion-related): the predictions made from the test are later confirmed by observations of behavior or by subsequent testing (e.g., subjects are successful in their career choice after tests indicated a high probability of happiness in that job).

*Concurrent* (criterion-related): the results of a test should be comparable to the results of other tests given about the same time.

*Construct:* the extent to which a test measures a hypothetical construct (e.g., about depression or anger). Often the results of several different tests will be employed to measure different components of the construct.

**Values:** "the way things should be" (Covey, 1990, p. 24); convictions or beliefs that prescribe or determine behavior in relation to goals or needs; basic "ideas and beliefs about what is right and good and what is wrong and bad" (Ajzen, 1973, p. 44); "multifactor or behavioral biases which mold and dominate the decision-making power of a particular individual" (Peters, 1962, p. 373).

**Variables:** elements of research that can vary or be varied. The two major types of variables are:

*Independent:* variables that are altered independently of any other variable. These are the variables that are manipulated to see what will occur (e.g., behavioral changes) in the dependent variables. Sometimes referred to as "predictor variables" or "stimulus variables."

*Dependent:* variables that are being measured or changed, and whose values are hypothesized to change as a result of changes in the independent variable. Sometimes referred to as "response variables" or "outcome variables."

**Visualization:** an inward picturing or image we make in our thoughts, something we see on the inside rather than the outside.

**Vocation:** a job or occupation; activities and positions of employment.

**Vocational development:** see Career development.

**Will to meaning:** Frankl's term for a person's primary motivation; an inward search for meaning in life; the striving to find a concrete meaning in personal existence.

**Will to power:** a term originally borrowed from Friedrich Nietzsche, but it has changed to mean a client's striving for superiority and dominance in order to overcome feelings of inadequacy and inferiority (associated with Adler).

**With-it-ness:** having "eyes in the back of your head"; the group leader's ability to have all group members know he or she is aware of what is going on with everyone in the group while talking to just one or two members; similar to "peripheral consciousness."

**Women's ontology:** a branch of philosophy dealing with existence and reality, adapted here to women's issues.

**Worker job obsolescence:** a change or trend in an occupation that renders a job obsolete and dislocates workers.

**Working through:** the process of resolving basic conflicts in the client's life or relationship with the counselor.

**World view:** how an individual perceives the world and his or her relationship to it, including its institutions, other people, things, and nature. World views are comprised of attitudes, values, opinions, and concepts and affect how we think, make decisions, behave, and define events.

**YAVIS:** acronym for a client who is "Young, Attractive, Verbal, Intelligent, Successful" (see also QUOID).

**Yin and yang:** the two complementing elements in Chinese philosophy; the yin is the feminine side, and the yang is the masculine side (associated with Jung).

**Zeitgeist counseling:** zeitgeist means "the spirit of the times; the prevailing cultural climate" (Corsini, 1984). Some have used this term in referring to eclectic counseling, as they see the trend toward its principles of integration and convergence gaining in popularity.

# REFERENCES

Ackerman, N. (1966). *Treating the troubled family*. New York: Basic Books.

Adler, M. (1977). *Reforming education: The schooling of a people and their education beyond schooling*. Boulder, CO: West Press.

Ajzen, R. (1973). Human values and counseling. *Personnel and Guidance Journal, 52*, 77–81.

Albanese, C. L. (1992). *America: Religions and religion (2nd ed.)*. Belmont, CA: Wadsworth.

American College Testing Foundation. (1984). *DISCOVER: A computer-based career development and counselor support system*. Iowa City: Author.

American Counseling Association. (1995). *Code of ethics and standards of practice*. Alexandria, VA: Author.

American Psychiatric Association. (1987). *Diagnostic and statistical manual of mental disorders (3rd ed., rev.)*. Washington, DC: Author.

American Psychiatric Association. (1994). *Diagnostic and statistical manual of mental disorders (4th ed.)*. Washington, DC: Author.

Ashton, P. (1985). Motivation and the teacher's sense of efficacy. In C. Ames & R. Ames (Eds.), *Research on motivation in education: Vol. 2. The classroom milieu.* San Diego: Academic.

Association for Specialists in Group Work. (1989). *Ethical guidelines for group counselors.* Alexandria, VA: Author.

Austin, L. A. (1982). *Factors influencing the academic success of adult college students after initial academic failure.* Unpublished doctoral dissertation, University of Wyoming, Laramie.

Austin, L. A. (1992). *Reality therapy in college counseling centers.* Unpublished manuscript.

Austin, L. A. (1993). *Reality therapy with freshmen issues.* Unpublished manuscript.

Averill, J. R. (1968). Grief: Its nature and significance. *Psychological Bulletin, 6,* 721–748.

Axelson, J. A. (1985). *Counseling and development in a multicultural society.* Monterey, CA: Brooks/Cole.

Bandler, R., & Grinder, J. (1975). *The structure of magic I.* Palo Alto, CA: Science and Behavior Books.

Bandura, A. (1989). Social cognitive theory. In R. Vasta (Ed.), *Six theories of child development.* Greenwich, CT: JAI Press.

Beck, A. (1976). *Cognitive therapy and emotional disorders.* New York: Meridian.

Becvar, D. S., & Becvar, R. J. (1982). *Family therapy: A systematic integration.* Needham Heights, MA: Allen & Bacon.

Beers, C. (1908). *A mind that found itself.* New York: Longman Green.

Belenky, M. F., Clenchy, B. M., Goldberger, N. R., & Torule, J. (1986). *Women's ways of knowing: The development of self and mind.* New York: Basic Books.

Belkin, G. S. (1988). *Introduction to counseling (3rd ed.).* Dubuque, IA: Wm. C. Brown.

Berne, E. (1964). *Games people play.* New York: Grove.

Berne, E. (1972). *What do you say after you say hello?* New York: Grove.

Blau, P. M., Gustad, J. W., Jessor, R., Parnes, H. S., & Wilcox, R. S. (1956). Occupational choices: A conceptual framework. *Industrial Labor Relations Review, 9,* 531–543.

Bolles, R. N. (1993). *What color is your parachute? A practical manual for job-hunters and career changers. (9ᵗʰ ed.).* Berkeley, CA: Ten Speed.

Bowen, M. (1978). *Family therapy in clinical practice.* New York: Jason Aronson.

Bowman, V. E. (1996). Counselor self-awareness and ethnic self-knowledge as a critical component of multicultural training. In J. DeLucia-Waack (Ed.), *Multicultural counseling competencies: Implications for training and practice.* Alexandria, VA: Association for Counselor Education and Supervision.

Boy, A. V., & Pine, G. J. (1982). *Client-centered counseling: A renewal.* Boston: Allyn & Bacon.

Brofenbrenner, U. (1986). Ecology of the family as a context for human development: Research perspectives. *Developmental Psychology, 22,* 723–742.

Bugental, J. (1978). *Psychotherapy and process.* Reading, MA: Addison-Wesley.

Cancian, F. M., & Gordon, S. L. (1988). Changing emotion norms in marriage: Love and anger in U.S. women's magazines since 1900. *Gender and Society, 2,* 308–342.

Caplan, G. (1970). *The theory and practice of mental health consultation.* New York: Basic Books.

Carkhoff, R. R. (1969). *Helping and human relations: A primer for lay and professional helpers. Volume I, Selection and training.* New York: Rinehart & Winston.

Carkhoff, R. R. (1980). *The art of helping (4ᵗʰ ed.).* Amherst, MA: Human Resources Development.

Carkhoff, R. R. (1983). *The art of helping (5ᵗʰ ed.).* Amherst, MA: Human Resources Development.

Carpenito, L. J. (1993). *Handbook of nursing diagnosis.* Philadelphia: J. B. Lippincott.

Carter, E. A., & McGoldrick, M. (1980). *The family life cycle: A framework for family therapy.* New York: Gardner.

Chamberlain, J. M. (1975). *Handbook for eliminating a self-defeating behavior.* Unpublished manuscript.

Chamberlain-Hayman, S. (1998). *Power and control in women's issues.* Unpublished manuscript, South Dakota State University, Rapid City.

Chapman, B., Condie, J., & Helgeson, M. (1995). *Feminist family therapy.* Unpublished manuscript, South Dakota State University, Rapid City.

Chapman, R. J. [chapman@lasalle.edu]. "Subject: Defining the profession." In CESNET-L. [CESNET-L@VM.SC.EDU]. 18 February 1997.

Chodorow, N. J. (1978). *The reproduction of mothering.* Berkeley: University of California Press.

Chodorow, N. J. (1989). *Feminism and psychoanalytic theory.* New Haven, CT: Yale University Press.

Chusmir, L. H. (1983). Characteristics and predictive dimensions of women who make nontraditional vocational choices. *Personnel and Guidance Journal, 62*(1), 43–48.

Combs, R. H. (1991). Marital status and personal well-being: A literature review. *Family Relations, 40,* 97–102.

Corbett, J. M. (1990). *Religion in America.* Englewood Cliffs, NJ: Prentice-Hall.

Corey, G. (1991a). *Case approach to counseling and psychotherapy (3rd ed.).* Pacific Grove, CA: Brooks/Cole.

Corey, G. (1991b). *Theory and practice of counseling and psychotherapy (4th ed.).* Pacific Grove, CA: Brooks/Cole.

Corey, G. (1995). *Theory and practice of group counseling (3rd ed.).* Pacific Grove, CA: Brooks/Cole.

Corsini, R. J. (1984). *Current psychotherapies (3rd ed.)*. Itasca, IL: Peacock.

Corsini, R. J., & Gross, D. (1991). *Introduction to counseling: Perspective for 1990s*. Boston: Allyn & Bacon.

Covey, S. (1990). *The seven habits of highly effective people*. New York: Simon & Schuster.

Crites, J. O. (1981). *Career counseling: Models, methods, and materials*. New York: McGraw-Hill.

Day, M. (1983). Margin: What it means for you. In A. Reeve (Ed.), *Changes, challenges, and choices*. Acton, MA: Tapestry.

DeLoache, J. S., Cassidy, D. J., & Carpenter, C. J. (1987). The three bears are all boys: Mothers' gender labeling of neutral picture book characters. *Sex Roles, 17,* 163–178.

Denmark, F. L. (1994). Engendering psychology. *American Psychologist, 49,* 329–334.

*DISCOVER: A computer-based career development and counselors support system*. (1984). Iowa City: American College Testing Foundation.

Egan, G. (1990). *The skilled helper (4th ed.)*. Pacific Grove, CA: Brooks/Cole.

Elkins, D. N., Hedstrom, L. J., Hughes, L. L., Leaf, J. A., & Saunders, C. (1988). Toward a humanistic-phenomenological spirituality. *Journal of Humanistic Psychology, 28,* 5–18.

Ellis, A. (1962). *Reason and emotion in psychotherapy*. Secaucus, NJ: Lyle Stuart/Citadel Books.

Ellis, A. (1980). Psychotherapy and atheistic values: A response to A. E. Bergin's "Psychotherapy and religious values." *Journal of Consulting and Clinical Psychology, 48,* 635–639.

Ellis, A. (1984). Rational-emotive therapy. In R. Corsini (Ed.), *Current psychotherapies*. Itasca, IL: Peacock

Ellis, A., & Harper, R. A. (1975). *A new guide to rational living*. Englewood Cliffs, NJ: Prentice-Hall.

Erickson, M. H. (1983). *Healing in hypnosis.* New York: Irvington.

Erikson, E. H. (1968). *Identity: Youth and crisis.* New York: W. W. Norton.

Erikson, E. H. (1972). Eight stages of man. In C. S. Lavatelli & F. Stendler (Eds.), *Readings in child behavior and child development.* San Diego: Harcourt Brace Jovanovich.

Ewing, D. B. (1977). Twenty approaches to individual change. *Personnel and Guidance Journal, 55*(6), 331–338.

Fowler, J. W. (1976). Stages in faith: The structural developmental approach. In T. Hennessy (Ed.), *Values and moral development.* New York: Paulist Press.

Frankl, V. (1959). *Man's search for meaning: An introduction to logotherapy.* New York: Washington Square.

Frankl, V. (1963). *Man's search for meaning.* Boston: Beacon.

Frankl, V. (1967). Logotherapy and existentialism. *Psychotherapy: Theory, Research, and Practice, 4,* 138–142.

Freud, A. (1946). *The ego and the mechanisms of defense.* New York: International Universities Press.

Freud, S. (1905). Fragment of an analysis of a case of hysteria. In *Collected Papers (Vol. 3).* New York: Basic Books.

Friere, P. (1985). *The politics of education.* Boston: Bergin & Garvey.

Gallup, G. H., Jr., & Bezilla, R. (1994, January 22). More find religion important. *The Washington Post,* p. G10.

Gallup, G., & Castelli, J. (1989). *The people's religion: American faith in the '90s.* New York: Macmillan.

Garfield, S., & Bergin, A. (1978). *Handbook of psychotherapy and behavior change (2nd ed.).* New York: Wiley.

Gelatt, H. B. (1989). Positive uncertainty: A new decision-making framework for counseling. *Journal of Counseling Psychology, 36*(2), 252–256.

Gendlin, E. (1981). *Focusing.* New York: Bantam.

Genia, V. (1990). Religious development: A synthesis and reformulation. *Journal of Religion and Health, 31,* 317–326.

George, R. L., & Cristiani, T. S. (1986). *Counseling: theory and practice (2nd ed.).* Englewood Cliffs, NJ: Prentice-Hall.

Gibran, K. (1968). *The prophet.* New York: Knopf.

Gilligan, C. (1982). *In a different voice: Psychological theory and women's development.* Cambridge, MA: Harvard University Press.

Gilligan, C. (1990). Teaching Shakespeare's sister. In C. Gilligan, N. Lyons, & T. Hanmer (Eds.), *Making connections: The relational worlds of adolescent girls at Emma Willard School.* Cambridge, MA: Harvard University Press.

Ginzberg, E., Ginsburg, S. W., Axelrad, S., & Herma, J. L. (1951). *Occupational choice: An approach to general theory.* New York: New American Library.

Glasser, W. (1965). *Reality therapy: A new approach to psychiatry.* New York: Harper & Row.

Glasser, W. (1984). In R. Corsini (Ed.), *Current psychotherapies.* Itasca, IL: Peacock.

Glasser, W., & Zunin, Z. M. (1973). Reality therapy. In R. Corsini (Ed.), *Current psychotherapies.* Itasca, IL: Peacock.

Gordon, D. (1978). *Therapeutic metaphor.* Capitola, CA: Meta Publications.

Gottfredson, L. S. (1981). Circumspection and compromise: A developmental theory of occupational aspirations. *Journal of Counseling Psychology, 28*(6), 545–579.

Gould, R. L. (1978). *Transformations: Growth and change in adult life.* New York: Simon & Schuster.

Hackney, H., & Cormier, S. (1994). *Counseling strategies and interventions (4th ed.).* New York: Simon & Schuster.

Haley, J. (1976). *Problem-solving therapy*. San Francisco: Jossey-Bass.

Hanna, S. M., & Brown, J. H. (1995). *The practice of family therapy: Key elements across models*. Pacific Grove, CA: Brooks/Cole.

Hansen, L. S. (1977). *An examination of the definitions and concepts of career education*. Washington, DC: National Advisory Council for Career Education.

Harris, T. (1969). *I'm OK, you're OK*. New York: Harper & Row.

Havinghurst, R. (1953). *Human development and education*. New York: Longman.

Helms, J. E. (1984). Toward a theoretical explanation of the effects of race on counseling: A black and white model. *The Counseling Psychologist, 12,* 153–165.

Helwig, A. A. (1992). *Study guide for the national counselor examination.* (Available from Andrew Helwig, 1154 Loch Ness Avenue, Broomfield, CO 80020)

Helwig, A. A. (1994). *Study guide for the national counselor examination.* (Available from Andrew Helwig, 1154 Loch Ness Avenue, Broomfield, CO 80020)

Holland, J. (1985). *Making vocational choices: A theory of careers (2nd ed.)*. Englewood Cliffs, NJ: Prentice-Hall.

Hollis, J. W. (1997). *Counselor preparation 1996–98 (9th ed.)*. Washington, DC: Taylor & Francis.

Hollis, J. W., & Wantz, R. (1971). *Counselor education directory, 1971: Personnel and programs*. Muncie, IN: Ball State University.

Hoppock, R. (1976). *Occupational information (4th ed.)*. New York: McGraw-Hill.

Horney, K. (1967). *Feminine psychology*. New York: W. W. Norton.

Huston, A. C. (1983). Sex-typing. In P. H. Mussen (Ed.). *Handbook of child psychology (Vol. 4, 4th ed.)*. New York: Wiley.

Jacobson, N. S., Holtzworth-Monroe, A., & Schmaling, K. B. (1989). Marital therapy and spouse involvement in the treatment of depression, agoraphobia, and alcoholism. *Journal of Consulting and Clinical Psychology, 57,* 5–10.

Jourard, S. M. (1963). *Personal adjustment.* New York: Macmillan.

Jung, C. G. (1954). *The development of personality. In The collected works of Carl Gustav Jung (Vol. I).* Princeton, NJ: Princeton University Press.

Kadushin, A. (1969). *Why people go to psychotherapists.* New York: Atherton.

Kelly, E. W. (1995). *Spirituality and religion in counseling and psychotherapy: Diversity in theory and practice.* Alexandria, VA: America Counseling Association.

Kempler, W. (1973). Gestalt therapy. In R. Corsini (Ed.), *Current psychotherapies.* Itasca, IL: Peacock.

Kiewra, K. A. (1989). A review of note taking; The encoding-storage paradigm and beyond. *Educational Psychology Review, 1,* 147–172.

Kirman, W. J. (1988). Emotional education in the classroom: A modern psychoanalytic approach. In G. S. Belkin (Ed.), *Introduction to counseling (3rd ed.).* Dubuque, IA: Wm. C. Brown.

Knefelkamp, L. L., & Slepitza, R. (1976). A cognitive developmental model of career development: An adaptation of the Perry scheme. *Counseling Psychologist, 6*(3), 53–58.

Kohlberg, L. (1958). *The development of modes of moral thinking and choice in the years 10 to 16.* Unpublished doctoral dissertation, University of Chicago.

Kohlberg, L. (1966). A cognitive-developmental analysis of children's sex-role concepts and attitudes. In E. E. Maccoby (Ed.), *The development of sex differences.* Palo Alto, CA: Stanford University Press.

Kohlberg, L. (1976). Moral stages and moralization: The cognitive-development approach. In T. Lickona (Ed.), *Moral development and behavior.* New York: Holt, Rinehart, & Winston.

Kohlberg, L. (1986). A correct statement on some theoretical issues. In S. Modgil & C. Modgil (Eds.), *Lawrence Kohlberg.* Philadelphia: Falmer.

Kubler-Ross, E. (1969). *On death and dying.* New York: Macmillan.

Kubler-Ross, E. (1974). *Questions and answers on death and dying.* New York: Macmillan.

Kurpius, D., Fuqua, D. R., & Rozecki, T. (1993). The consulting process: A multidimensional approach. *Journal of Counseling and Development, 71*(6), 601–606.

Lamb, M. E. (1986). *The father's role: Applied perspectives.* New York: Wiley.

Lanning, Wayne. [lanning@nevada.edu]. "internet counseling." In CESNET-L. [CESNET-L@UM.SC.EDU]. 13 September 1997.

Lazarus, A. A. (1984). In R. Corsini (Ed.), *Current psychotherapies.* Itasca, IL: Peacock.

Lee, D. (1984). Counseling and culture: Some issues. *Personnel and Guidance Journal, 62,* 592–597.

Lee, O., & Anderson, C. W. (1993). Task engagement and conceptual change in middle school science classrooms. *American Educational Research Journal, 30,* 585–610.

Levinson, D. J. (1978). *The seasons of a man's life.* New York: Knopf.

Levy, D. R. (1985). White doctors and black patients: Influence of race on the doctor-patient relationship. *Pediatrics, 75,* 939–643.

Lewin, K. (1946). Action research and minority problems. *Journal of Social Issues, 2,* 34–46.

Luria, A., & Herzog, E. (1985, April). *Gender segregation across and within settings.* Paper presented at the biennial meeting of the Society for Research in Child Development, Toronto.

Lyddon, W. J. (1990). First and second order change: Implications for rationalist and constructivist cognitive therapies. *Journal of Counseling and Development, 69,* 122–127.

Maccoby, E. E. (1989, August). *Gender and relationships: A developmental account.* Paper presented at the meeting of the American Psychological Association, New Orleans.

Madanes, C. (1981). *Strategic family therapy.* San Francisco: Jossey-Bass.

Mahler, M. (1979). *Separation-individuation (Vol. 2).* London: Jason Aronson.

Marshall, J. (1995). *Educational evaluation and research.* Unpublished manuscript. South Dakota State University, Ellsworth.

Maslow, A. H. (1954). *Motivation and personality.* New York: Harper & Row.

Maslow, A. H. (1971). *The farther reaches of human nature.* New York: Viking.

Maslow, A. H. (1987). *Motivation and personality (3rd ed.).* New York: Harper & Row.

Masters, W. H., & Johnson, V. E. (1970). *Human sexual inadequacy.* Boston: Little, Brown.

Maxwell, N. A. (1978). *Things as they really are.* Salt Lake City: Bookcraft.

Maxwell, N. A. (1988). *Not my will, but thine.* Salt Lake City: Bookcraft.

McConkie, B. R. (1979). *Mormon doctrine.* Salt Lake City: Bookcraft.

Mehrabian, A. (1971). *Silent messages.* Belmond, CA: Wadsworth.

Meichenbaum, D. (1977). *Cognitive-behavior modification.* New York: Plenum.

Meichenbaum, D. (1986). Cognitive behavior modification. In F. H. Kanfer & A. P. Goldstein (Eds.), *Helping people change: A textbook of methods* (pp. 346–380). New York: Pergamon.

Meier, P. D., Minirth, F. B., Wichern, F. B., & Ratcliff, D. E. (1995). *Introduction to psychology and counseling: Christian perspectives and applications (2nd ed.).* Grand Rapids, MI: Baker.

Minuchin, S. (1974). *Families and family therapy.* Cambridge, MA: Harvard University Press.

Mitchell, L. K., & Krumboltz, J. D. (1990). Social learning approach to career decision making: Krumboltz's theory. In D. Brown & L. Brooks (Eds.), *Career choice and development: Applying contemporary theories to practice (2nd ed.)* (pp. 145–196). San Francisco: Jossey-Bass.

Moreno, J. L. (1946). *Psychodrama: Volume 1.* New York: Beacon House.

Mosak, H. H. (1984). Adlerian psychology. In R. Corsini (Ed.), *Current psychotherapies (3rd ed.)*. Itasca, IL: Peacock.

Muxen, M. (1995). *Grief in the family*. Unpublished manuscript. South Dakota State University, Brookings.

Myers, J. E. (1998). Bibliotherapy and DCT: Coconstructing the therapeutic metaphor. *Journal of Counseling and Development, 76,* 243–260.

Naranjo, C. (1970). Present-centeredness: Technique, prescription, and ideal. In J. Fagan & I. L. Shepherd (Eds.), *Gestalt therapy now*. Palo Alto, CA: Science & Behavior Books.

National Board for Certified Counselors (1997, December 1). Standards for the ethical practice of web counseling. Available at http://www.nbcc.org/wcstandards.htm.

Nichols, M., & Schwartz, R. (1991). *Family therapy: Concepts and methods (2nd ed.)*. Needham Heights, MA: Allyn & Bacon.

Norcross, J. C. (1986). Eclectic psychotherapy: An introduction and overview. In J. C. Norcross (Ed.), *Handbook of eclectic psychotherapy* (pp. 3–24). New York: Brunner/Mazel.

Norcross, J. C., & Prochaska, J. O. (1988). A study of eclectic (and integrative) views revisited. *Professional Psychology: Research and Practice, 19,* 170–174.

Ormond, J. E. (1998). *Educational psychology: Developing learners*. Englewood Cliffs, NJ: Prentice-Hall.

Packer, B. K. (1989, August). The decision of life. *New Era, 19,* 4.

Parkes, C. M. (1972). *Bereavement: Studies of grief in adult life*. New York: International University Press.

Parsons, F. (1909). *Choosing a vocation*. Boston: Houghton Mifflin.

Paul, G. L. (1967). Strategy of outcome research in psychotherapy. *Journal of Consulting Psychology, 31,* 109–118.

Pedersen, P. (1991). Multiculturalism as a generic approach to counseling. *Journal of Counseling and Development, 70*(1), 6–12.

Perls, F. (1969). *Gestalt therapy verbatim.* Moab, UT: Real People Press.

Perry, W. G. (1970). *Forms of intellectual and ethical development in the college years.* New York: Holt, Rinehart & Winston.

Peters, H. J. (1962). *Counseling: Selected readings.* Columbus, OH: Charles E. Merrill.

Peterson, G. W., Sampson, J. P., & Reardon, R. C. (1991). *Career development and services: A cognitive approach.* Pacific Grove, CA: Brooks/Cole.

Peterson, J. V., & Nisenholz, B. (1995). *Orientation to counseling (3rd ed.).* Boston: Allyn & Bacon.

Pfeifle, D. (1997). *Gestalt therapy.* Unpublished manuscript, South Dakota State University, Rapid City.

Piaget, J. (1954). *The construction of reality in the child.* New York: Basic Books.

Piaget, J. (1970). Piaget's theory. In P. H. Mussen (Ed.), *Carmichael's manual of psychology.* New York: Wiley.

Pietrofesa, J. J., Bernstein, B., Minor, J., & Stanford, S. (1980). *Guidance: An introduction (2nd ed.).* Chicago: Rand McNally.

Pietrofesa, J. J., Hoffman, J., & Splete, H. H. (1984). *Counseling: An introduction (2nd ed.).* Boston: Houghton Mifflin.

Pintrich, P. R., Marx, R. W., & Boyle, R. A. (1993). Beyond cold conceptual change: The role of motivational beliefs and classroom contextual factors in the process of conceptual change. *Review of Educational Research, 63,* 167–199.

Polster, E., & Polster, M. (1973). *Gestalt therapy integrated.* New York: Brunner/Mazel.

Prochaska, J. O., DiClemente, C. C., & Norcross, J. C. (1992). In search of how people change. *American Psychologist, 47,* 1102–1113.

Pucci, A. (1997, February). Cognitive-behavioral therapy [Letter to the editor]. *Counseling Today,* p. 4.

Reik, T. (1952). *Listening with the third ear.* New York: Farrar Strauss.

Remley, T. P., Jr. (1993). Toward common standards. *Guidepost, 36*(4), 4.

Robinson, F. (1965). Counseling orientations and labels. *Journal of Counseling Psychology, 12,* 338.

Rockwood, G. F. (1993). Edgar Schein's process versus content consultation models. *Journal of Counseling and Development, 71*(6), 636–638.

Roe, A. (1956). *The psychology of occupations.* New York: Wiley.

Rogers, C. R. (1942). *Counseling and psychotherapy.* Boston: Houghton Mifflin.

Rogers, C. R. (1951). *Client-centered therapy.* Boston: Houghton Mifflin.

Rogers, C. R. (1957). The necessary and sufficient conditions of therapeutic personality change. *Journal of Consulting Psychology, 22,* 95–103.

Rogers, C. R. (1959). A theory of therapy, personality, and interpersonal relationships, as developed in the client-centered framework. In S. Koch (Ed.), *Psychology: A study of a science Vol. III. Formulations of the person and the social context* (pp. 184–256). New York: McGraw-Hill.

Rogers, C. R. (1961). *On becoming a person.* Boston: Houghton Mifflin.

Rogers, C. R. (1980). *A way of being.* Boston: Houghton Mifflin.

Rotter, J. B. (1966). Generalized expectations for internal versus external control of reinforcement. *Psychological Monographs, 80*(609).

Santrock, J. W. (1992). *Life-span development (4th ed.).* Dubuque, IA: Wm. C. Brown.

Satir, V. (1967). *Conjoint family therapy (rev ed.).* Palo Alto, CA: Science & Behavior Books.

Satir, V. (1972). *Peoplemaking.* Palo Alto, CA: Science & Behavior Books.

Schein, E. H. (1978). The role of the consultant: Content expert or process facilitator? *Personnel and Guidance Journal, 56*(6), 346–350.

Schlessinger, L. (1997). *How could you do that: The abdication of character, courage, and conscience.* New York: HarperCollins.

Schlossberg, N. K., & Pietrofesa, J. J. (1978). Perspectives on counseling bias: Implications for counselor education. In L. S. Hansen & R. S. Rapoza (Eds.), *Career development and counseling of women.* Springfield, IL: Charles C. Thomas.

Schmidt, J. J. (1996). *Counseling in the schools: Essential services and comprehensive programs.* Boston: Allyn & Bacon.

Segedin, F. P. (1994). *Hypnotherapy with college-aged students.* Unpublished manuscript, University of Evansville, Evansville, IL.

Selvini Palazzoli, M., Boscolo, L., Cecchin, G., & Prata, G. (1980). Hypothesizing, circularity, neutrality: Three guidelines for the conduct of the session. *Family Process, 19*(1), 7–19.

Shafranske, E. P., & Gorsuch, R. L. (1984). Factors associated with the perception of spirituality in psychotherapy. *Journal of Transpersonal Psychology, 16,* 231–241.

Shafranske, E. P., & Malony, H. N. (1990). Clinical psychologists' religious and spiritual orientation and their practice of psychotherapy. *Psychotherapy, 237,* 72–78.

Sheehy, G. (1976). *Passages: Predictable crises of adult life.* New York: Dutton.

Sheridan, M. J., Bullis, R. K., Adcock, C. R., Berlin, S. D., & Miller, P. C. (1992). Practitioners' personal and professional attitudes toward religion and spirituality: Issues for education and practice. *Journal of Social Work Education, 28,* 190–203.

Shertzer, B., & Stone, S. (1980). *Fundamentals of counseling, (3rd ed.).* Boston: Houghton Mifflin.

Shipman, S., & Shipman, V. C. (1985). Cognitive styles: Some conceptual, methodological, and applied issues. In E. W. Gordon (Ed.), *Review of research in education (Vol. 12).* Washington, DC: American Educational Research Association.

Simkin, J. S., & Yontef, G. M. (1984). Gestalt therapy. In R. Corsini (Ed.), *Current psychotherapies (3rd ed.).* Itasca, IL: Peacock.

Skinner, B. F. (1953). *Science and human behavior.* New York: Macmillan.

Smith, D. S. (1982). Trends in counseling and psychotherapy. *American Psychologist, 37,* 802–809.

Spotnitz, H. (1963). The toxoid response. *Psychoanalytic Review, 50*(4), 81–94.

Spotnitz, H. (1968). *Modern psychoanalysis and the schizophrenic patient.* New York: Grune & Stratton.

Spotnitz, H. (1976). *Psychotherapy of preoedipal conditions.* New York: Jason Aronson.

St. Clair, M. (1986*). Object relations and self psychology.* Pacific Grove, CA: Brooks/Cole.

Steenbarger, B. N. (1991). All the world is not a stage: Emerging contextualist themes in counseling and development. *Journal of Counseling and Development, 70,* 288–297.

Steiner, C. (1974). *Scripts people live.* New York: Grove.

Sternberg, R. J. (1988). *The triangle of love.* New York: Basic Books.

Stuart, R. B. (1976). An operant interpersonal program for couples. In D.H.L. Olsen (Ed.), *Treating relationships* (pp. 119–132). Lake Mills, IA: Graphic Publishing.

Super, D. (1980). A life-span, life-space approach to career development. *Journal of Vocational Behavior, 16,* 282–298.

Super, D. (1990). A life-span, life-space approach to career development. In D. Brown & L. Brooks (Eds.), *Career choice and development.* San Francisco: Jossey-Bass.

Tiedeman, D. V., & O'Hara, R. P. (1963). *Career development: Choice and adjustment.* Princeton, NJ: College Entrance Examination Board.

Trotzer, J. P. (1977). *The counselor and the group: Integrating theory and practice.* Monterey, CA: Brooks/Cole.

Tuckman, B. (1965). Developmental changes in small groups. *Psychological Bulletin, 63,* 384–399.

Unikel, I. P. (1973). Issues in behavior therapy. In H. E. Adams & I. P. Unikel (Eds.), *Issues and trends in behavior therapy* (pp. 43–56). Springfield, IL: Charles C. Thomas.

Vaillant, G. E. (1977). *Adaption to life.* Boston: Little, Brown.

Van Deurzen-Smith, E. (1990). *Existential therapy.* London: Society for Existential Analysis.

Vessey, J. T., & Howard, K. I. (1993). Who seeks psychotherapy? *Psychotherapy, 30,* 546–553.

Vosniadal, S., & Brewer, W. F. (1987). Theories of knowledge restructuring in development. *Review of Educational Research, 57,* 51–67.

Walz, G., & Benjamin, L. (1978). A change agent strategy for counselors functioning as consultants. *Personnel and Guidance Journal, 56*(6), 331–334.

Watson, J. B. (1963). Psychology as the behaviorist views it. *Psychological Review, 20,* 159–170.

Whitaker, C. & Bumberry, W. (1988). *Dancing with the family: A symbolic-experiential approach.* New York: Brunner/Mazel.

Williamson, E. G. (1939). *How to counsel students: A manual of techniques for clinical counselors.* New York: McGraw-Hill.

Williamson, E. G. (1970). A concept of counseling. In W. Van Hoose & J. J. Pietrofesa (Eds.), *Counseling and guidance in the twentieth century.* Boston: Houghton Mifflin.

Wolpe, J. (1958). *Psychotherapy by reciprocal inhibition.* Palo Alto, CA: Stanford University Press.

World Health Organization. (1994). *International Classification of Diseases: ICD-9-CM.* Albany, NY: Author.

Wrenn, C. G. (1962). *The counselor in a changing world.* Washington, DC: Personnel and Guidance Assocaition.

Wuthnow, R. (1994). *Sharing the journey: Support groups and America's new quest for community.* New York: Free Press.

Yalom, I. (1985). *Theory and practice of group psychotherapy (3rd ed.).* New York: Basic Books.

Yalom, I. (1989). *Love's executioner and other tales of psychotherapy.* New York: HarperCollins.

Young, M. E., & Feller, F. (1993). Theoretical trends in counseling: A national survey. *Guidance and Counseling, 9,* 4–9.

Young, M. E., Feller, F., & Witmer, J. M. (1989). *Eclecticism: New foundation for recasting the counseling profession.* Unpublished manuscript, Station University, Deland, FL.

Zook, A., & Walton, J. M. (1989). Theoretical orientations and work settings of clinical and counseling psychologists: A current perspective. *Professional Psychology: Research and Practice, 20,* 23–31.

Zunker, V. G. (1994). *Career counseling: Applied concepts of life planning (4th ed.).* Pacific Grove, CA: Brooks/Cole.

# INDEX

# ABOUT THE AUTHOR

Leonard A. Austin is an assistant professor at Black Hills State University in South Dakota, near Mt. Rushmore. His master's degree is in Adult Education, and his doctoral degree is in Educational Psychology and Counseling from the University of Wyoming.

Dr. Austin has been a Licensed Professional Counselor and is active in the American Counseling Association. He has administered the National Counselor Examination to master's-level students and maintains a small private counseling practice. He has taught courses to aspiring counselors and psychologists in such areas as the theories of counseling, educational psychology, processes of groups, and orientation to the counseling profession. He continues to supervise counselors in the field who are seeking further training prior to becoming Licensed Professional Counselors.

Dr. Austin presents workshops nationwide for adult and adolescent audiences on topics such as: dealing with difficult youth, being optimistic in a pessimistic world, enhancing one's spiritual life, teaching adult students, entrepreneurism in counseling, and basic counseling skills for nontherapists. He currently is completing a second book titled Counseling Clients from Different Religious Backgrounds, which examines the history, culture, and important constructs of various religious denominations in the United States. This new text will offer intervention strategies for counselors who work with clients who are affiliated with specific religious denominations, while giving insights into how clients' spirituality and religiosity can be used effectively in the healing process.

Dr. Austin and his wife, Margaret Kubler Austin, met on the night of their graduation from the same high school in Napa, California. Both taught high school in Australia and are the parents of Melissa, Sierra, and Eli.